BEYOND BLACK AND WHITE

Number Thirty-five:

Walter Prescott Webb Memorial
Lectures

BEYOND BLACK & WHITE

Race, Ethnicity, and Gender in the U.S. South and Southwest

Edited by Stephanie Cole & Alison M. Parker

Introduction by Nancy A. Hewitt

*By Laura F. Edwards, William D. Carrigan, Clive Webb,
Stephanie Cole, Sarah Deutsch, and Neil Foley*

Published for the
University of Texas at Arlington
by Texas A&M University Press
College Station

The paper used in this book meets the minimum requirements
of the American National Standard for Permanence
of Paper for Printed Library Materials, Z39.48-1984.
Binding materials have been chosen for durability.
∞

Library of Congress Cataloging-in-Publication Data

Beyond black and white : race, ethnicity, and gender in the U.S. South and Southwest / edited by
Stephanie Cole and Alison M. Parker, introduction by Nancy A. Hewitt ; by Laura F. Edwards . . .
[et al.]— 1st ed.
 p. cm. — (Walter Prescott Webb memorial lectures ; 35)
Includes bibliographical references.
 ISBN 1-58544-297-6 (cloth : alk. paper) — ISBN 1-58544-319-0 (pbk. : alk. paper)
 1. Southern States—Race relations. 2. Southwest, New—Race relations. 3. Southern States—
Ethnic relations. 4. Southwest, New—Ethnic relations. 5. Ethnicity—Southern States.
6. Ethnicity—Southwest, New. 7. Sex role—Southern States. 8. Sex role—Southwest, New.
9. Southern States—Social conditions. 10. Southwest, New—Social conditions. I. Cole, Stephanie,
1962– II. Parker, Alison M. (Alison Marie), 1965– III. Edwards, Laura F. IV. Series.
F220.A1 B49 2003
305.8'00975—dc21
      2003010130

To Laverne Prewitt

Contents

Preface

I n March, 2000, the University of Texas at Arlington Department of History held the Thirty-fifth Annual Walter Prescott Webb Memorial Lectures, focusing on the theme, "Beyond Black and White: Race, Ethnicity, and Gender in the U.S. South and Southwest." The following chapters emerged from that conference. Walter Prescott Webb, whom these lectures honor, pioneered the history of the West, and his work helped to place Texas within that context. Seeking to meet Professor Webb's challenge to think innovatively about regional history—though not his specific regional distinctions—this volume explores the connections between Texas, southwestern, and southern history. Beginning with the notion that residents of the United States too often look at race relations in terms of "black" and "white," the authors here attempt to uncover and disrupt the assumptions that lie behind that habit, in part by linking ideas and events within southwestern history to that of the South. Their chapters illustrate that elites' common (and inaccurate) use of dichotomous categories to describe social relationships—not only black and white, but also male and female, slave and free, dependent and independent—shored up white power in both regions. Together, they reveal social diversity within places, times and events generally analyzed with a black and white (or otherwise simplistic) framework, and they demonstrate that acceptance then and now of simple categories has impeded efforts by groups outside those categories to claim rights and privileges on their own terms. Although the topics covered range from law in the South in the nineteenth century to political activism by Mexican Americans in the twentieth century, they begin with a common viewpoint: If we are to understand the complexity of race in the United States, we must go beyond thinking in terms of black and white.

This volume would not have been possible without the generous support of many people and institutions. First, on behalf of the Department of

History at the University of Texas at Arlington, we acknowledge the generous grants and endowments that have kept the Webb Lecture Series going, providing the funding necessary to sponsor the conference, subsidize an essay competition to accompany the conference, and help to publish the subsequent collection. The late C. B. Smith, Sr., of Austin, Texas, the Rudolf Hermann Endowment for the Liberal Arts, and Jenkins and Virginia Garrett of Fort Worth have been especially important contributors. We are also grateful for the continued support of UTA's administration and our library, especially Kit Goodwin of Special Collections. Second, as editors, we have relied on the cooperation of our contributors, as well as the help of friends and colleagues. We are especially grateful to Nancy Hewitt for taking time out of a busy schedule to write the introduction and to Chris Morris, Geoffrey Hale, and Steven Reinhardt for their insights and assistance. After many years of serving as chair of the Webb Lectures Committee, Professor Reinhardt is stepping down from that post with the publication of this volume; we trust that this convergence of events does not imply that we tried his nerves more than our predecessors. In any event, we want to commend him for his service to the department, and thank him for his helpful advice and quiet good humor in organizing the lectures and guiding this publication. Lastly, we wish to commemorate the many years of service Laverne Prewitt has given to the Department of History and UTA. We appreciate her dedication and wish her well in her retirement.

—Stephanie Cole and Alison M. Parker

Introduction

Nancy A. Hewitt

When Barbara Fields published her now classic essay on ideology and race in American history in 1982, her claims were met with skepticism, criticism, and caution.[1] Within a decade, however, her basic premise—that race is socially and culturally, not biologically, constructed—took hold in the academy. Indeed, there is now a mini industry among scholars focused on the making of race in America. Yet despite the radical implications of Fields's argument, the works her intervention generated break down largely along a black-white divide. Scholars of African American life have probed ways that region, color, class, ethnicity, gender, and sexuality mark blackness within both African American and white communities, while historians of whiteness have explored the process by which Irish, Italians, Jews, and other immigrant groups became white. This rich and provocative work has complicated our understandings of race, but has, at the same time, etched racial dichotomies more deeply into the historical, and historiographical, record.

The following chapters join a small but growing literature that moves beyond the black-white binary in American history by exploring social groups and historical developments that cut across or contested a biracial system. Scholars such as Gary Nash, Peggy Pascoe, Martha Hodes, James Barrett and David Roediger, Kirsten Fischer, and others, including the authors in this volume, have explored *mestizaje,* miscegenation, "in-between peoples," and "suspect relations" as ways of opening up discussions of racial constructions on the North American continent from the seventeenth century to the present.[2] Yet with few exceptions, such as Hodes and Fischer, this work has focused on the West or the Northeast, leaving the South as the first and last bastion of biracialism. The authors in this volume take on that critical terrain, probing moments and spaces of conflict where diverse populations confronted each other and, in the process, challenged the ideological and institutional constructions of southern society. These crises were most frequent and most visible in the Southwest, particularly Texas and Oklahoma, where large populations of American Indians and Mexicans and smaller communities of Asian and southern European immigrants confounded attempts to impose a black-white template on multiracial communities.

The focus on the South's geographical margins is not surprising. As Geraldine Pratt has argued, and a wide range of scholars have demonstrated, borderlands are especially useful spaces for exploring complex identities, because they are "saturated with inequality, domination and forced exclusion; they are social and political constructions that are used to construct differences. But they are also relational places where individuals live and construct themselves in relation to each other."[3] This volume centers on the Southwest but also pushes beyond it to argue persuasively for a recasting of race throughout the entire South. And if the South cannot sustain conventional understandings of black and white, then our conceptualizations of race in the United States and the North American territories must be dramatically recast.

The complex dynamics of race in the United States are rooted in the nation's long history of enslavement, conquest, and immigration. Millions of Africans were forcibly transplanted to North American soil and, despite cultural and later legal prohibitions on sex and marriage between them and Anglo Americans, large numbers of blacks were coerced into sexual relations with their white owners and a far smaller number crossed racial lines voluntarily. Moreover, Africans and African Americans did not engage in intimate intercourse only with Euro-Americans. They also formed sexual liaisons and long-term relationships with American Indians, Mexicans, Mexican Americans, and other groups considered not quite white.[4] By the eighteenth and early nineteenth centuries, mixed-race and multiracial communities had formed throughout the South, most notably in the Carolinas, Florida, and the Southwest, even as white legislatures and courts worked with increasing diligence to impose a biracial order on the region.[5]

By pushing groups once isolated from each other—Indians, African Americans, and Mexicans—into intimate proximity, military and political efforts to dominate the North American continent contributed mightily to creating the very racial heterogeneity that civic leaders sought to eradicate or obscure. In addition, massive immigration from Europe, Asia, the Caribbean, and elsewhere assured that racial mingling would increase even if the particular forms of race mixing differed by region and over time. Finally, late-nineteenth-century imperial ventures added territories such as Puerto Rico, the Philippines, and Hawaii, with their own complex racial traditions, into the American fold, bringing more "people of color" under U.S. authority.

Despite this history, the ability of economically and politically powerful whites to insist on biracial categories as the bedrock of U.S. society meant that challenging the black-white dichotomy and the power relations it was intended to enforce was fraught with peril. Indians, for example, who forged communal and familial bonds with African Americans, found themselves having to choose between traditions of racial assimilation and conflicts with the federal government—resulting in warfare in the nineteenth century and struggles over tribal recognition and limited benefits in the twentieth. Poor Mexicans whose agricultural labors marked them as "like blacks" in the South's racial and economic hierarchy were subject to forms of discrimination and abuse similar to those visited upon African Americans. Thus, as racism in the United States continued to be framed in black and white, those who identified with these bifurcated categories and those who did not embraced a variety of strategies to function within and against such dichotomous constraints. Still, the system of domination was never total, a fact that was especially clear in areas inhabited by large numbers of Caribbean, Mexican, and/or American Indian peoples.

My own research on conditions in late-nineteenth- and early-twentieth-century Tampa, Florida, brought me face to face with both the stubborn grip of the South's black-white divide and persistent challenges to it. Teaching at the University of South Florida in Tampa during the 1980s, I was introduced to a South marked by bilingualism more than biracialism, tobacco and tourism more than cotton and textiles, Caribbean more than Confederate influences, and the attractions of Disneyland more than Dixieland. These differences from southern orthodoxy were not, however, simply the effects of the late-twentieth-century Sunbelt boom. Florida, along with a broad swath of the Gulf Coast region, formed part of the Spanish empire from the sixteenth through the early nineteenth century. Distinct ideas about race, religion, and empire were forged in North America's Spanish colonies as Catholic traditions converged with harsh New World conditions. Writing on slavery in early Florida, Jane Landers notes that, as in other Spanish colonies, "slavery was not exclusively based on race. A slave's humanity and rights and liberal manumission policy eased the transition from slave to citizen."[6] Because of the sparse settlement and wilderness environment of Florida in the seventeenth and eighteenth centuries, a significant number of Africans and African Americans in the region remained free, gained high-status occupations, and took up arms in defense of Spanish interests. In addition, intermarriage was fairly common, especially between black women and Spanish men, creating a free community that incorporated individuals across a broad spectrum of race, color, and class.

Only in the early to mid-1800s did military conquest bring the Gulf Coast territories under U.S. authority; Spanish, Caribbean, and Mexican influences remained powerful in the region long after its official incorporation into the United States. For example, even when Florida was written into southern American history, it was largely as a refuge for runaway slaves and recalcitrant Indians. After Andrew Jackson's 1817 raid convinced Spain to cede Florida to the United States, the Seminole Nation continued to harbor fugitive slaves, some of whom had married into the tribe. When the U.S.

government sought to resettle Florida Seminoles in the Indian Territory of Oklahoma, a minority refused to go. Under the leadership of Osceola, they fought a seven-year guerrilla war (1835–42) against federal troops. Seeking to end the conflict in 1838, General Thomas Sidney Jessup offered to send mixed-race insurgents, that is, those with African American and Indian blood, to Oklahoma and allow the "pure-blood" Seminoles to remain in Florida. Assuming that such racial divides existed and could be turned to political advantage, Jessup was surprised when the Seminoles refused his offer. Fighting continued until U.S. forces used deceit to capture Osceola.[7]

Even then, the defeated Seminoles moved to Oklahoma en masse, keeping their racially mixed community together and providing a haven in Indian territory for slaves held by the Cherokee, Choctaw, and other southern tribes. Moreover, one Seminole chief, Wild Cat, led some two hundred Indians and African Americans into Coahuila, Mexico, in 1850, where they established a colony in the Santa Rosa Mountains, eighty miles southwest of the Rio Grande. The existence of this community attracted other fugitives from Texas and the Plains Indians and increased tensions between Mexico and the United States over the next decade. As a consequence, white Texans increased their attacks on and deportations of Mexicans residing in ten southwestern counties, whom they feared were "instilling false notions of freedom" in slaves and making them "discontented and insubordinate."[8]

While the removal of the Seminoles intensified racial conflicts in the Southwest, it eased tensions back east. The end of the Seminole War increased settlement by U.S.-born whites and led to statehood in 1845, suggesting that Florida might take on a more conventional southern cast. Yet Spanish cultural, religious, and legal traditions maintained a hold on the population well beyond the territory's official transfer to the United States. Under Spanish law, for instance, women could inherit, hold, and distribute property, which could not be seized to pay debts owed by their husbands. Women could enter into a wide variety of legal contracts and could testify in court on their own behalf. Even slave women were allowed some of these rights, because Spanish law recognized them as legal persons instead of chattel, as in Anglo American law. The Catholic Church reinforced legal statutes by supporting the right of slaves to choose their spouses and opposing the breakup of families through the sale of slave children or parents. In addition, significant numbers of Africans and African Americans in Florida and other Gulf Coast cities retained or gained their freedom, creating a large population of free people of color, a majority of whom were women. Finally, children born out of wedlock—including daughters of free black women and Spanish men—could inherit goods and property from their fathers.[9]

Certainly, many slaves and free blacks were treated brutally by Spanish owners and employers; many wives and concubines were abused by fathers, husbands, and lovers. Nevertheless, women and people of color in Spanish territories that came under U.S. authority in the early nineteenth century expected to maintain the rights they had historically enjoyed. For example, Andrew Jackson, who was appointed territorial governor of Florida in 1821, was immediately swept into a legal challenge that pitted Mercedes and Carolina Vidal, free women of color, against the executor of their father's estate, John Innerarity.[10] The father, a Spanish colonial official, had left behind property in Louisiana and Florida for his daughters, who were born out of wedlock to two different free women of color. Innerarity, with the apparent acquiescence of the Spanish courts, had refused to turn over the property or its proceeds to them. Clearly in this case, colonial Spanish authorities had refused to recognize the rights of women and free people of color granted under law, and the women sued. Under Anglo American law, the women had no right to inherit their father's property; indeed, they would not have been acknowledged as legitimate heirs or allowed to sue in court on their own behalf. Yet Jackson chose to assist them, and when the former Spanish governor refused to turn over requested documents, the newly appointed governor had his predecessor jailed for violating agreements between the United States and Spain over the transfer of territory, including all documents related to property rights.

The Vidal case was one of many in which women and people of color claimed rights recognized in Spanish law after Florida had become part of the United States. The Vidal sisters and others gained the support of U.S. authorities, who were interested mainly in imposing their domination over former Spanish territories. In the process, Governor Jackson and others ended up protecting "rights" not accorded under Anglo American law and thereby sustaining residents' belief that their "traditional" rights would be recognized.

Despite the state's complex heritage, white Floridians did gradually embrace the values, politics, and legal structures of the Old South. Florida's slave codes and miscegenation laws were increasingly modeled on those of the cotton South, and contests that pitted women and people of color against Spanish authorities soon waned. In spring, 1861, Florida was among the first six states to follow South Carolina in seceding from the Union. In the aftermath of the Civil War, its history paralleled that of other Confederate strongholds. A brief stint with racially progressive government quickly gave way to white supremacy and Jim Crow legislation.[11]

Still, in southern Florida especially, biracialism dominated the social and political landscape for only a brief period—during the Civil War and Reconstruction. By the late 1870s and 1880s, Cuban immigrants flooded into Key West and Tampa in response to Spain's defeat of the Cuban independence movement and the relocation of dozens of cigar factories from the island to the peninsula. According to the 1900 census, more than 3,500 Cubans resided in Tampa along with nearly 1,000 Spaniards and 1,300 Italians; most of these immigrants lived in the ethnic enclave of Ybor City. Based on linguistic and cultural similarities, these groups came to think of themselves as Latin.[12] Another 2,500 residents were second-generation immigrants, including Germans and Rumanians as well as descendants of the various Latin groups. At the same time, the city's black population exceeded 4,300, including several hundred Cubans, Bahamians, and other Afro-Caribbeans. The 4,557 native-born whites with native-born white parents—that is, Anglos—clearly formed the minority in this multiracial metropolis at the beginning of the twentieth century.[13]

The racially and ethnically diverse population of Tampa and other South Florida cities and towns created havoc with the state's Jim Crow regulations and with more general assertions of white supremacy. The largest cohort of wage-earning immigrants in Tampa and Key West, for instance, were cigar workers and members of radical interracial and mixed-sex labor unions that staged periodic industry-wide strikes. Although Anglo Tampans viewed the mass of Latin workers as docile exotics, they feared "foreign agitators," who, they claimed, sought to impose "a transplanted despotism" on the city.[14] By the early twentieth century, prolonged cigar strikes, massive parades of workers, and frequent demands for improved public services illustrated the power of Tampa's Latin community to maintain a sense of solidarity across lines of ethnicity, race, and gender and to wield significant political clout. Yet so concerned were white civic leaders to maintain the enormous economic benefits of the cigar industry that they allowed Afro-Cuban women and men to work alongside whiter Cubans, Spaniards, and Italians in the cigar factories and the union halls. Indeed, until 1901, even the social clubs and mutual aid societies of Ybor City were racially integrated, and the neighborhoods, coffee shops, restaurants, and stores remained so for considerably longer.

These challenges to Jim Crow were never confined simply to the ethnic enclaves but repeatedly spilled over into Tampa proper. In 1899, for instance, thousands of cigar workers marched in the Labor Day parade, while thousands of local residents—white, black, and Latin, lined the streets. A white reporter noted that one float honored the "'Queen of Labor,' a very dark brunette," who was surrounded by her court and sitting beneath a sign that read "Labor Knows No Color, Creed or Rank." The reporter was moved by the tableau but claimed that it "would have met with more approval from the discerning public had the attendants been colored and the queen white." "The dusky belle," he declared, "was somewhat of a startling innovation."[15] Both the language of the report and the impact of the float suggest the ease with which black-white distinctions could be challenged by the mere presence of other racial or ethnic groups. Despite the clear implication that the queen was Afro-Cuban, the reporter described her only as "dusky" and "a very dark brunette," shying away from any direct accusation that Jim Crow restrictions had been violated. At the same time, his assertion that "the discerning public" would have preferred a different racial ordering made clear that neither African Americans nor Latins were part of that public from an Anglo perspective, even though they likely constituted a majority of parade spectators. Perhaps it is not surprising that shortly after this event, civic leaders barred blacks from participation in the annual parade and insisted as well that racial segregation be enforced in El Club Nacional Cubano, resulting in the organization's division into two separate associations—one "black" and one "white."[16]

Still, the complications introduced by the existence of multiracial communities under a Jim Crow regime could not be easily resolved. In 1902, the Tampa Electric Company decided to impose segregated seating on the streetcars running along the Port Tampa route, which carried wealthy white residents back and forth between the city center and their Hyde Park homes along with large numbers of African American domestics and day laborers. Three years later, the state legislature mandated segregated seating on all streetcars throughout the state. H. H. Hunt served as manager of TECO in 1902 and in 1905 as a liaison with the Boston firm, Stone and Webster, Inc., that owned numerous southern streetcar lines. Hunt voiced concern about the ability of conductors to enforce segregation given the multiracial character of Tampa. After an inspection tour in July, 1905, he wrote his superiors that only "the really black Cubans . . . are not riding the cars." The "balance of Cubans," he claimed, "do not seem to mind . . . but on the contrary appear rather pleased at the fact that they are permitted to keep the same portion of the car as the white people." A year earlier, however, he had taken a more pessimistic (and perhaps more realistic) stance. "As you know," he wrote, "the Cubans comprise many shades of color, from the white man to the black man, and any attempt to separate the colored from the white people" on streetcars "would necessarily result in trouble." He referred to an earlier attempt, probably in 1902 on the Port Tampa line, which "resulted in the separation of husband and wife in some cases, and it had to be ultimately abandoned as an absolute failure."[17]

For Tampa civic leaders, the possibility of angering Cubans who rode the streetcars was serious. Cigar workers formed a significant portion of riders on a daily basis, and the cigar unions had earlier threatened to boycott the line if their needs were not given due consideration. But, of course, this experiment could not be abandoned; state law now mandated segregation. In some Florida cities, such as Jacksonville, African Americans organized extended and effective boycotts; Hunt was no doubt concerned that such efforts could be sustained much longer in Tampa if supported by immigrants as well as African Americans. Instead, the implementation of segregation in Tampa proved easier than in Jacksonville, suggesting the limits of racial solidarity.

Some Afro-Cubans and African Americans refused to ride the streetcars in summer, 1905, as a protest against second-class seating. Unfortunately, the two groups had little history of cooperation or collective action, limiting their ability to sustain a coalition. Although forced together by racial segregation, most older Afro-Cubans continued to identify as Cubans and to speak Spanish as their primary language; many considered themselves superior to African Americans economically and culturally. At the same time, Afro-Cubans formed less than twenty percent of the city's Cuban population in the early 1900s, and lighter-skinned counterparts were willing, even happy, according to Hunt, to ride the newly segregated cars. Hunt believed that light-skinned Cubans recognized the benefits of being categorized as white and therefore accepted Jim Crow regulation of the streetcars without protest. It is just as likely that Tampa conductors enforced the regulation selectively, assuring fewer protests, at least by Latin riders. For whatever reasons most cigar workers declined to join the boycott, and their absence assured that the strategy would prove ineffective. As long as the vast majority of Cubans and Italians continued to ride, the impact of African Americans and Afro-Cubans not riding was minimized.[18]

The streetcar episode makes clear the difficulty of forging alliances among people of color despite the common ground they seemed to share in the face of native-born white claims of racial superiority. In the Tampa case, however, this cannot be explained simply by pointing to the different ways in which Anglos treated Latins and African Americans, or even by the fact that in some instances Anglos were willing to grant that some Latins were white. There were simply too many cases in which immigrants and African Americans were lumped together, sharing similar modes of rhetorical denigration, legal discrimination, and vigilante justice. Although Anglos claimed attacks against Latin immigrants were justified by labor agitation rather than the violation of social and sexual norms used to rationalize anti-black violence, the effects were similar. Anglo citizens' committees, organized by some of the wealthiest and most powerful men in Tampa, formed in response to the industry-wide cigar strikes that erupted throughout the early twentieth century. The committees threatened and arrested strikers; kidnapped and deported labor organizers; attacked soup kitchens, union halls, and the labor press; and tarred, feathered, and beat labor leaders. In 1910, a bookkeeper was shot and gravely wounded outside a cigar factory during a prolonged strike. Six days later two Italian workers—Angelo Albano and Castenge Ficarrotta—were arrested. While they were being transferred to the jail in West Tampa, the two were taken from sheriff's deputies by a group of twenty to thirty white men. They were discovered a short time later, handcuffed together and hanging from a tree with a sign warning other strikers to take note. As with so many lynchings in the South, no evidence connected the victims to their supposed crime, but the horrific violence perpetrated by native-born whites certainly linked Latin workers to their African American neighbors.[19]

A dozen years earlier, the first race riot in Tampa already suggested that the fates of African Americans and recently arrived immigrants were intertwined. In spring, 1898, thousands of U.S. troops arrived in Tampa, which served as the staging area for American military intervention in Cuba. Both African American and white soldiers encamped in the area, leading to a series of confrontations between army units and local residents and between black and white soldiers. The mixed-race composition of the Cuban independence movement quickly raised concerns among some white civic leaders; according to the *Tampa Tribune,* the "colored infantrymen" had "made themselves very offensive to the people of the city" by "insist[ing] on being treated as white men are treated."[20] Although local Anglos applauded rowdy white troops, including Theodore Roosevelt's Rough Riders, for their martial spirit, they met simple demands for fair treatment by African American soldiers with hostility. Efforts by black troops to order food at a white-owned restaurant, get a shave at a white-owned barbershop, or buy a drink at a white-owned saloon led to refusals, ejections, curses, and physical violence. The sight of black men in uniform simultaneously inspired pride in African American residents and aroused antipathy in white residents and white soldiers.

The mixed-race environs of Ybor City might have provided a haven for black troops, especially because Cuban insurgents had created an explicitly interracial movement to assure Spain's defeat. Unfortunately, white soldiers viewed the ethnic enclave as a playground for themselves, an opportunity to visit bars and brothels with little fear of being reprimanded by local authorities or their own officers. It is not surprising, then, that it was on the streets of Ybor City where Tampa's first race riot erupted. It began on June 6, 1898, when a group of drunken white Ohio volunteers decided to use a two-year-old black boy, most likely an Afro-Cuban, for target practice. Grabbing the boy from his horrified mother on the streets of Ybor City, they handed him back only after a bullet had pierced his small sleeve. In response to this latest injustice, African American soldiers poured into the streets demanding retribution. With pistols drawn, white and black troops wreaked havoc on saloons, cafes, brothels, and other local businesses as they fought each other to a bloody standstill. The riot ended when U.S. forces were hastily loaded onto transport ships for the voyage to Cuba; however, the message to Tampa residents was clear.[21] Whites, whether local or outsiders, viewed as an outrage any attempt by "colored" people—Latin or African American, soldiers or citizens—to claim equality. The people of color, on the other hand, considered themselves partners in the war against Spain and expected their political and military efforts to be rewarded with rights and respect.

It was in the year following the race riot that Latin workers chose a "dusky belle" as their "Queen of Labor" and local authorities began insisting that Cuban residents abide by at least some of the strictures of Jim Crow. It would be another twenty years before Latin and African American residents forged meaningful alliances; even then, it was largely Afro-Cubans, Black Bahamians, and African Americans who found common ground. Lighter-skinned Latins generally remained more flexible in their conceptions of and attitudes toward racial difference than Anglos, but as the failure of the streetcar boycott in 1905 showed, most came to accept Jim Crow customs and laws.[22]

The articles in this volume expand upon the issues and themes raised by the Tampa case. They appear in roughly chronological order and indicate how the differences present in Florida resonated across time and throughout the South and Southwest. Together these authors move the discussion beyond black and white and beyond dichotomous categories more generally. Laura Edwards examines the other side of southern "justice." She explores court-based claims for protection in the heart of the antebellum South and suggests that there was room even here for black and white women to maneuver for control. They could do so, in part, because the boundaries between dependents and patriarchs were in flux, allowing legal understandings of race and gender dichotomies and hierarchies to be challenged. Focusing on extralegal activities of redress, William Carrigan and Clive Webb recast the history of lynching by incorporating western as well as southern Mexican and also African American victims of vigilante violence into their analysis. Sarah Deutsch and Stephanie Cole explore turn-of-the-century Boley, Oklahoma, and Dallas, Texas, respectively, settings with racial dynamics at least as complex as those in South Florida. Finally, Neil Foley traces some of the most significant political implications of the developments discussed in the preceding articles. He demonstrates how the logic of multiracial communities living for more than a century under a biracial order shaped, and distorted, campaigns for Mexican civil rights in the late twentieth century.

In "The People's Sovereignty and the Law," Edwards focuses on the Old South, both geographically and chronologically. She demonstrates the ramifications of upending sharp dichotomies in a place and time that supposedly relied on them so fundamentally. Arguing that racial and gender hierarchies were contested within the legal system even before the eruptions of Civil War and emancipation, Edwards analyzes a series of court cases in antebellum North and South Carolina to suggest the mutability of purportedly fixed relations of power. She then questions the standard concepts that historians have used to understand racial dynamics in the South and claims that scholars "have taken legal categories too literally." On that basis they have assumed that all white men wielded authority over all dependents—slaves, women, children, and employees. Here, too, however, overlapping hierarchies and competing sets of rules and understandings challenged neat distinctions between women and men, blacks and whites, even slaves and free people. This study does not focus on the multiracial diversity or the legacies of Spanish laws and customs that upset the white patriarchal order in Florida and Texas. Rather, Edwards explores contradictions within that order that allowed women, slaves, and other dependents to gain some leverage by positing one authority—the court—against another—individual husbands, owners, and employers.

Edwards traces the new possibilities provided by the legal system back to its incomplete transformation following the American Revolution. Combining British common law with colonial traditions and precedents and new constitutional mandates, Carolina courts both embraced and reinforced tensions between white male household heads and those supposedly dependent on them. Challenging a too-easy reliance on race, class, and gender differences to explain legal battles and their outcomes, Edwards shows how local circumstances shaped the specific dynamics of particular cases. Even a slave-owning male head of household, for instance, could be vulnerable to accusations of wife beating if his holdings were relatively small and his wife's family had sufficient standing. Also, a white man, unable to control a slave woman on loan from his father, might be forced to sue in court to impose his will on her, despite the fact that he supposedly already had "complete" authority over her.

These openings in the legal system were never large enough to endanger seriously white patriarchal authority in the heart of the slave South. Yet the examples illustrate why other disruptions of the existing order posed such severe threats. The legacy of Spanish law and custom in Florida and the Southwest, or the power of the southeastern Indian tribes before and after their removal to Oklahoma, or the challenges to biracialism posed by Cubans, Mexicans, Chinese immigrants, Indians, Italians, and other "others" were layered on top of an established order that was already laced with fractures of various sorts. As "the people" came to occupy the legal position once reserved for the monarch, it was increasingly critical to define precisely which people had access to legal rights and protections.

In "*Muerto por Unos Desconocidos* (Killed by Persons Unknown)," Carrigan and Webb make clear that Mexicans often shared with African

Americans the absence of such rights and protections. Yet the authors are not claiming that Mexican Americans simply need to be added to the existing literature on extralegal violence against blacks, but that the comparative analysis of Mexican or Mexican American and African American cases will transform the historical understanding of both lynching and resistance to it. When whites in the South felt most directly threatened, they turned to brutal forms of racial control, including lynching. A weapon used throughout the South, it was wielded primarily but not solely, against African Americans. As Carrigan and Webb show, the attention to white-on-black violence in the South, for instance, led the principal collectors of lynching statistics to undercount cases in the Southwest and to obscure ethnic differences among nonblack victims by categorizing them all as white. Although individuals from many backgrounds—Italian, Chinese, American Indian, and Anglo American as well as Mexican American and African American—died at the hands of vigilantes, Mexican Americans were the only group to suffer lynching in roughly the same proportion to their population as blacks. By comparing these two groups, scholars can also explore similarities and differences between western "frontier justice" and southern lynching and raise questions about the standard interpretations of each. In addition, this investigation reveals that African Americans and Mexicans challenged extralegal violence in distinct ways: blacks emphasized their rights under the law as U.S. citizens; Mexicans asserted their rights as persons legally recognized as white. As this article suggests, such differences had and have important implications for relations among people of color.

Having mined numerous archives and reports as well as local newspapers throughout the South and Southwest, Carrigan and Webb paint a detailed portrait of the chronology, geography, justification, economics, racial dynamics, and forms of execution that characterized lynching of blacks and Mexicans. They note some key differences between the two sets of cases, including the diplomatic issues raised by those involving Mexicans and the greater focus on alleged crimes of property rather than sexuality in these lynchings. Still, the authors clarify that racism and fear of economic competition played key roles in attacks on both blacks and Mexicans. Despite the shared dangers of vigilante violence, the two groups rarely forged coalitions to address the problem. Indeed, in the late nineteenth and early twentieth century, racial conflict more often characterized relations between Mexicans and African Americans. Members of the former group viewed themselves as white and often as superior to blacks, while African Americans resented the attention given to Mexican victims by a federal government more concerned with cross-border relations than with domestic persecution. The comparative analysis of lynching, then, opens a window on a fundamental problem in southern and American history: what defines an American, and what rights and protections does being an American guarantee?

Stephanie Cole's "Finding Race in Turn-of-the-Century Dallas" offers a fine-grained analysis of the subtle distinctions made by residents of one southern city, as they sought to answer this question. Cole opens her story with a series of telling examples from the 1900 census that illustrate census takers' difficulty in fitting the local populace into the federal government's four official categories: White, Negro, Mongolian, and American Indian. Chinese residents, for instance, were alternately listed as white and Chinese; and despite the so-called "one drop" rule, the daughter of a Chinese father and an African American mother was listed as Chinese. The children of a black woman married to a Mexican, however, were designated black. Despite this seeming confusion of categories, native-born whites in Dallas were determined to draw clear boundaries between themselves and a variety of "others." In the process, those who were clearly not African American but were also not quite white—Mexican Americans, Russian Jews, Asian immigrants—became caught in the high-stakes game of gaining or disclaiming white privilege. As Cole contends, "the flexibility of racial identity worked both for and against" groups living on the racial margins.

As those in power, mostly long-time residents who claimed deep white southern roots, sought to draw definitive lines between whites and non-whites, the impossibility of the task became obvious. As in Tampa, it proved difficult in Dallas to impose Jim Crow regulations on streetcars given the presence of Mexican, Indian, and Chinese riders. The complicated history of the "separate cars" law in Texas suggests the racial self-consciousness of white leaders who sought to implement segregation without offending possible "white" voters. The concerns were largely confined in Dallas to Asian and Mexican residents. Unlike New Orleans and Tampa, where Italians became the victims of vicious lynchings in 1891 and 1910, respectively, European immigrants in Dallas seem to have been readily accepted as thoroughly white. Clearly, then, the issue had more to do with demographics than bloodlines. The relatively small and acculturated Italian community in Dallas posed no threat, and local newspapers discussed the brutal lynching in New Orleans in 1891 in terms of flawed legal procedures rather than racist indignation. Indeed, the *Dallas Morning News* claimed that officials must "maintain safeguards for foreigners as well as themselves."

Attitudes toward Asian immigrants also suggested contradictory impulses. Certainly white Texans absorbed fears of the "yellow peril," but they also demonstrated their fascination with Chinese and Japanese culture. Some of the most fashionable local ladies hosted parties and fund-raisers with "Oriental" themes, while the editor of one of the city's smaller papers voiced his support for Filipino leader Emilio Aguinaldo. Still, such fads among wealthy residents who felt assured of their racial status did not mean that Chinese and Japanese residents could necessarily gain access to the everyday privileges of whiteness, such as equal employment and pay.

Economic success was certainly one way for Asians to claim whiteness. So, too, Mexicans, or rather "Spaniards," could be incorporated into elite circles with sufficient wealth. Russian Jews, too, once established in the city, were recognized as white even though they continued to be noted—in city directories, voluntary associations, and society pages—as Hebrew. For African Americans, however, affluence could not blur the color line, assuring that biracialism would be maintained in practice as well as law. Of course, the apparent immutability of blackness and the use of class to mark race also meant that poorer members of "white" ethnic groups were in danger of slipping over the line by failing to maintain the power and privilege that supposedly defined the race.

By examining one city in detail, Cole reminds us that even as southern whites employed a black and white lens to order their world, they could never fully contain the multiracial amalgam that continually challenged— sometimes overtly, sometimes implicitly—that biracial system. It was not only whites, however, who sought to simplify and control racial dynamics. As African Americans moved west in hopes of gaining economic power and personal autonomy in the late nineteenth century, they too constructed racial hierarchies as a means of gaining status and asserting order.

In "Being American in Boley, Oklahoma," Sarah Deutsch traces the process by which African Americans, Creek Indians, Creek freedmen, and Afro-Creeks negotiated the racial identities and relations in the "black township" of Boley. Locating events there in the context of the Spanish-American War, she suggests the war's importance to developments in the Southwest as well as the Southeast. The war fostered—and was nurtured by—a new imperial culture of colonization that marked a dramatic shift from older notions of territorial incorporation. In this context, concepts of "race," "citizenship," and "manhood" were reconstructed with the critical distinction being drawn between "whites" and "others." The international expositions that were so popular in the late nineteenth and early twentieth century linked southern blacks, frontier Indians, and newly colonized Caribbean and Pacific Islanders in exhibits that claimed to reproduce "native" cultures in their "natural" primitive surroundings. In these sites, whites assumed superiority and maintained seemingly clear definitions of who was white.

In real towns and cities, however, residents from varied racial and ethnic backgrounds faced more complicated situations. Boley, Oklahoma, had been settled in 1903 on land purchased by African Americans from Creek freedmen. Creek freedmen were those of African descent formerly enslaved by the Creek, who held Creek citizenship in 1901 when the federal government alloted Creek lands. As Deutsch shows, there was no easy way to force African Americans, Creek Indians, Creek freedmen and Afro-Creeks into the new system of racial dichotomies. In this case, it was not only whites that sought to impose racial categories on others. Here native-born blacks considered themselves the dominant group and their relations with Creeks echoed in many ways those between African Americans and Afro-Cubans in Tampa. Those who celebrated the "black" township, such as Booker T. Washington, embraced the classic white narrative of the "disappearing Indian," refusing to recognize either the importance of Creeks to Boley's development or the existence of a substantial mixed-race population. At the same time, the Oklahoma Constitution recognized only persons of African descent and whites, thereby offering a white identity to those Creeks without visible African ancestry. Creeks themselves were divided not only by differences in their racial lineage but also by class (measured mainly in landholdings), political affiliation (Union versus Confederate in the Civil War era), and gender. (By the 1890s, Creek men could no longer marry black women, but Creek women could marry black men.) By excavating the multifaceted racial histories of the residents of Boley and tracing them through the town's political and economic struggles in the early twentieth century, Deutsch demonstrates the process by which a rigid biracialism was imposed on and sought to erase a multiracial past. She illustrates as well the ways that Jim Crow became entrenched in the West and the concomitant subjugation of Creek and African American women to the dominant white patriarchal order.

More often included in western than in southern history, Oklahoma was in fact a regional hybrid, created specifically to ease land and racial tensions in the Southeast by providing for Indian resettlement on the frontier. From the beginning, however, the "native" Americans who settled in the "Indian Territory" included people of African ancestry. These settlers also mixed with "whites" of European descent and Mexicans. This racial tapestry was not only evident in the rural landscapes and small towns of Oklahoma but also in the burgeoning cities of Texas. Although much history is still written as though the masses of immigrants who entered the United States in the late nineteenth and early twentieth century avoided the South, studies of Tampa, Miami, New Orleans, Dallas, El Paso, and other cities along what became known as the Sunbelt suggest otherwise.

Tensions and conflicts among white property-owning men over the definition of racial categories and the distribution of rights and protections often created a gap between the stated authority of those in power and their actual ability to rule. Perhaps if all of those who were relatively less powerful had banded together, especially in the late nineteenth century when political, economic, and demographic transformations necessitated change on all sides, white privilege and power could have been thwarted. As these articles demonstrate, however, groups excluded from power do not necessarily see their interests in common. Those that do forge alliances at one moment may not be able to sustain them as circumstances change. Creek Indians, African Americans, and Afro-Creeks created some of the strongest bonds across barriers of race in the nineteenth century United States. Yet amid the shifting political and economic struggles of the early twentieth century, the links were broken, or crushed. Jim Crow laws created the potential for collective action among all those considered nonwhite, yet only rarely did Cubans, Mexicans, Asians, or other immigrants join protests against these racist regulations. Mexican Americans and African Americans, both facing mob violence, developed different—sometimes competing—strategies of resistance. White women and slaves, equally dependent under the law on white male heads of households, most often fought their battles on different terms and with different chances of success.

In "Partly Colored or Other White," Neil Foley traces the implications of these earlier patterns of thwarted cross-racial alliances into the present. Documenting the growing importance of Latinos in the United States—demographically, economically, and politically—he demonstrates the way that "the black-white binary stubbornly continues to shape thinking about the racial place and space of Latinos in the United States." He then explores how the persistence of biracialism shaped, and distorted, Mexican American civil rights struggles in the last half of the twentieth century. From the Treaty of Guadalupe Hidalgo in 1848 on, Mexicans were eligible to become U.S. citizens and, at least from the Mexican perspective, were recognized as white. In embracing Louisiana lawmakers' definition of blackness, the *Plessy* v. *Ferguson* decision of 1896 accepted Mexican Americans' whiteness. As noted above, Texas laws that mandated segregation differentiated only between whites and those of African ancestry. Foley explores how this "long history of black-white racial thinking has not only impinged upon the freedom of Mexican Americans and other Latinos, but it has also stifled the ability of all Americans to reconsider and reconfigure racial discourses in new and productive ways."

Beginning in the 1930s, Mexican American civil rights activists fought their second-class status by emphasizing their whiteness and stressing the importance of assimilation. This set them at odds with African American activists, who argued for justice and equality based on their uniquely American heritage, which they believed should negate differences of race. Responding in part to the immigration restriction debates of the 1920s and the insertion of the category "Mexican" in the 1930 federal census, middle-class, urban Mexican Americans forged a distinct identity and formed organizations to protest de facto discrimination. In El Paso, for instance, members of the League of United Latin American Citizens successfully challenged efforts to register the births and deaths of Mexican-descent residents as "colored" rather than "white." Other actions were directed at the U.S. Treasury Department when it requested that applicants for social security cards who were not "white" or "Negro" write in their "color or race" and used as examples "Mexican, Chinese, Japanese, Indian, Filipino, etc." In protesting this debasement of their racial heritage, Mexican American civil rights activists accepted the notion that "colored" people were inferior and sought to secure their own rights by maintaining their whiteness.

Foley's piece carries forward questions about citizenship highlighted by Carrigan and Webb and by Edwards. For Foley, Mexican American assertions of whiteness were tied in part to the ambiguities that continued to surround their nationality into the twentieth century. Whereas African Americans were clearly U.S. citizens, Mexican Americans, whether or not they were born in the United States, were, and still are, often perceived as foreigners. The fact that most Anglo Americans identified Mexican Americans with illegal aliens, "wetbacks," and the poor more generally nurtured concerns among affluent Hispanics about the dangers of slipping into nonwhite categories. This largely forestalled the building of coalitions with those groups who were denied white racial status: African Americans, Asian Americans, and Native Americans, the last especially relevant because so many Mexican Americans historically intermarried with Indians in the Southwest. In the post–World War II era, when civil rights itself became closely identified with blacks, some Mexican Americans, such as those in the American GI Forum, refused to use the term for their own efforts at achieving first-class citizenship. By tracing civil rights cases brought to state and federal courts by Mexican Americans in the 1950s, Foley demonstrates the distinct logic of a group that could claim whiteness to challenge discrimination in schools, courts, and other public institutions. Yet he also laments the opportunities thus lost to define a "transnational multi-racial identity that acknowledges the Indian and African heritage of Latinos."

Despite the continued power of the black-white binary in American and southern history, the following chapters demonstrate the limits of such dichotomous categories. Clearly there has been extensive racial mixing among a variety of supposedly distinct groups—African Americans, Mexican Americans, Native Americans, Asian Americans, and Euro-Americans. Yet by distributing rights and resources according to a rigid biracialism, "whites" in power have been able to sustain their privileges and to nurture internecine struggles among all those categorized as "others." By accepting culturally constructed categories of racial identification as "real," many historians, often inadvertently, helped to obscure the complex and tumultuous relations that defined race in America. Certainly other scholars, reaching back to Barbara Fields and forward to the authors included here, have now examined the process by which diverse peoples were forced into bifurcated racial categories. Many of these researchers built on the work of Winthrop Jordan and others, whose intimate explorations of slavery in America revealed the ethnic and linguistic differences among those Africans and Afro-Caribbeans who forged an African American culture.[23]

Too often, however, southern historians have been reluctant to move beyond black and white. They have feared, sometimes with good reason, that muting these categories might obscure our understanding of their power to fuel the most brutal forms of oppression and the most exhilarating models of resistance in the region. This volume makes clear that biracialism distorted as well as shaped the South's past and challenges us to unravel the complex racial legacies that molded the region's history and continue to influence its development. Today we are faced with new and powerful dichotomies: evil terrorists versus innocent victims, Muslim fundamentalists versus Christians and secular humanists, American democracy versus anti-American tyranny. We will remain hostage to the political and social constraints imposed by such bifurcated categories until we acknowledge and embrace the transnational and multiracial character of our own past. *Beyond Black and White* contributes to that critical process.

Notes

1. Barbara J. Fields, "Ideology and Race in American History," in *Region, Race, and Reconstruction: Essays in Honor of C. Vann Woodward*, ed. by J. Morgan Kousser and James MacPherson (New York: Oxford University Press, 1982), pp. 143–77.

2. Gary Nash, "The Hidden History of Mestizo America," *Journal of American History* 82 (1995): 941–64; Peggy Pascoe, "Miscegenation Law, Court Cases, and Ideologies of 'Race' in Twentieth-Century America," *Journal of American History* 83(June, 1996): 44–69; Martha Hodes, *White Women, Black Men: Illicit Sex in the Nineteenth-century South* (New Haven, Conn.: Yale University Press, 1997); James Barrett and David Roediger, "Inbetween Peoples: Race, Nationality and the New Immigrant Working Class," *Journal of American Ethnic History* 16 (Spring, 1997):3–44; Kirsten Fischer, *Suspect Relations: Sex, Race, and Resistance in Colonial North Carolina* (Ithaca, N.Y.: Cornell University Press, 2002); and Neil Foley, *The White Scourge: Mexicans, Blacks, and Poor Whites in Texas Cotton Culture* (Berkeley: University of California Press, 1997). Work by scholars in women's studies—especially by Chicana feminists—American studies, and cultural studies has been critical in shaping many of these historical analyses.

3. Geraldine Pratt, "Spatial Metaphors and Speaking Positions," *Environment and Planning D: Society and Space* 10 (June, 1992): 243–44.

4. Martha Hodes, ed., *Sex, Love, Race: Crossing Boundaries in North American History* (New York: New York University Press, 1999).

5. See, especially, Kirsten Fischer, *Suspect Relations*; Neil Foley, *White Scourge*; Sarah Deutsch, *No Separate Refuge: Culture, Class, and Gender on an Anglo-Hispanic Frontier in the American Southwest, 1880–1940* (New York: Oxford University Press, 1987); Claudio Saunt, *A New Order of Things: Property, Power, and the Transformation of the Creek Indians, 1733–1816* (Cambridge: Cambridge University Press, 1999); and Nancy Hewitt, *Southern Discomfort: Women's Activism in Tampa, Florida, 1880s–1920s* (Urbana: University of Illinois Press, 2001). There is, in addition, a large and growing literature on Native Americans and on Mexican Americans, Chicano/as, Latino/as, and Hispanics, reaching back to the sixteenth century and up to the present, that implicitly challenges the idea of North America or the United States as biracial at any time in its history.

6. Jane L. Landers, *Black Society in Spanish Florida* (Urbana: University of Illinois Press, 1999), p. 2. For material in rest of paragraph, see also Larry E. Rivers, *Slavery in Florida: Territorial Days to Emancipation* (Gainesville: University Press of Florida, 2000), chapter 1.

7. Kenneth Wiggins Porter, "Florida Slaves and the Free Negroes in the Seminole War, 1835–1842," *Journal of Negro History* 28 (1943): 390–421; Rivers, *Slavery in Florida*, chapters 8–10.

8. Quintard Taylor, *In Search of the Racial Frontier: African Americans in the American West, 1528–1990* (New York: W. W. Norton, 1998), pp. 60–66, quote, 61.

9. Jane Landers, "'In Consideration of Her Enormous Crime': Rape and Infanticide in Spanish St. Augustine," in *The Devil's Lane: Sex and Race in the Early South*, ed. by Catherine Clinton and Michele Gillespie (New York: Oxford University Press, 1997), pp. 205–17.

10. Virginia Meacham Gould, "'A Chaos of Iniquity and Discord': Slave and Free Women of Color in the Spanish Ports of New Orleans, Mobile, and Pensacola," in *The Devil's Lane*, ed. by Clinton and Gillespie, pp. 232–46.

11. See, for instance, Jerrell H. Shofner, *Nor Is It Over Yet: Florida in the Era of Reconstruction, 1863–1877* (Gainesville: University Presses of Florida, 1974), and J. Morgan Kousser, *The Shaping of Southern Politics: Suffrage Restriction and the Establishment of the One-Party South, 1880–1910* (New Haven: Yale University Press, 1974), especially pp. 91–103.

12. "Latin," rather than "Latino," was the preferred term in Tampa, and in much of the coun-

try throughout the late nineteenth and early twentieth century. For example, Rudolf Valentino, the "Latin Lover," suggests this popular understanding of the term. Later in the twentieth century, especially in the Southwest, the term Latino or Chicano was more widely used.

13. Gary Mormino and George Pozzetta, *The Immigrant World of Ybor City: Italians and Their Latin Neighbors in Tampa, 1885–1985* (Urbana: University of Illinois Press, 1987), especially pp. 55–57.

14. *Cigar Makers' Official Journal,* Nov., 1900. On labor agitation and anti-labor violence in Tampa, see Robert P. Ingalls, *Urban Vigilantes in the New South: Tampa, 1882–1936* (Knoxville: University of Tennessee Press, 1988).

15. *Tampa Morning Tribune,* Sept. 5, 1899. For a thorough discussion of this incident, see Hewitt, *Southern Discomfort,* chapter 4.

16. On this division, which many white Cubans accepted without protest, see Susan Greenbaum, *The Afro-Cubans of Ybor City: A Centennial History* (Tampa: Tampa Printing Co., 1986), p. 7.

17. H. H. Hunt to Stone and Webster, July 17, 1905, and July 11, 1904, George J. Baldwin Papers, #850, Southern Historical Collection, Wilson Library, University of North Carolina, Chapel Hill.

18. For a detailed discussion of this episode, see Hewitt, *Southern Discomfort,* chapter 5. On African American and Afro-Cuban relations more generally, see Nancy Raquel Mirabal, "Telling Silences and Making Community: Afro-Cubans and African Americans in Ybor City and Tampa, 1899–1915," in *Races and Empire: African-Americans and Cubans before the Cuban Revolution,* ed. by Lisa Brock and Digna Castañeda Fuertes (Philadelphia: Temple University Press, 1998), pp. 49–69.

19. See Ingalls, *Urban Vigilantes,* especially pp. 95–97, on lynching.

20. Quoted in Willard Gatewood, "Negro Troops in Florida, 1898," *Florida Historical Quarterly* 49 (July, 1970): 3–4. On these racial confrontations more generally, see Hewitt, *Southern Discomfort,* chapter 4.

21. Gatewood, "Negro Troops in Florida," pp. 8–10; *Tampa Morning Tribune,* June 8, 1898; and Hewitt, *Southern Discomfort,* pp. 108–11.

22. Nancy A. Hewitt, "Becoming Black: Creating a Shared Identity among African Americans and Afro-Cubans in Tampa, Florida, 1880s–1920s," in *Black Women's History at the Intersection of Knowledge and Power: ABWH's Twentieth Anniversary Anthology,* ed. by Rosalyn Terborg-Penn and Janice Sumler-Edmond (Acton, Mass: Tapestry Press Ltd., 2000), pp. 101–13; and Mirabal, "Telling Silences and Making Community."

23. Winthrop Jordan, *White Over Black: American Attitudes toward the Negro, 1550–1812* (Chapel Hill: University of North Carolina Press, 1968).

Beyond Black and White

CHAPTER 1

The People's Sovereignty and the Law

Defining Gender, Race, and Class Differences
in the Antebellum South

LAURA F. EDWARDS

M ost historians of the Old South begin their analyses assuming the presence of a black-white binary. To the extent that racial multiplicity enters into the historiography, it is linked with geography and the national incorporation of western territories. The multiracial societies that characterized the Old Southwest—Louisiana, Mississippi, Alabama, and western Tennessee and Georgia—soon disappeared as white, U.S. settlers flooded in, dragging their slaves, their racial practices, and their political institutions behind them. By extension, racial multiplicity disappeared in southern states along the eastern seaboard long before the Revolution's first shots were fired. All that, to a certain extent, is true. Between the Revolution and emancipation, lawmakers in the Old South states did fortify existing binary differences between slave and free, black and white, drawing on equally polarized conceptions of gender and class in the process. This process, however, reveals as much about the inherent instability of these binary categories as it does about their entrenchment in the culture and institutions of these states. In the very places that supposedly provided the racial blueprint for the rest of the nation, at the very moment when that racial structure seemed the most stable, it was not. Indeed, the historiographical tendency to focus on definitive statements of binary racial categories in law and by the region's elite commentators tends to obscure the process that necessitated them in the first place. There is perhaps no better way to begin to understand these dynamics than through the stories of two women who became enmeshed in legal cases that defy historiographical assumptions based on oppositional conceptions of race, gender, and class.

In 1824, Sarah Chandler swore out a complaint against her husband. One of the magistrates in Granville County, North Carolina, listened to her story and then issued a peace warrant. Sarah Chandler, he wrote, "is afraid that Thomas Chandler . . . will beat, wound, maim, kill or do her some bodily hurt." The magistrate omitted the details, but Sarah described the incident at length in a divorce petition the following year. Her husband, she claimed, "beat her first with a bridle and large green corn stalk in the yard where all the family were about except two of the children . . . he then drove her and the children into the house which he nailed up on the inside when he struck her several times violently with a hammer after he had tormented her for a considerable time and declared with dreadful implications that he would kill her." Then "he turned her children out; when he had her alone he compelled her [to] strip off her clothes except her shift and with hot tongs punched her flesh." Thomas Chandler posted bond, but he failed to "keep the peace towards Sarah" and the "good citizens" of the state of North Carolina as he had promised to do. The following month, Sarah swore out another complaint. This time the magistrate charged her husband with assault and battery. Unable to give bond, Thomas Chandler was jailed. One year later, the court granted her a full divorce on the basis of her husband's abuse.[1]

Thirty years later in Spartanburg District, South Carolina, Thomas Burgess brought assault charges against Violet, a slave of his father's who was on loan to him. Violet, as one of the Burgess daughters later testified, "generally done as she pleased." Polly Burgess, Thomas's wife and Violet's new mistress, decided to change that: "I ordered her to go off about her own bissness [sic] or I would strike her and she come at me." In response, Polly Burgess "struck" Violet. "But," Polly continued, "the slave took the weapon out [my] hand and knocked [me] down and struck [me] again, when the girls lifted me up [she] struck me again, [she] struck Mr. T[homas] Burgess when he attempted to secure me, he called on the girls to assist and tied [her]. . . . I never whipped her before, I struck her onst [sic] before with a switch for her saucy talk . . . the girl thought she was an eaqual [sic]." Although Thomas Burgess whipped Violet and tied her down, Violet untied her bonds, left, and stayed away for a few days before she came back. Defeated, Thomas Burgess filed charges, hoping that the court system would succeed where he had failed. Convicted of assault, Violet was sentenced to fifty lashes at the public whipping post.[2]

These two cases seem completely backward. Legal officials in the antebellum South were not supposed to prosecute white men for disciplining their wives. The law was supposed to support their authority over all their dependents. Yet neither were white men supposed to need the law to excercise that authority, particularly in disciplining their own slaves. They were supposed to do that themselves.

So what do these cases say about the Old South? One answer is nothing. Most white men did not find themselves in these circumstances. Therefore, the few who did might be exceptions that proved the rule. Conventional historical wisdom, which emphasizes the authority that white men held over all domestic dependents and the race, class, and gender differences that supported their power, would suggest such a reading. By disciplining one patriarch who abused his power and stepping in to uphold power of another the courts actually affirmed existing relations. From this perspective, Sarah Chandler's and Violet's cases would be only extraordinary incidents that say nothing new about southern society generally.

The other answer, and the one this chapter will explore, is that these two cases and others like them in North and South Carolina between 1787 and 1840 say a great deal about the antebellum South. They did not form the majority of cases on court dockets. Nor did the specific conflicts typify social relations. Still, these cases are representative of power relations in southern society at this time. Specifically, they show that racial, gender, and class differences were not as fixed or as polarized as historians now assume.

The Revolution exposed profound contradictions in the legal definition of authority and difference. By replacing the sovereignty of the king with the sovereignty of "the people" and thereby elevating former subjects to the place previously occupied by the king, these changes carried the potential to increase "the people's" authority and legal discretion. These changes also opened up the possibility that "the people" might include *all* former subjects, recasting the significance of gender, race, and class differences. Even domestic dependents—white women, slaves, and children—might be able to claim the full range of civil rights as part of "the people." That, of course, did not happen. The extended individual sovereignty ultimately used differences of race, class, and gender to distinguish between those who could be full members of the polity and all those who could not. Recognition of white, propertied men's sovereignty actually increased their relative authority over their domestic dependents, who remained subjects because of their race, class, and gender.

That outcome, however, emerged slowly, in a fitful dialog with other elements of the law that are not usually associated with either Revolutionary ideology or democratic change. After the Revolution, southern states continued to rely on common law rules that had developed within the English monarchical system. One important strand of common law treated *everyone* as subordinate subjects of the sovereign king. In their application during the colonial period, these legal rules had upheld the authority of propertied white men. They did this so effectively that many men at that time assumed that they held this power in their own right. But in the theoretical logic that structured these legal rules, white men also were subjects, who exercised their power at the king's behest. Other subjects could make claims on the king's power as well, demanding protection even from their own heads of household. Of course, that theoretical option was irregularly allowed in practice, particularly in the colonial South. It rarely applied to slaves, who were denied the status of subjects by colonial legal officials.[3] Yet the possibility remained within existing legal practice, and it played a key role in shaping the handling of many different kinds of cases after the Revolution. The operation of common law in the lower courts emphasized other kinds of differences than those that emerged from Revolutionary ideology. The major line of differentiation was between household head and domestic dependent, but those two groups were not categorized in binary terms: they were still similar in the sense that both were also subjects. So even as common law upheld the authority of white propertied men, it also could undercut it by treating them as subjects and accentuating their similarities to those they also ruled. The rigidly hierarchical elements of common law logic thus had unexpected, potentially radical implications when they were applied within the particular context of the post-Revolutionary South.

These conflicting tendencies existed in constant tension. New forms of governance reinforced old hierarchies of power, just as old legal rules accentuated new political possibilities. This dynamic cautions against easy, linear generalizations about change over time. Consequently, this chapter does not try to determine whether gender, race, and class differences became more or less meaningful in this period or whether the power differential between white propertied men and domestic dependents increased or decreased as a result. Focusing on local and state court records in North and South Carolina in the years 1787 through 1840, it explores the contradictory results of change. In so doing, it also questions the emphasis on oppositional conceptions of gender, race, and class differences that drives so much of the recent historiography as well as the related presumption that those binaries explain inequality. As this paper argues, the construction and meaning of these particular differences were far more historically specific and politically contingent than historians have heretofore imagined. Nor did these differences constitute the whole story, particularly at this time and place in history. If anything, historians need to be far more careful about the analytical reliance on binary constructions of gender, race, and class differences, because they can obscure as much about power relations as they reveal.

Difference, Power, and the Historiography of the Antebellum South

The historiography of the Old South relies heavily on dichotomous categories of difference to explain the operation of power. Traditionally, southern historians have emphasized race and class in these terms. Within this framework, for instance, historians might explain Sarah Chandler's case in terms of oppositional differences based in class among white men. Although

Thomas Chandler owned land and a few slaves, his position did not compare with that of the substantial slaveholders who ran the county. His marginality, then, disposed court officials to charge him with assault and, later, to grant his wife a divorce. Thomas did not have the class status necessary to protect him. Had he been more prominent, the court never would have dared to question his authority.[4]

For Violet, historians would point to racial and class differences, contructed in binary terms, to explain both the denial of full citizenship rights to African Americans and the development of a strong culture of resistance within the slave community. The racial ideology of the time characterized African Americans as inherently inferior and incapable of self-governance. As such, it fell to white slaveholders to direct their labor and to keep them from becoming a danger to the larger community. Such a view not only justified the Burgesses' violence but even obligated them to use it. They were justified because there was no other way to return Violet to her "natural" position of subordination. They were obligated, because, if unchecked, her unruly behavior established a dangerous example that threatened all masters' authority. The jury of slaveholders who heard the case had a vested interest in upholding the social order based on these racial and class differences. By convicting Violet and then sentencing her to a severe public whipping, the court punished Violet and set an example for other slaves in the area.[5]

Yet, as historians who focus on slave culture would point out, Violet's punishment did not necessarily convey the lesson that slaveholders intended, because dichotomies of race and class differences also created a separate culture in the slave quarters. Violet, like other slaves in the antebellum South, lived within strong communities that encouraged slaves to pursue their own goals. Violet, for instance, had clearly worked around the slave system with some success before the fight with the Burgesses. As one of the Burgess daughters testified, Violet "generally done as she pleased." More than that, Violet acted as if "she was an eaqual." Of course, the Burgesses likely exaggerated Violet's unruliness to make their case stronger in court. Even so, their characterization of Violet carries a grain of truth. The fight began because Polly Burgess tried to exert more control than usual over Violet, ordering her to "go off about her own bissness"—to do, in other words, her assigned chores. It was because Violet refused the order that Polly Burgess struck her. Then Violet fought to defend herself. Afterward, she ran away, still refusing to submit. Violet's actions were not unusual. As the scholarship on slavery indicates, the culture of the slave quarters supported such resistance; masters failed to eradicate it; and the resulting tensions framed relations between masters and slaves.[6]

Recent work on gender has taken issue with traditional scholarship, arguing that it oversimplifies by focusing on certain differences and excluding others. Above all, these historians argue that the scholarship has ignored gender difference, cast in binary terms as the authority that propertied, white men wielded as *men* over all women. Although highlighting gender, these historians combine it with racial and class differences in a single analytical lens. The racial and class position of white men was linked to their gendered position as heads of household with authority over a range of dependents—white women and children as well as slaves. Marriage and slavery were analogous institutions that grounded the South's social and political relations. White women, according to this logic, belonged within households as wives, just as African Americans belonged within households as slaves. Although bound by responsibilities, wives and slaves could demand—at least in theory—maintenance and protection from their husbands and masters. Their claims then became the domestic duties of their husbands and masters, who acquired full civil and political rights to fulfill their domestic obligations. The South's governing institutions did more than uphold that authority; they were built around it.[7]

Although the immediate focus has been on gender, racial, and class differences, framed in oppositional terms, another important implication of this work lies in the similarities among parts of southern society previously presumed to be unrelated. Perhaps most important is the connection between private households and public governing structures. Earlier scholarship drew a sharp line between private and public, emphasizing either the consequences of racial and class differences in public arenas or the efforts of slaves and white women to construct meaningful relations in their own lives despite their powerlessness within the larger society. As we have seen, this work would look to differences in the class standing among white men to explain Thomas Chandler's inability to advance his interests in public, legal forums. Similarly, such scholarship would emphasize either Violet's inability to claim rights in public arenas controlled by whites or the ways that the slave community nurtured her sense of independence despite her inability to realize it. By contrast, the work on gender posits a dynamic connection between private households and the public order, showing how difference and inequality *within* households reveal a good deal about southern society.[8]

At the same time, the new work on gender also highlights similarities among various groups of domestic dependents. Slaves were obviously in a far different position than wives, both in terms of their legal rights and their actual social conditions. However, the legal logic underlying the two groups' subordination was similar. Those similarities are most evident in extreme incidents of domestic violence, such as the violence that Sarah Chandler experienced. Even when husbands turned physically abusive, most southern courts refused to intervene. Instead, they stood by the common law "rule of thumb" that allowed husbands to beat their wives as long as the instrument used was not larger in diameter than an average man's thumb. Even when husbands breached that rule, higher courts routinely gave them broad disciplinary discretion.[9]

Why? Because much more was at stake than a wife's pain or an individual man's personal affairs. Questioning a household head's domestic authority, even in its most sadistic forms, challenged the foundations of the entire social edifice. That logic held true for wives as well as slaves, because slavery and marriage were linked in the logic of the South's governing structures. To allow wives redress against their husbands would open up the possibility of allowing the same for slaves. Acknowledging conflicts within households, moreover, would imply that wives and slaves had interests separate from and even in conflict with their husbands and masters. Admitting that would then undermine the legal logic that subsumed domestic dependents' interests within those of their household heads, that gave household heads public rights as the representatives of their dependents, and that denied domestic dependents rights in their own names. Even if Sarah Chandler's physical wounds outraged and repelled public officials, they—at least in their minds—could not acknowledge them without inflicting great damage on the public body.[10]

Yet the reliance on a binary construction of gender difference ultimately limits this scholarship's explanatory power. By revealing connections between households and the state, the work on gender does trace the actions of domestic dependents, like Violet and Sarah Chandler, into the larger social order. But this work then assumes that preexisting, oppositional, racial, class, and gender differences defined power relations there. Where household heads had public power, domestic dependents did not. They were, by definition, unable to participate in the existing social order in any substantive way, although they clearly were connected to it and often disruptive of it. We thus are left with a long line of defiant, disorderly folks who continually were crushed under the inevitable affirmation of patriarchal power. If anything, the actions of these people seem utterly futile, because they always failed to produce any noticeable change in the existing order. Violet's heroic struggle only reinforced the subordination of all slaves. Sarah Chandler released herself from a bad marriage without producing any change in the power relations between husbands and wives generally. The conclusions are similar to those in work that does not use gender as an analytical tool: propertied white men in this period had the power to shape the social order because of who they were and what they had; everyone else did not, because of who they were and what they did not have.

But if binary constructions of racial, class, and gender differences defined power relations in this way, Violet's and Sarah Chandler's cases would not exist. Given the unlikelihood for success, it is surprising that they and others like them bothered to assert themselves at all. Yet they did. Why? Why did Sarah Chandler ever think she could file charges against her husband or obtain a divorce based on his abuse? Why could Violet do "as she pleased" up until the point she was convicted in court? In fact, given her actions, Violet seems to have thought she might continue to do "as she pleased." Why else would she make such a bold stand? Thomas Burgess apparently feared as much himself. Why else would he call in the law to help discipline her?

Sarah Chandler's and Violet's cases only make sense if we push beyond differences cast in binary terms. Binaries alone do not explain either the relations between white, male household heads and their domestic dependents or the relative power that any of these groups wielded in the larger society. In fact, the oppositional definitions of racial, class, and gender differences articulated so clearly and so forcefully in some legal matters were just one trajectory of legal theory and practice in the post-Revolutionary era. Although distinctions among white, propertied men, white women, and enslaved men and women had long been important features in the South's social landscape, the *meaning* and *operation* of those differences had to be re-explained and redefined to fit within new, post-Revolutionary systems of governance. That process took several decades to accomplish, and, even then, other legal principles and practices continued to contradict the logic of those decisions. In these cases, similarities were as important as differences in adjudicating conflicts. Nowhere was this more evident than in the laws governing violence.

New Changes, Old Patterns

One implication of locating sovereignty in "the people," was to enhance male household heads' legal discretion, particularly over their dependents. Common law rules governing violence, as they had developed in the eighteenth century, presumed that all people were subjects of the king, whose sovereign body represented the public order. No violent act became a "public wrong"—a criminal matter that threatened the public order—unless it injured the king's metaphorical body, by breaking the peace of his realm. By contrast, injuries done to individuals' bodies were "private wrongs"—civil matters involving conflicts between individuals that did not necessarily involve the public interest. As Robert Kitchin explained in his seventeenth-century legal treatise, assaults had to involve bloodshed to rise to the status of criminal matters. The seriousness of the crime had less to do with the injury to the individual than the harm done to the king's metaphorical body. Only if "the King's people were disturbed," Kitchin wrote, did the assaults become "more than particular" matters. The same logic led Sir William

Blackstone to place assault under the category of "private wrongs" in his mid-eighteenth-century codification of English common law. Blackstone qualified this categorization, noting that assaults "savour something of the criminal kind, being always attended with some violation of the peace; for which, in strictness of law a fine ought to be paid to the king, as well as private satisfaction to the party injured." By this logic, assault had distinct but related civil and criminal components. The civil offense was the injury done to the private individual. The criminal offense was the disturbance of the public order.[11]

Of course, legal practice did not always follow legal theory. This disjuncture actually constituted a central, accepted feature of common law, which was intended to be flexible enough to allow for differences in local customs. Colonial southerners, who were a litigious lot when given the opportunity, routinely filed charges when they were physically threatened or injured. Legal officials then determined whether incidences of violence were serious enough to constitute a public threat on a case-by-case basis. Assault cases thus appear in the colonial records as either civil or criminal matters or both. The results defy easy categorization, as legal historians who have studied these cases all note with considerable frustration. They are probably best explained by specific local concerns and conditions that went unrecorded and are now lost to historians.[12] Yet it is likely that magistrates considered a number of factors, including social status and personal reputation as well as the race, class, and gender of those involved, in determining whether to make violent acts criminal. A habitual rabble-rouser who inflicted random violence was different from an otherwise upstanding citizen who happened to lose his temper with a particularly obstreperous neighbor. A husband who beat his wife overstepped his acknowledged authority, whereas a wife who beat her husband or even defended herself from him exercised power that was not rightfully hers.[13]

Regardless of these individual peculiarities, the legal logic that applied to household heads and dependents in cases of violence was similar in the sense that their injuries were not the basis of criminal charges. Both groups were subjects. Dependents could claim the king's protection, because their household heads exercised authority at the king's behest. If they did so improperly, they could be disciplined. This legal logic, for instance, guided Sarah Chandler's assault case against her husband, although in her case the state's interests were defined as those of "the people" and not the king. The local magistrate considered her injuries serious enough to qualify as a public threat. Her suffering, alone, was not the basis of the criminal charge. It was the injury to the public order that mattered legally. Still, Sarah Chandler had room to pursue her own interests. As a subject under the state's protection, she could mobilize the law to address her problematic domestic circumstances. The state could intervene because her husband was also a subject. As such, his authority was conditional, granted to him at the state's behest in the interest of the larger public order. He did not exercise it unconditionally in his own right.

Yet, at the same time, existing laws and their application took on new meanings after the Revolution. It was not so much the laws or even people's actions that changed. Rather, because the political context was so different, the logic underpinning those laws had different implications for the routine legal handling of violence and the public status of those involved. After the Revolution, "the people" replaced the king as sovereign members of the polity. Now that their bodies made up the body politic, their physical injuries were, in theory, "public wrongs." What followed was a slow but dramatic evolution in the actual legal treatment of violence, as officials began to place "the people" in the legal position formally occupied by the king.

The effects rippled slowly through the legal system, cropping up unexpectedly as particular cases revealed both divergences and convergences between common law practices and Revolutionary political ideals. Reconciling the two occupied North and South Carolina's legislatures and state appellate courts well into the nineteenth century. In cases of violence, state courts began categorizing a wider range of violent acts as criminal matters. Most significantly, the emphasis on the public order as the basis of the offense receded. Instead, it was the injury to the individual that defined the criminal charge.[14]

The fact that "the people" remained undefined in the states' governing documents opened up the possibility that wives and slaves were included among "the people." Legislatures and state courts, for instance, sometimes leaned in this direction as they tried to define "the people" and which rights applied to which groups of people. Both North and South Carolina, for instance, repealed petty treason, which likened a wife's murder of her husband to the murder of the king. Of course, that particular offense had fallen out of use anyway. Its logic—which elevated a particular kind of murder over other kinds based on an analogy that blatantly replicated power relations under a monarchical regime—no longer made sense in a country built around the sovereignty of "the people." The same issues shaped cases involving slavery. They were particularly pronounced in North Carolina, where the state applied the common law to slaves. Instead of enacting a code that specifically outlined slaves' status, the state appellate court adapted the rules governing domestic dependents to slaves on a case-by-case basis. Doing so opened a series of troubling questions, because the common law positioned slaves as subjects, who could claim certain rights from the state. For instance, did the right to trial by jury, longstanding in common law and recently enumerated in the state's bill of rights, extend to them? Could slaves claim the common law right to self-defense? Did a master's discipline ever become murder, as it did for other domestic dependents? That, combined with natural rights philosophy so central to Revolutionary rhetoric, led some judges to apply a more generous definition of common law rights to slaves and even to consider granting them constitutionally defined rights.[15]

Nevertheless, decisions in other cases undercut these possibilities by clearly differentiating all domestic dependents from white, propertied men.[16] In cases of violence, for instance, state courts limited the extent to which domestic dependents' injuries qualified as public crimes. Certainly, in practice, judges had always done that, but they had done so without disturbing the logic that characterized everyone as subjects and that made the power of male household heads conditional. Now judges began refusing domestic dependents legal protection on the basis that the sovereignty of a household head placed all his actions toward his dependents beyond legal question. The disruptive, public effects of a household head's violent actions no longer mattered. Instead, judges presumed that these men, by definition, *always* acted in the interests of their dependents and the public. Even when "discipline" resulted in death, higher courts routinely struck down convictions. Although this trend is best documented for slaves, the same logic held for wives as well. After Alvin Preslar beat his wife, for instance, she sought shelter at her father's house. She never made it. On the way, she stopped to rest. The next morning, she was dead. The prosecution argued that Preslar was responsible: his actions, beating his wife and then forcing her out of the house to suffer the elements, directly caused her death. The North Carolina Supreme Court disagreed. Alvin Preslar's actions did not end his wife's life or even endanger it. To the contrary, she was in no immediate danger when she left the house. Nor did her decision to leave indicate any immediate danger. If anything, her actions suggested her general refusal to submit to his authority. Alvin Preslar was simply exercising his disciplinary rights within the bounds of moderation. The court, therefore, would not intervene to punish him.[17]

The courts also extended these principles to cases where the parties were not in the same household. The higher courts considered white women's and African Americans' disobedience, verbal insults, and even defiant gestures sufficient to provoke violence from all white men. These actions were legally considered "violence," similar to a drawn knife or a direct blow, in the sense that they allowed white men to defend themselves using physical force without bearing criminal responsibility for their acts. Such was the experience of Mrs. Allison. Her husband and a man named Roberts were gambling at the Allisons' house. For some unknown reason, Mrs. Allison ordered Roberts to leave. Perhaps she was intervening in an argument between the two men. Perhaps she had tired of her husband's gambling away the family resources. Perhaps they were just in her way. Whatever the reason, Mrs. Allison threw water on Roberts and then knocked off his hat, a symbolic offense to his honor and, admittedly, a rather gutsy move on Mrs. Allison's part. In response, Roberts whacked her with a rifle, knocking her to the ground. Mrs. Allison's husband then advanced on Roberts and, in the ensuing fight, was killed. The Supreme Court of North Carolina, however, refused to charge Roberts with murder, because Mrs. Allison "certainly commenced" the fight "by her rudeness." None of Mrs. Allison's actions would have constituted legal provocation had she been a man. Because she was a woman, though, "rudeness" alone was sufficient justification for Roberts's assault on her and, ultimately, his murder of her husband.[18]

These rulings, by implication, gave white men more latitude in using violence, particularly against those who were supposed to be domestic dependents. They cast almost any assertive act of an injured dependent as malicious provocation that justified violence—even deadly violence—from a white man. Mrs. Preslar's efforts to escape her husband's abuse became legal evidence of her lack of wifely submission. Mrs. Allison's efforts to get a disruptive man off her property opened the door for legally justified violence. If a household head or even if another white man used force, it was the domestic dependent's fault for pushing him over the edge.[19]

The legal handling of violence at the local level followed changes at the state level in key respects. By the turn of the nineteenth century, assault cases involving all free people began appearing in local courts as criminal matters only. Local officials effectively consolidated the civil and criminal component of assault cases, prosecuting them under the single criminal offense of "trespass, assault, and battery." There were no formal decisions directing this change. It took place at different times in different counties in North and South Carolina, an unevenness that suggests both the localized, particular nature of the change in the actual legal process and wide-spread, general character of the ideas that underlay it.[20]

In practice, moreover, courts tended to define the criminal matter in terms of the individual injury. A range of people at the local level had always used the courts to obtain redress for violence, both before and after the Revolution. That did not change. In court, they tried to turn their private disputes into public matters, as victims advanced their understandings of the seriousness of their injuries and defendants argued for the legitimacy of their acts. That did not change either. However, now their claims acquired different meanings. Instead of becoming public through the king, their physical injuries acquired public meaning in their own right. As legally recognized individuals who were sovereign members of the public order, their own bodies and not the king's had been injured. Legal officials, in turn, began construing the cases in this way.

Changes in legal practice at the local level at this time also tended to increase the authority of white men by distinguishing them from domestic dependents, just as rulings at the state level did. Only free white men, particularly those with property, could claim sovereign membership in the polity. Domestic dependents and even men without property could not. More than that, placing white, propertied men in the legal position formerly occupied by the king had the effect of closing down all domestic dependents' access to legal arenas.

Wives were subordinate parties in criminal assaults. Technically, injuries to them were public crimes. The injuries also constituted crimes against their husbands, whom the law identified as equally "injured" because it subsumed wives' legal interests under those of their husbands. The effect was to make wives' injuries public through their husbands and fathers, just as they had once become public through the king. Without the active participation of their husbands, wives could not become legally visible.[21]

This situation did not mean that wives could not initiate a legal process that resulted in criminal proceedings. Many, like Sarah Chandler, appealed to justices and the lower courts for protection from their husbands and other people as well. If court officials proceeded with peace warrants or even assault charges, they did so because the offense breached the public peace, not because of the individual who had been threatened or hurt. Thus the physical injuries of wives who suffered at the hands of their husbands still became public through white men: it was the damage done to the collective public body, composed of white men, that made wives' injuries a crime.[22]

Wives and free children, however, still had more legal visibility than slaves. Slaves could not bring complaints to justices like other domestic dependents. In North Carolina, however, their place among those protected by the government was ambiguous, and local officials did entertain complaints made on their behalf.[23] Nor were slaves recognized parties in criminal offenses, even in the subordinate way that wives were. In North Carolina, where common law governed master-slave relations, the courts prosecuted violence against slaves as assaults. Yet, as in the case of wives, the slaves' injuries acquired criminal status through the damage to the larger public. From there, the slaves' presence was unnecessary: it was the master who filed charges, whose name appeared on the documents, and whose word mattered in court. The situation tended to transform the slaves' physical injury into the master's legal injury and to make that into the breach of the peace.[24]

Assaults against slaves only entered South Carolina courts as criminal matters in cases of slave-on-slave violence. Masters prosecuted these cases, which were defined in terms of the masters' interests and injuries, effectively erasing the legal import of the damage sustained by the slaves themselves. For most of the antebellum period, violence by whites against slaves did not rise to the level of a crime in South Carolina at all. Such incidents were civil offenses that entitled masters to sue for damages to their property, a situation that did not even include slaves within the public peace in the limited way that North Carolina did.[25]

Together, these legal changes constituted a major transformation in the public status of domestic dependents and household heads. By 1840, the law gave free white men broad discretionary rights to use violence and defend themselves from it. That freedom, moreover, became a defining right of citizenship. Where the state had once protected free white men from physical harm, white men now had the right to protect themselves and to demand the state's intervention to uphold that right. At the same time, domestic dependents' ability to call on the state for protection diminished. Before the Revolution, they could ask the state to discipline their household heads, who were also subjects. Afterward, that changed because the public order was defined as the interests of white, male household heads. Even the act of self-defense in the most extreme, threatening circumstances was conditional. Dependents could look to the state for protection. They could even ask forgiveness if they took matters into their own hands. Unlike white men, however, they had no absolute legal right to defend their own bodies and their own interests. Instead, their injuries remained private matters that became public only through the damage done to the social order. Nor could domestic dependents legally assert their interests physically.

The laws governing violence thus polarized the differences between white men and all domestic dependents, enhancing the authority of white men and, by implication, closing down legal access that domestic dependents had formally enjoyed—in theory, if not always in practice. The two results are different sides of the same coin. In fact, the new authority of white men—what many historians have seen as the defining characteristic of democracy in the new nation—is what allowed southern lawmakers to apply the principle of domestic dependency in particularly expansive, repressive ways.

Old Patterns, New Possibilities

Yet, as Sarah Chandler's case indicates, the transformation of free white men's authority and the separation of household heads from dependents along the lines of gender, race, and class was not complete. Although firmly entrenched in some areas of the legal system and the South's governing structures by 1840, it was not in others. After all, the decisions that established free white men's difference from domestic dependents were built around the same legal logic that affirmed basic similarities between these two groups. At the same time, local officials and community members used this same legal logic in ways that made white men, even those with property, subjects in ways similar to their domestic dependents.

As other historians have noted, southern communities did step in to discipline errant patriarchs and enforce local notions of appropriate patriarchal behavior. As these historians have argued, such cases certainly represented a suspension of legal decisions—like those discussed in the previous section—that upheld a man's power over his household.[26] At the same time, however, such cases also were sanctioned within existing common law traditions that characterized all men as subjects of the state, rather than sovereign members of it. When the local court disciplined Thomas Chandler for overstepping his authority, for instance, it treated him as an errant subject, not unlike the dependents over whom he supposedly had mastery. Like his wife and his slaves, he also had to answer to a higher, sovereign power. In fact, Sarah Chandler could take her husband to court because the legal differences that supposedly upheld all white men's domestic authority did not *only* work in that way. Local officials still regularly placed the public interest over those of individual, free white men. Issuing peace warrants or assault charges against husbands for beating their wives and even masters for abusing their slaves was only one example.[27] Local officials did not always acknowledge all white men's sovereignty by granting their individual injuries public, criminal status either. Instead, magistrates often issued peace warrants, which affirmed the notion that no individual was sovereign, that the public injury took precedence over individual one, and that everyone was subject to the discipline of a higher authority.[28]

The similarities among people as subjects did not just exist in the theoretical realm of law. When the court interceded to shore up the authority of individual men, it unwittingly reinforced similarities between household heads and dependents in social practice. Violet whacked her master and mistress with an axe handle because the legal differences that supposedly defined their authority over their slaves did not necessarily establish it in actuality.

Indeed, as Violet's case suggests, the differences between household heads and domestic dependents were not as clear or as dichotomous as they were in legal rulings at the state level. The law of domestic relations, as it developed in the higher courts, purposefully overstated the authority that individual patriarchs exercised in their communities. It defined patriarchal authority in terms of isolated households, abstracted from social context, where individual white men exercised unchecked power over their domestic dependents. That legal fiction, however, distorted the actual position of household heads and dependents in the early nineteenth century. No husband stood alone, unencumbered by other social ties. Nor was any wife or slave completely isolated within a single household. A dense web of social relations actually shaped the operation of patriarchal authority in daily life. Relations between household heads and dependents were deeply rooted within local contexts, shaped by kin ties, community networks, and personal reputation as well as gender, race, and class. As a result, individual patriarchs were always subject to other men and to other women.[29]

Like Violet, Thomas Burgess was himself dependent. Violet was actually the property of John Burgess, Thomas Burgess's father. He had only recently loaned Violet to his son and daughter-in-law. That situation compromised Thomas Burgess's authority by accentuating his economic dependence on his father. After the fight with Violet, Thomas Burgess went to his father for assistance. As he later testified, he "would have been sattisfied if his father had have corected [*sic*]" Violet. But the father refused to discipline Violet. Perhaps he believed that his son needed a lesson in mastery. Perhaps he thought that Thomas Burgess treated Violet badly and was sympathetic toward her. Perhaps he knew it was fruitless to try to control her. Any of these possibilities would help explain why Violet had done "as she pleased" before. Without his father's support, Thomas Burgess had no alternative but the courts. There, he hoped, a jury of slaveholding men would do what he could not do and what his father would not do.[30]

Thomas Chandler also had to answer to a host of people in the community. These included his wife's brothers and her widowed mother, who controlled her father's estate. They had a sense of obligation for Sarah's welfare. They also had a direct economic interest in preserving family property that would go, through Sarah, to her children. Their authority annoyed Thomas Chandler. As he later testified in the divorce case, "he verily believes that the disquiet which has existed in his family and the differences existing between [him and his wife] have been principally created by the mischievous and malicious interferences of his said wife's mother & her friends." These friends were Sarah's brothers and other community members who also found Thomas Chandler's behavior problematic. When neighbors and kin withdrew their support, Thomas Chandler's authority collapsed.[31]

If the legal fiction of domestic authority overstated the power of individual patriarchs by obscuring their dependence on others, it also overstated the subordination and isolation of dependents within the domestic sphere. The law defined patriarchal authority as the power of an abstract, individual man over an abstract, individual domestic dependent. In law, then, domestic violence of the kind Sarah Chandler and Violet experienced *only* involved the husband and wife or the master and slave, whose opposing interests were easily and completely separable from their communities. Yet neither Sarah's nor Violet's cases were only about such abstract entities.

That Sarah Chandler was able to proceed with her legal suits at all indicates the presence of community support. In their depositions, neighbors

and kin emphasized the ways Thomas Chandler's behavior negatively affected the larger community. There was the severity of the abuse, which
clearly transgressed community norms. Then there was his neglect of his
duties, as a neighbor as well as a husband. He fought constantly, introducing
unnecessary conflict into the community and threatening important social
networks. He drank to excess and neglected to work his property as he
should, failing to support his family and to fulfill his part in the web of economic relations that knit together the members of this rural community. He
also squandered the property that Sarah had brought into the marriage,
threatening the patrimony of her family and their efforts to provide for their
heirs, Sarah's children. Neighbors and kin lined up on Sarah Chandler's side
against Thomas Chandler because they were all involved in the conflict in direct, tangible ways.[32]

Violet's actions also were predicated on the support of both blacks and
whites in her community. The local court records in the South Carolina upcountry where Violet lived indicate the presence of cohesive slave communities—built by blacks and tolerated by whites—that transcended individual plantations. In this region, slaves customarily left their own small
plantations in evenings and on weekends to gather at the houses of their
friends and kin. The practice of hiring out slaves or sending them to work on
the farms of their masters' neighbors and kin reinforced these patterns. Upcountry slaves built their social networks openly. Whites did try to limit
what they considered to be disruptive, illicit activities—drinking, gambling,
trading, and fighting. Nevertheless, they still accepted a good deal of mobility as long as it did not result in open disorder. In fact, mobility was so common that white slaveholders did not always bother to keep track of their
slaves' whereabouts. For slaves, however, mobility translated into autonomy
in ways that whites did not always intend, even though their own actions
supported these expectations.[33]

This context helps explain Violet's actions. Although Violet pushed the
limits of accepted custom, she assumed that she had every right to make
such claims. Like many slaves in the area, Violet worked both on and off her
master's plantation. She was on loan to Thomas Burgess, even though she
was owned by Burgess's father. While on Thomas Burgess's plantation, she
hired "out or [worked as] a field hand, but milk[ed] night & morning." Given
the customs of the white community, Violet expected to have a certain
amount of control over her work and her life. She claimed these rights
openly and assertively precisely because she had exercised them before and
had every expectation that she might continue to do so in the future. Her
actions presumed a level of support from whites for the substance of her
claims, if not her expression of them. Violet also assumed a level of support
from other slaves. After the fight, she disappeared for a week. The court

record does not say where she went, but it is likely that slaves in the area sheltered her. They could do so because they, like Violet, had established a certain level of autonomy. To them, Violet was not an outlaw who stepped outside existing social patterns to defy authority in heroic, yet ultimately self-destructive, ways. Rather, her claims were an extension of those that defined the lives of all slaves in the area. They supported her because her cause was their own. Of course, Violet overplayed her hand. She reached beyond what whites in her community would accept. Ultimately, the slave community could not protect her. That does not erase the presence and importance of these networks, which are what made Violet think that she could play her hand in the first place.[34]

The law, however, stripped cases from the social networks that defined them and gave them meaning. Then the law universalized from the particulars, so that each case involved the position of all household heads versus the position of all domestic dependents. Given that legal context, recognizing the right of wives and slaves to speak for themselves and act for themselves was a slippery slope. It meant the unraveling of coverture and slavery in ways that made it difficult to deny white women and African Americans other citizenship rights implied by direct access to governing institutions. In the theoretical realm of law, particularly the law of domestic relations, the actions and words of wives and slaves thus acquired threatening meanings that reached well beyond the circumstances of the specific cases and the intent of those directly involved. They became a threat to the power of all patriarchs.

Yet neither Sarah Chandler, nor Violet, nor those who supported them directly opposed patriarchal authority. To the contrary, they were firmly enmeshed within patriarchal social relations. This dynamic is most clear in Sarah Chandler's case, because she was more invested in the system and had far more to gain from it than Violet. Patriarchy is what allowed Sarah Chandler the possibility of checking her husband's particular, and particularly abusive, expression of authority. It is also what gave her supporters legitimacy and leverage. Sarah's brothers carried weight because they had a recognized interest in their sister's life and obligations to her. So did her mother. As the widow and eldest member of the family, she was also a recognized representative of her dead husband's interests. The opinions of other community members mattered as well, because Thomas Chandler's abuse of his authority imposed responsibilities on them and threatened community stability.[35]

Unlike Sarah Chandler, Violet had little to gain within the existing system. But the overlapping hierarchies that characterized the operation of patriarchy at the local level worked to her advantage far more than the legal notion of a sovereign patriarch with complete authority over his household. She capitalized on the power differential between fathers and sons, challenging the son because she knew the father still held control over him. Violet also used the overlapping hierarchies that held all patriarchs accountable to each other and the larger social order. If the father controlled the son, the father himself was dependent on others in the community. All this allowed Violet to carve out an area of autonomy for herself long before her mistress tried to rein her back in. Violet, who hired out her time, likely had resources of her own. She certainly insisted that she control her own work pace, deciding where she would work and when she would do the chores that Thomas Burgess and his wife expected of her. Apparently, she even thought of herself as an "eaqual." What, specifically, did that mean in this context? To be an "eaqual" to whites meant that Violet was still enmeshed in the larger patriarchal social structures that made everyone dependent in some regard. Ironically, those structures, which blurred the stark differences between household heads and all dependents, actually allowed this black woman to see herself as an "eaqual" in the first place. Had her master, either the father or the son, actually exercised absolute authority as defined in law, such equality would have been far more difficult for Violet even to imagine, let alone claim.[36]

All these people's definitions of the social operation of patriarchal authority and its political purposes differed greatly from those defined in other arenas of the law, particularly those cases that placed the authority of household heads beyond question. Nor did everyone involved in Sarah Chandler's and Violet's cases agree on these matters. All these people advanced specific ideas about the duties of husbands and wives and masters and slaves to each other and to the larger community, about limits of a household head's authority and the proper expression of it, and about the community's role in regulating that authority.

The family members who were present when Thomas Chandler turned violent hesitated. They watched while Thomas beat Sarah Chandler with a bridle and switches in the yard. They watched him drive her into the house and nail the door shut. They ignored her screams as he beat her with a hammer and burned her flesh with hot tongs. Perhaps they feared Thomas Chandler themselves. If so, they had good reason, given what he was doing to Sarah and his reputation as a fighting man. Perhaps they believed that Sarah had done something to provoke him, a judgment that kept onlookers from intervening in separate, similar cases. Yet, others were not so hesitant. They sheltered Sarah Chandler and supported her legal proceedings. For them and for the magistrate who heard her complaint, the incident was about both the seriousness of the beating and Thomas Chandler's failure to fulfill his duties to his household and community. The combination made the incident part of larger, socially problematic pattern instead of an isolated, excusable outburst.[37]

There were also discernable differences within the community over Violet's situation. Thomas Burgess and his wife responded violently to Violet's demands. The court ultimately backed him. The law of the state, which forbade any physical aggression by a slave against a white person, was clearly on his side. But community standards differed. Thomas Burgess's father refused to "discipline" Violet further as the son requested. In their testimony, moreover, the Burgesses had to justify their use of force to the slaveholders who decided the case. They had to work hard to convince the jurors that Violet was the one who instigated the fight and that they were only disciplining an unruly slave who needed correction.[38]

White women and slaves, like Sarah Chandler and Violet, had their own, particular interests. White women tried to limit physical expressions of a household head's authority. They refused to submit to men they considered morally errant and economically irresponsible. They insisted that their voices be heard; they demanded access to public arenas to air their grievances. Slaves pushed further in all these matters. Violet's response to Polly Burgess's orders is indicative. Violet did not think that Polly Burgess could exert that much authority. When Polly threatened to use force to make her obey, Violet held her ground and struck back.[39]

Still, domestic dependents, even slaves, did not act alone. They were participating in a larger debate over the nature of patriarchal power. From this perspective, domestic dependents and their interests are distinctive, but not completely separable, from those of their communities generally. In fact, their concerns are part of larger, political concerns. This perspective, in turn, changes our understanding of domestic dependents' political agency. It is not sufficient to say that they failed in court, which they usually did. Here Sarah Chandler's situation provides an exception. The outcome of Violet's case is more representative. That they tried at all and were successful in that effort opens a window on a larger debate about authority that affected *all* southerners.

Local matters, in turn, ultimately reshaped the legal construction of patriarchal power in the antebellum South, although not in ways the people involved intended. Conflicts over the nature of patriarchal power and local uses of traditional legal practices to resolve these conflicts blurred the distinctions between household heads and dependents that were being made in other areas of the legal system. Both domestic dependents and household heads used the local courts to obtain redress from violence. Both tried to turn their private disputes into public matters, as victims advanced their understandings of the seriousness of their injuries and defendants attempted to legitimize their acts. At the local level, the differences between the two groups were not always apparent, even in law. After all, the distinction between an assault prosecuted as a breach of the peace and one prosecuted on the strength of the individual injuries was not necessarily clear in the handling or outcome of the case. Nor was it always obvious that a man bound over to keep the peace and the wife who charged him were legally different. As a result, cases against white men still moved through the local courts in ways that made them appear similar to domestic dependents.

That blurring had larger implications in the theoretical realm of law. The injuries to domestic dependents' bodies might constitute a public crime, just as they increasingly did for free white men. Other rights of citizenship might then apply to domestic dependents as well. That seemed dangerously close to happening with Sarah Chandler's legal cases and in the life Violet managed to carve out for herself, before her master's son took her to court. Conversely, all white men might still be subjects in law as they had once been. That certainly seemed to be true in the legal handling of Thomas Chandler's cases and in Thomas Burgess's experience with Violet before the law's intervention. Nor did legal changes that elevated free white men and distinguished them from domestic dependents automatically clarify matters, because these changes were based, in part, on the same legal logic that once cast them as subjects and that opened the possibility that *all* former subjects might now be sovereign members of the polity. The results were contradictory. One differentiated legally between free white men and domestic dependents. The other collapsed the legal treatment of the two groups in ways that emphasized their legal similarities.

The ways local practice made those larger legal contradictions apparent resulted in the repeated, categorical statements about the authority of household heads, the subjection of dependents, and the racial, class, and gender differences that defined that configuration of power in other areas of the legal system. Sarah Chandler's and Violet's cases remained at the local level. The legal ambiguities revealed in similar cases moved them into the higher courts. Those ambiguities allowed room for appeal. They also caught the interest of higher court judges, who took on these cases because they necessitated statements about the limits of post-Revolutionary change and clarification on who would be citizens and who would remain subjects. That the courts had to repeat themselves over and over again during this period suggests how new and how fragile this order was.

Ironically, the very legal decisions that contain these complications also deny them. That is the point. The courts introduced dramatic changes in the legal construction of patriarchal authority under the cover of tradition, erasing domestic dependents' uses of the law and community discussions about patriarchal authority. The result made the agency of free white men, as household heads, visible, while making the agency of domestic dependents and other community members invisible. On one level little difference existed among household heads and domestic dependents: they beat up other people and they got beat up; they defended themselves and asserted their interests; they marched off to public institutions of governance and demanded intervention. Yet, another level illustrated only difference. As the law developed in the early-nineteenth-century South, only the injuries and actions of free white men carried public weight in their own right. In the historical documents of the time, only their actions are visible and politically meaningful.

The notion that domestic dependents and free white men were so fundamentally different as to occupy opposite poles has profoundly shaped historiography of the South and the early nineteenth century generally. This is not surprising, because legal records are a primary source base for the antebellum South. Yet Southern historians have taken legal categories too literally. As a result, we presume the existence of a particular kind of social order based around particular kinds of differences between free white men and domestic dependents. We presume, for instance, that free white men acted differently—more violently and more assertively—than white women and African Americans. We presume that they acted out of different motives. We presume that their actions carried different weight. We presume that it was always that way. But we presume too much. These presumptions hide important changes in the construction of authority in the early-nineteenth-century South. Those who appeared politically marginal because of their differences actually played a politically important role in the law's continued effort to subordinate them. What has appeared timeless, namely free white men's power both within and outside their households, was undergoing significant revision at this time. So, too, was this particular differentiation of white male household heads from domestic dependents, along the binary lines of gender, race, and class.

Notes

1. *State* v. *Thomas Chandler,* 1825, Criminal Action Papers, Granville County, North Carolina Department of Archives and History (NCDAH). *Sarah Chandler* v. *Thomas Chandler,* 1826, Divorce Papers, Granville County, NCDAH. Chandler sat in jail for some time before he was able to post bond the second time. The amount had doubled. Beyond that, Chandler probably had more difficulty convincing friends to risk their property a second time. Those who came to his aid soon had reason to regret their decision, because Chandler did his best to evade further prosecution. Constables tried, unsuccessfully, to bring him into court on four different occasions. He finally turned up in August of 1825, although the case disappears from the records after that, probably because he and Sarah were in the process of divorcing.

2. *State* v. *Violet,* 1854, case #160, 2921; Trial Records, Magistrates and Freeholders Court, Spartanburg District, South Carolina Department of Archives and History (SCDAH).

3. Although the British never tried to include slaves as subjects within the empire as comprehensively as either the French or the Spanish, they did try to do so in the late colonial period, as part of the effort to consolidate the empire. That produced conflict between British officials and colonials, who were unwilling to cede de facto authority over their slaves to the crown's representatives. See Christopher L. Brown, "Empire without Slaves: British Concepts of Emancipation in the Age of the American Revolution," *William and Mary Quarterly* 56 (Apr., 1999): 273–306; Jeffrey Robert Young, *Domesticating Slavery: The Master Class in Georgia and South Carolina, 1670–1837* (Chapel Hill: University of North Carolina Press, 1999). Colonials themselves debated the extent to which it was necessary to include slaves within the legal structure as subjects to check abuses of power and to promote social stability; see, for instance, Robert Olwell, *Masters, Slaves, and Subjects: The Culture of Power in the South Carolina Low Country, 1740–1790* (Ithaca: Cornell University Press, 1998).

4. Lacy K. Ford, Jr., *Origins of Southern Radicalism: The South Carolina Upcountry, 1800–1860* (New York: Oxford University Press, 1988); Steven Hahn, *The Roots of Southern Populism: Yeoman Farmers and the Transformation of the Georgia Upcountry, 1850–1890* (New York: Oxford University Press, 1983); James Oakes, *The Ruling Race: A History of American Slaveholders* (New York: Knopf, 1982); Oakes, *Slavery and Freedom: An Interpretation of the Old South* (New York: Knopf, 1990); J. Mills Thornton, III, *Politics and Power in a Slave Society: Alabama, 1800–1860* (Baton Rouge: Louisiana State University Press, 1978). Also see Stephanie McCurry, *Masters of Small Worlds: Yeoman Households, Gender Relations, and the Political Culture of the Antebellum South Carolina Low Country* (New York: Oxford University Press, 1995) for a gendered rereading of the ideology that connects planters and yeomen.

5. See, in particular, the work on slavery and the law: Edward L. Ayers, *Vengeance and Justice: Crime and Punishment in the Nineteenth-Century American South* (New York: Oxford University Press, 1984), especially pp. 132–36; Andrew Fede, *People Without Rights: An Interpretation of the Fundamentals of the Law of Slavery in the U.S. South* (New York: Garland, 1992); Daniel J. Flanigan, "Criminal Procedure in Slave Trials in the Antebellum South," *Journal of Southern History* 40 (Nov., 1974): 537–64; Eugene D. Genovese, *Roll, Jordan, Roll: The World the Slaves Made* (New York: Vintage Books, 1976), pp. 25–49; Michael Stephen Hindus, *Prison and Plantation: Crime, Justice, and Authority in Massachusetts and South Carolina, 1767–1878* (Chapel Hill: University of North Carolina Press, 1980); Arnold Edmund Keir Nash, "Negro Rights and Judicial Behavior in the Old South," Ph.D. dissertation, Harvard University, 1967; Philip J. Schwarz, *Twice Condemned: Slaves and the Criminal Laws of Virginia, 1705–1865* (Baton Rouge: Louisiana State University Press, 1988); Christopher Waldrep, *Roots of Disorder: Race and Criminal Justice in the American South, 1817–80* (Urbana: University of Illinois Press, 1998), pp. 15–58; Mark V. Tushnet,

The American Law of Slavery, 1810–1860: A Consideration of Humanity and Interest (Princeton: Princeton University Press, 1981). Recent work has begun revising this view, pointing out that slaves actually did exercise more legal agency, although in indirect ways, than previous scholarship allowed, see, for instance, Ariela Gross, *Double Character: Slavery and Mastery in the Southern Courtroom, 1800–1860* (Princeton: Princeton University Press, 2000).

6. See, for instance, John Blassingame, *The Slave Community, Plantation Life in the Antebellum South* (New York: Oxford University Press, 1972); Ira Berlin, *Many Thousands Gone: The First Two Centuries of Slavery in North America* (Cambridge: Harvard University Press, 2000); Herbert G. Gutman, *The Black Family in Slavery and Freedom, 1750–1925* (New York: Pantheon Books, 1976); Charles Joyner, *Down by the Riverside: A South Carolina Slave Community* (Urbana: University of Illinois Press, 1984); Lawrence Levine, *Black Culture and Black Consciousness: Afro-American Folk Thought from Slavery to Freedom* (New York: Oxford University Press, 1977); Philip Morgan, *Slave Counterpoint: Black Culture in the Eighteenth-Century Chesapeake and Lowcountry* (Chapel Hill: University of North Carolina Press, 1998); George P. Rawick, *From Sundown to Sunup: The Making of the Black Community* (Westport, Conn.: Greenwood Press, 1972); Brenda E. Stevenson, *Life in Black and White: Family and Community in the Slave South* (New York: Oxford University Press, 1996). Also see Genovese, *Roll Jordan Roll;* although emphasizing the relationship between masters and slaves and arguing that the hegemony of masters shaped slave culture, he also separates the culture of the slave quarters from public arenas of governance.

7. Peter Bardaglio, *Reconstructing the Household: Families, Sex, and the Law in the Nineteenth-Century South* (Chapel Hill: University of North Carolina Press, 1995); Victoria Bynum, *Unruly Women: The Politics of Social and Sexual Control in the Old South* (Chapel Hill: University of North Carolina Press, 1992); Laura F. Edwards, *Gendered Strife and Confusion: The Political Culture of Reconstruction* (Urbana: University of Illinois Press, 1997); Elizabeth Fox-Genovese, *Within the Plantation Household: Women in the Old South* (Chapel Hill: University of North Carolina Press, 1988); McCurry, *Masters of Small Worlds;* LeeAnn Whites, *The Civil War as a Crisis in Gender: Augusta, Georgia, 1860–1890* (Athens: University of Georgia Press, 1995). Some of the important conceptual models in southern history do not focus on the nineteenth century, see the following: Kathleen M. Brown *Good Wives, "Nasty Wenches," and Anxious Patriarchs: Gender, Race, and Power in Colonial Virginia* (Chapel Hill: University of North Carolina Press, 1996); Kirsten Fischer, *Embodiments of Power: The Racial Politics of Illicit Sex in Colonial North Carolina* (Ithaca, N.Y.: Cornell University Press, 2002); Glenda Elizabeth Gilmore, *Gender and Jim Crow: Women and the Politics of White Supremacy in North Carolina, 1896–1920* (Chapel Hill: University of North Carolina Press, 1996); Nancy MacLean, *Behind the Mask of Chivalry: The Making of the Second Ku Klux Klan* (New York: Oxford University Press, 1994).

8. Bardaglio, *Reconstructing the Household;* Bynum, *Unruly Women;* Edwards, *Gendered Strife and Confusion;* Fox-Genovese, *Within the Plantation Household;* Whites, *The Civil War as a Crisis in Gender.* This work actually builds on the insights of Eugene Genovese, who also posited a connection between the domestic authority of planters and the basis of their public authority. See, in particular, *Roll, Jordan, Roll.*

9. Existing work focuses on the higher courts' refusal to deal with domestic violence in the South. Bardaglio, *Reconstructing the Household,* pp. 33–34, Bynum, *Unruly Women,* pp. 70–72; Laura F. Edwards, "Women and Domestic Violence in Nineteenth-Century North Carolina" in *Lethal Imagination: Violence and Brutality in American History,* ed. by Michael A. Bellesiles (New York: New York University Press, 1999), pp. 114–36. Work on violence by husbands against wives in the nineteenth century generally tends to emphasize community controls over legal ones, affirming the idea that the issue remained outside official structures of governance. The exceptions, the implications of which will be discussed later, include Stephanie Cole, "Keeping the Peace: Domestic Assault and Private Prosecution in Antebellum Baltimore," in *Over the Thresh-*

old: Intimate Violence in Early America, ed. by Christine Daniels and Michael V. Kennedy (New York: New York University Press, 1999), pp. 148–69; Laura F. Edwards, "Law, Domestic Violence, and the Limits of Patriarchal Authority in the Antebellum South," *Journal of Southern History* 65 (Nov., 1999): 733–70. Northern courts and legislatures were also slow to deal with this particular issue, although they did begin intervening in other domestic matters long before southern courts; see Michael Grossberg, *Governing the Hearth: Law and the Family in Nineteenth-Century America* (Chapel Hill: University of North Carolina Press, 1985). Also see David Peterson del Mar, *What Trouble I Have Seen: A History of Violence against Wives* (Cambridge: Harvard University Press, 1996); Linda Gordon, *Heroes of Their Own Lives: The Politics and History of Family Violence* (New York: Viking Press, 1988); Pamela Haag, "The 'Ill-Use of a Wife': Patterns of Working-Class Violence in Domestic and Public New York City, 1860–1880," *Journal of Social History* 25 (Spring, 1992): 447–77; Jerome Nadelhaft, "Wife Torture: A Known Phenomenon in Nineteenth-Century America," *Journal of American Culture* 10 (fall, 1987): 39–59; Elizabeth Pleck, *Domestic Tyranny: The Making of Social Policy Against Family Violence from Colonial Times to the Present* (New York: Oxford University Press, 1987); Christine Stansell, *City of Women: Sex and Class in New York, 1789–1860* (Urbana: University of Illinois Press, 1987), pp. 78–83. The reluctance of southern courts to intervene in domestic violence against slaves is well documented; see the literature in note 4.

10. See note 7.

11. Quote from Kitchin in Bradley Chapin, *Criminal Justice in Colonial America, 1606–1660* (Athens: University of Georgia Press, 1983), p. 131. Also see Sir William Blackstone, *Commentaries on the Laws of England,* ed. by St. George Tucker (Philadelphia: William Young Birch and Abraham Small, 1803), vol. 4, pp. 119–22; vol. 5, pp. 142–44, 144–47, 149, 216–17. The difference between assault and other criminal categories of violence underscores the logic that determined whether violent acts were "private wrongs" or "public wrongs." Murder, rape, and mayhem (or maiming) were always criminal acts. On one level, the seriousness of the injuries gave these offenses public implications. As Blackstone explained, they violated "the laws of nature . . . the moral as well as political rules of right," they always included a "breach of the peace," and they "threaten[ed] and endanger[ed] the subversion of all civil society" by "their example and evil tendency." But it was not the individual's suffering, per se, that made murder, maim, and rape criminal. Were any of "these injuries . . . confined to individuals only, and did they affect none but their immediate objects," wrote Blackstone, "they would fall absolutely under the notion of private wrongs." By implication, it was the extent to which these offenses infringed on the king's sovereign power over his realm and his subjects' lives that made them public wrongs. Quotes from Blackstone, *Commentaries,* vol. 5, pp. 176, 177; also see vol. 5, pp. 176–204; vol. 4, p. 121, for murder; vol. 5, pp. 205–207, for mayhem, vol. 5, pp. 209–16, for rape. Blackstone is particularly useful in describing the logic that structured the treatment of these crimes. Also see Cynthia Herrup, *The Common Peace: Participation and the Criminal Law in Seventeenth-Century England* (New York: Cambridge University Press, 1987), pp. 2–5; that did not negate the importance of local participation in applying these rules.

12. For the legal handling of assault in colonial North Carolina, see Donna J. Spindel, *Crime and Society in North Carolina, 1663–1776* (Baton Rouge: Louisiana State University Press, 1989), pp. 46, 49–50, 52, 55–59, 93–94, 135–37. In colonial South Carolina, the routine handling of assault cases is less clear, because the centralization of the court system meant that minor criminal matters remained in the hands of magistrates, who left no records. Until 1769, magistrates could try misdemeanors and civil matters with damages of twenty pounds or less, and they probably handled most common assault and battery cases. After the Circuit Court Act of 1769 decentralized the system, most assault cases still would have fallen within their jurisdiction as either minor civil matters or criminal misdemeanors. See Rachel N. Klein, *Unification of a Slave State: The Rise of*

the Planter Class in the South Carolina Backcountry, 1760–1808 (Chapel Hill: University of North Carolina Press, 1990), pp. 38–41, 74; M. Eugene Sirmans, *Colonial South Carolina: A Political History, 1663–1763* (Chapel Hill: University of North Carolina Press, 1966), pp. 12, 38, 142–44, 166, 250–52, 170–76. Also see William Simpson, *The Practical Justice of the Peace and Parish-Officer, of His Majesty's Province of South Carolina* (Charleston, 1761), pp. 1–3.

13. It is also likely that court officials would have considered violence against free white men to be more of a public threat than violence against domestic dependents, particularly if they were attacked by someone of subordinate status. Personal reputation also determined which cases magistrates decided to pursue. Magistrates in the nineteenth century, for instance, were more willing to prosecute a known brawler for beating his wife than a man of unimpeachable character. They were also more willing to listen to a woman known as a hard worker and good neighbor than one who neglected her responsibilities to her family and community. For further discussion of these points, see Laura F. Edwards, "Women and Domestic Violence."

The legal system's definition of personal violence—as a minor offense against individuals that did not always involve the public order—was not entirely accurate. Indeed, North and South Carolina's treatment of violence was, in part, an effort to contain the disruptive, public actions of their contentious, irreverent inhabitants. It was not the people's direct defiance of authority that was so threatening: most common brawlers did not fight with the specific intent of defying their social betters. Rather, the threatening aspect resided in the way they bypassed established authority and assumed public status in their own right when they routinely asserted themselves physically in defense of their own interests. They acted as sovereign individuals, instead of subjects who depended on the king and his representatives to protect them. The unruly settlers in North and South Carolina stepped over this line frequently, as the bellyaching of colonial officials and elite commentators abundantly illustrates. The legal categorization of violence as "personal" rather than "public" matters diffused the potential political threat to some degree. By personalizing the injury done to the individual, the law stripped violent actions of any wider implications. When physical damage to an individual's body only became public through the injury to the king's metaphorical body, neither the conflicts that ultimately resulted in violence nor those involved were constitutive components of the polity, in their own right. Only the ancillary damage to the king's peace mattered.

The law's purposeful depoliticization of violence was a legal fiction. The law could not completely contain the political implications of violence in the colonial South, as statutes that extended the definition of maiming suggest. Legislatures in North and South Carolina redefined maiming to include the destruction of ears and noses, body parts traditionally excluded from mayhem, which covered only those limbs necessary for a man to defend himself in a fight. These statutes addressed the pervasive, ritualized fighting among southern men, white and black, which included gouging eyes as well as biting off noses and ears. They also suggest the political threat such fighting posed to the fragile authority of the colonial elite. If unchecked, such physical assertions could acquire legitimacy and lead to the politically problematic notion that individuals had the right to act for themselves and represent their own interests in other ways as well. The political threat posed by violence probably also explains the willingness of colonial authorities to try violence as criminal matters. When the lower orders used violence too freely, they not only broke the king's peace; they also moved in on his sovereign territory. For maiming, see *Laws of North Carolina, 1754,* chapter 15, in *The State Records of North Carolina,* ed. by Walter Clark (Goldsboro, 1904), 23: 420. The penalties were later downgraded, see Act of 1791, Rev., ch. 339. As Zephaniah Swift, *A System of Laws of the State of Connecticut* (Windham, 1796), vol. 2, pp. 178–79, explains, the destruction of limbs was a felony because it meant men were unable to perform their military duties in defending the realm. For fighting, see Elliott J. Gorn, "'Gouge and Bite, Pull Hair and Scratch': The Social Significance of Fighting in the Southern Backcountry," *American*

Historical Review 90 (Feb., 1985): 18–43; Kenneth Greenberg, *Honor and Slavery: Lies, Duels, Noses, Masks, Dressing as a Woman, Gifts, Strangers, Humanitarianism, Death, Slave Rebellions, the Pro-slavery Argument, Baseball, Hunting, and Gambling in the Old South* (Princeton: Princeton University Press, 1996); Ted Ownby, *Subduing Satan: Religion, Recreation, and Manhood in the Rural South, 1865–1920* (Chapel Hill: University of North Carolina Press, 1990); Bertram Wyatt-Brown, *Southern Honor: Ethics and Behavior in the Old South,* (New York: Oxford University Press, 1982).

14. In 1824, for instance, the North Carolina State Supreme Court decided that firing guns at an individual's house and killing a dog was best treated as a criminal, not a civil matter, substituting the offense against the individual for that done to the public. *State* v. *Langford* 10 N. C. 381 (1824). For other cases that also privilege personal injuries as the basis of criminal offenses, see *State* v. *Irwin,* 2 N. C. 151 (1794) and *State* v. *Evans* 2 N. C. 368 (1796). Key civil cases also emphasized the injury, itself, rather than contextualizing it within a broader context to determine its seriousness; see *Barry* v. *Inglis et al.* 1 N. C. 147 (1799) and *White* v. *Fort,* 10 N. C. 251 (1824).

15. For cases that centered on this issue, see *State* v. *Weaver,* 2 Haywood 54 (1798); *State* v. *Hall* 1 N. C. 150 (1799); *State* v. *Boon,* 1 N. C. 169 (1801); *State* v. *Reed* 9 N. C. 454 (1823). North Carolina statutes also extended laws prosecuting physical violence to slaves, making the willful killing of a slave murder unless done in resisting or under moderate correction in 1791 (Haywood, *Manual of the Laws of North Carolina,* vol. 2, p. 141); extending trial by jury to them (Laws of 1793, chapter 5); giving the right of appeal to slaves at all levels of the system (Laws of 1807, chapter 10); making manslaughter a crime against slaves (*Session Laws of North Carolina, 1817,* pp. 18–19). But these rights were undercut by decisions, discussed below, that clearly differentiated slaves from other free people. The way North Carolina applied the common law to slaves was unusual, but the logic that structured the legal status of slaves was not. South Carolina also drew heavily on the same common law rules for domestic dependents in its statutory slave code. See John Belton O'Neall, *The Negro Law of South Carolina* (Columbia, S. C., 1848). For similar questions in regard to women, see Linda K. Kerber, "The Paradox of Women's Citizenship in the Early Republic: The Case of *Martin vs. Massachusetts,* 1805," *American Historical Review* 97 (Apr., 1992): 349–78.

16. Christopher Morris, *Becoming Southern: The Evolution of a Way of Life, Warren County and Vicksburg, Mississippi, 1770–1860* (New York: Oxford University Press, 1995), especially pp. 56–61, 63–83, notes a similar development in the disappearance of opportunities for wives, in particular, to pursue their interests in court and the increasing emphasis on the sovereignty of male household heads.

17. *State* v. *Alvin Preslar,* 48 N. C. 421 (1856). As Tapping Reeve explained, household heads were supposed to prevent the development of "vicious habits" in their dependents that might prove "a nuisance to the community." As long as they acted "from motives of duty," "no verdict ought to be found against" them. Although writing about children and free servants, the point applied generally to all domestic dependents in the South. Quote from Tapping Reeve, *The Law of Baron and Femme,* 3rd ed. (Albany: William Gould, 1862; rpt. New York: South Book Press, 1970), p. 420. Reeve was actually talking about a parent's disciplinary authority, but that power also extended to masters and servants, see p. 535. Southern jurists drew on the same logic as Reeve when they considered masters' violence toward slaves, even using the exact words at times. Also see Morris, *Southern Slavery and the Law,* pp. 161–81. For slaves, the opinions of Justice Thomas Ruffin, whose influential cases involving slaves and violence shaped the law in the South as a whole, are representative. Ruffin's decision in *State* v. *Mann* 13 N. C. 263 (1829) is often cited by historians as the most extreme interpretation of a master's authority. In it, Ruffin argued that the master's (or in this instance the hirer of the slave who temporarily assumed the role of master) shooting of his slave could not be assault because the "power of the master must be absolute, to render the submission of the slave perfect." But he refused to intervene for the same reasons that Reeve refused to gainsay the intent of masters and fathers when disciplining their

servants and children. "The danger would be great indeed," wrote Ruffin, "if the tribunals of justice should be called on to graduate the punishment appropriate to every temper and every dereliction of menial duty." Ten years later in *State* v. *Hoover,* 20 N. C. 500 (1839), Ruffin seemed to backtrack from his position in *Mann,* arguing that a master's authority was not absolute to the point where he could take a slave's life at will and upholding the conviction of a master for the murder of his slave. But the two decisions are both consistent with the logic laid out by Reeve. In *Hoover,* Ruffin gave masters the same kind of latitude with their slaves that Reeve gave to parents and masters of servants. "'If death unhappily ensue from the master's chastisement of his slave, inflicted apparently with a good intent, for reformation for example, and with no purpose to take life or to put it in jeopardy," argued Ruffin, "the law would doubtless tenderly regard every circumstance which, judging from the conduct generally of masters towards slaves, might reasonably be supposed to have hurried the party into excess." In this case, however, Ruffin believed that there was ample proof of "*malus animus,*" the only evidence that would make a household head's killing of a domestic dependent into murder. Also see *State* v. *Weaver,* 3 N. C. 77 (1798); *State* v. *Walker,* 4 N. C. 471 (1817); *State* v. *Mann,* 13 N. C. 169 (1829); *State* v. *Robbins,* 48 N. C. 250 (1855); *State* v. *Fleming* 2 Strob. 464 (S. C., 1848); *State* v. *Bowen,* 2 Strob. 574 (S. C., 1849); Thomas R. R. Cobb, *An Inquiry into the Law of Negro Slavery in the United States of America* (Philadelphia and Savannah, 1858), pp. 84–96, 98–99.

18. *State* v. *Roberts* 8 N. C. 349 (1821). The range of behavior considered provocative for a slave was even greater. The North Carolina court laid out the standard in *State* v. *Tackett* (1820): "It exists in the very nature of slavery, that the relation between a white and a slave is different from that between free persons, and, therefore, many acts will extenuate the homicide of a slave which would not constitute a legal provocation if done by a white person." This same standard also applied to assault, as the court wrote in *State* v. *Hale* (1823): "*Every* battery on a slave is not indictable, because the person making it may have matter of excuse or justification, which would be no defense for committing a battery on a free person. Each case of this sort must, in a great degree, depend on its own circumstances." See *State* v. *Roberts* 8 N. C. 185 (1821); *State* v. *Tackett* 8 N. C. 210 (1820); *State* v. *Hale* 9 N. C. 582 (1823). In North Carolina, where the common law governed all homicides as well as third-party violence against slaves, charges of murder and manslaughter could be filed when slaves were killed. In South Carolina, where these matters were governed by statute, only murder charges could be filed. The South Carolina court occasionally interpreted the law broadly to allow for manslaughter charges. There, a 1740 statute explicitly included "undue correction" along with "heat of passion" within manslaughter, although a subsequent 1821 statute did not. The South Carolina court interpreted this omission to mean that "undue correction" was no longer a criminal offense; see *State* v. *Raines,* 3 McCord 315 (S. C., 1826). The results made it nearly impossible to secure a conviction against any white for killing a slave. The court later reversed itself, however, arguing that "undue correction" was covered by "heat of passion" in the 1821 statute; *State* v. *Gaffney,* Rice 431 (S. C., 1839); *State* v. *Fleming,* 2 Strob. 464 (S. C., 1848); *State* v. *Motley et al.,* 7 Rich. 327 (S. C., 1854). But the courts in both states explicitly stated that whites were often "justified" in using violence against slaves and, by extension, free blacks. For slaves, also see: *State* v. *Piver* 2 Haywood 79 (1798); *State* v. *Boon,* 1 N. C. 191 (1801); *State* v. *Hale,* 9 N. C. 582 (1823); *State* v. *Reed,* 9 N. C. 454 (1823); *State* v. *Jarrott,* 23 N. C. 76 (1840); *State* v. *Caesar,* 31 N. C. 391 (1849). Also see Cobb, *Law of Negro Slavery,* pp. 84–96, 98–99; Morris, *Southern Slavery and the Law,* pp. 161–208, 262–302. North Carolina was unusual in allowing the charge against a slave who had killed a free white person to be reduced from murder to manslaughter if the slave killed in self-defense. Nevertheless, that did not deny the free white assailant's right to beat the slave in the first place if "provoked." In South Carolina, this issue was resolved by statute and assumed "wicked intent" whenever a slave physically harmed a white person; killing was always murder, and assault was never justified. Although upholding the general

rule that provocation consists in actual violence or direct threats of it in fights among free white men, the higher courts also tended to loosen the definition of provocation in these instances as well, see: *State* v. *Norris*, 2 N. C. 556 (1796). These changes in the definition of provocation supports the general trend of allowing free white men more discretion to use violence to defend themselves and their interests, rather than requiring them to seek state protection.

19. In *The Southern Judicial Tradition: State Judges and Sectional Distinctiveness, 1790–1890* (Athens: University of Georgia Press, 1999), Timothy S. Huebner argues that southern courts' handling of violence did not deviate from that in northern courts. Huebner maintains that southern courts followed traditional common law rules that circumscribed their discretion in using violence, although the code of honor would suggest otherwise. Although there may not have been much difference between North and South in these matters, southern courts did apply common law rules in ways that gave white men more latitude in using violence. But that trend only becomes visible when the standard of comparison is the legal treatment of violence involving domestic dependents. For an expanded discussion of the issues and the cases involved, see Edwards, "Law, Domestic Violence, and the Limits of Patriarchal Authority in the Antebellum South."

20. This change in form did not necessarily imply a change in the public status of the individual's injury. Indeed, the form of "trespass, assault, and battery" had long been in use, although it was among several modes of prosecution and was often tried as a civil offense. Actual use in the nineteenth century, however, tended to define the criminal matter in terms of the individual injury. For instance, John Faucheraud Grimké, in *The South Carolina Justice of the Peace* (Philadelphia, Penn., 1788), p. 23, still separated the injury to the individual from the injury to the state. Assault, it claimed, is "an action, at the suit of the party, wherein he shall render damages, and also to an indictment, at the suit of the State, wherein he shall be fined, according to the heinousness of the offence." But by 1808, John Haywood, *The Duty and Office of Justices of the Peace, Sheriffs, Coroners, Constables, &c. According to the Laws of the State of North Carolina* (Raleigh, N. C., 1808), p. 16, no longer made this distinction. Assaults were "breaches of the peace, an affront to the government and a damage to the citizens—they are indictable and punishable by fine and imprisonment in the county court." In collapsing the civil and criminal components this manual made *all* individual injuries crimes, regardless of their seriousness. Charges of "trespass," "assault and battery," and "trespass, assault, and battery" were still being handled as civil offenses in the 1790s. Cases appealed through the system as civil matters in the state supreme courts as well; see, for instance, *Greer* v. *Sheppard*, 2 N. C. 129 (1794); *Barry* v. *Inglis et al.* 1 NC 147 (1799); *Elisha Stockstill* v. *John Shuford et al.;* 5 N. C. 37 (1804). The handling of assault underwent a similar transition in northern states as well, although the timing and specifics varied. For the merger of the civil and criminal components of assault in the North, see Swift, *A System of Laws of the State of Connecticut*, vol. 2, pp. 178–89. For the merger at the local level in North Carolina, see, for example, Superior Court Minutes, Randolph County; Superior Court Minutes, Granville County; Superior Court Minutes, Orange County; all in NCDAH. For South Carolina, see Brent H. Holcombe, comp., *Edgefield County, South Carolina, Minutes of the County Court, 1785–1795* (Easley, S. C., 1979); Brent Holcomb, comp., *Winton (Barnwell) County, South Carolina: Minutes of County Court and Will Book 1,* (Easley, S. C., 1978); Laurence K. Wells, comp., *York County, South Carolina, Minutes of the County Court, 1786–1797* (N.p., 1981); *Newberry County, South Carolina, Minutes of the Country Court, 1785–1798* (Easley, S. C., n.d.); Journals of the County and Intermediate Court, 1790–93, Pendleton District, SCDAH; County and Intermediate Court, Indictments, 1790–99, Pendleton District, SCDAH.

21. For husbands filing charges for wives, see *State* v. *Phillip Roberts*, 1803, *State* v. *Nimrod Ragsdale, Jones W. Ragsdale, Pleasant Ragsdale, Samuel Peace, Flemming Peace and John Oliver,* 1814; *State* v. *Dicy Jones, Ben Wheeler, Winny Wheeler, John Stem,* 1814; *State* v. *Richard Arnold,* 1819;

State v. *Bridgett Harris*, 1828; *State* v. *Hansel Guy*, 1828; all in Criminal Action Papers, Granville County, NCDAH. *State* v. *Edward Hall*, 1829, fall term, #12; *State* v. *Alexander Gaillard, Chanley Gaillard Jr., Peter C. Gaillard, Hobson Pinckney, Shulbrick Pinckney, Oakley Grant, John Huger, and John Gibby*, 1829, spring term, #3; *State* v. *Daniel H. Cochran*, 1830, fall term, #5; *State* v. *Daniel H. Cochran, James Crawford, Joshua Reeves, Joshua Crosley, and George Taylor*, 1834, fall term, #7; all in Court of General Sessions, Session Rolls, Anderson District, SCDAH. Male household heads also acted for children, mothers, and others under their care, see, for instance, *State* v. *Hiram G. Kellers, David Champ, John Adams*, 1834, spring term, #22; *State* v. *Benjamin Dupree*, 1837, fall term, #2; *State* v. *John Low*, 1837, fall term, #7; Court of General Sessions, Session Rolls, Anderson District, SCDAH. Also see *State* v. *John Washington and Woodson Washington*, 1827; *State* v. *William Hicks and Jacob Hicks*, 1829; Criminal Action Papers, Granville County, NCDAH. For a discussion of the legal principles that guided these cases, see Reeve, *The Law of Baron and Femme*, pp. 137–41. The continued use of civil suits in cases of assault against wives and children accentuated the effect. Although the merger of the civil and criminal component of the crime eliminated separate civil suits for damages sustained by the immediate injury, antebellum husbands and fathers could and did initiate separate civil proceedings for damages sustained by the loss of labor and sexual services.

22. Legally, wives and children were members of the public. Indeed, it was their place there, under the government's protection that allowed them to make complaints to local officials. Haywood defined the public peace in his justice's manual as "a quiet and harmless behavior towards the government, and all the citizens under its protection." Quote from Haywood, *The Duty and Office of Justices of the Peace*, p. 191; for discussion of peace warrants, see pp. 28–32. Grimké, *The South Carolina Justice of the Peace*, pp. 450–58.

Both Haywood's and Grimké's manuals made it clear that free servants, wives, and children could all swear out peace warrants, even against their masters, husbands, and fathers. There are twenty-five peace warrants sworn out against husbands by wives and seven assault cases against husbands in Granville County; see Criminal Action Papers, Granville County, NCDAH. The antebellum peace bonds for South Carolina are separated from the other court records, unsorted, and extremely voluminous. A sampling of these records for Anderson and Pendleton Districts indicates that numerous bonds were sworn out against husbands and fathers on complaints by their wives and daughters. Some of these bonds also suggest that criminal charges of assault were attached; see Anderson County, Court of General Sessions, Peace Bonds, 1828–1905, SCDAH. There is also one assault case, *State* v. *Andrew Oliver*, spring term 1839, #6, Court of General Sessions, Session Rolls, Anderson District, SCDAH. Although these numbers may not seem impressive, they are vastly under-representative of the actual number of peace warrants issued, because most remained in the hands of justices and were not saved. In North Carolina, for instance, only those warrants that ultimately made their way into a higher court, for one reason or another, were saved. Justices were also more likely to discipline poor men who were known troublemakers in other ways. Most of the men who gave bond for peace warrants were poor. Many either had been arrested for other offenses before their wives filed charges against them or were arrested for other offenses subsequently. Thomas Chandler was from a family that was constantly in and out of court for various offenses, from common brawling to drinking to womanizing. Chandler himself was accused of assaulting another man during the time he was dodging the constables charged with arresting him for beating his wife. Considering her husband's local reputation, it is not surprising that Sarah Chandler found a sympathetic ear in the local justice. For justices' willingness to prosecute marginal men, see Cole, "Keeping the Peace"; Edwards, "Women and Domestic Violence." For an application of the legal logic that made violence against wives criminal only through their husbands, see *State* v. *Joseph Martin, et al.*, 7 N. C. 533 (1819).

23. *State* v. *Harry,* 1820; *State* v. *Edward,* 1828; *State* v. *Simmon Clark,* 1839; Criminal Actions Concerning Slaves and Free Persons of Color, Granville County, NCDAH. Peace warrants were also sworn out against slaves, see *State* v. *Jack,* 1827; *State* v. *Richmond,* 1841, Criminal Actions Concerning Slaves and Free Persons of Color, Granville County, NCDAH.

24. This was exactly the argument that Justice Taylor made in *State* v. *Hale* (1823) in defending the applicability of assault and battery in cases involving slaves, even though it was not defined as a criminal offense by statute or in common law. As he explained, the criminal component did not rest either in the slave's injuries or the actual property damage suffered by the master. "An assault and battery," he explained, "is not indictable in any case to redress the private injury, for that is to be effected by a civil action; but because the offence is injurious to the citizens at large by its breach of the peace, by the terror and alarm it excites, by the disturbance of that social order which it is the primary object of the law to maintain, and by the contagious example of crimes." *State* v. *Hale* 9 N. C. 582 (1823). For assault and battery cases involving slaves at the local level, see *State* v. *Willie Howington,* 1802; *State* v. *Joseph Crews,* 1818; *State* v. *Vincent Day,* 1818; *State* v. *Charles Robertson,* 1825; *State* v. *John Prewett and John Jenkins,* 1828; *State* v. *Robert Rolleston,* 1829; Criminal Action Papers, Granville County, NCDAH. *State* v. *Abington Kimbel,* 1815–16, Criminal Actions Concerning Slaves and Free Persons of Color, Granville County, NCDAH.

25. In the 1850s, the South Carolina Supreme Court began extending a statute prohibiting "unjustified" abuse by masters to include violence against slaves by other whites as well, although the application was limited and still allowed "justified" violence: *State* v. *Wilson,* Cheves (Law, 1839–40), 163 (S. C., 1840); *State* v. *Boozer,* 5 Strob. 22 (S. C. 1850); *State* v. *Harlan,* 5 Rich. 471 (S. C. 1852). South Carolina never recognized the assault of slaves as a criminal offense in common law, though; *State* v. *Maner,* 2 Hill 355 (S. C., 1834). These decisions were an extension of the logic previously applied in civil cases, which allowed masters damages when third parties abused slaves without justification: *White* v. *Chambers,* 2 Bay 71 (S. C., 1796); *Witsell* v. *Earnest,* 1 N. and McC. 183 (S. C. 1818); *Richardson* v. *Dukes,* 4 McCord 93 (S. C. 1827); *Grimké* v. *Houseman,* 1 McMul. 132 (S. C., 1841); *Caldwell ads. Langford,* 1 McMul. 277 (S. C., 1841). Also see Morris, *Southern Slavery and the Law,* pp. 201–202.

26. Peter Bardaglio, "'An Outrage upon Nature': Incest and the Law in the Nineteenth-Century South," in *In Joy and in Sorrow: Women, Family, and Marriage in the Victorian South, 1830–1900,* ed. by Carol Bleser (New York: Oxford University Press, 1991), pp. 32–51; Charles Bolton, *Poor Whites of the Antebellum South: Tenants and Laborers in Central North Carolina and Northeast Mississippi* (Durham, N. C.: Duke University Press, 1994), pp. 61–63; Bill Cecil-Fronsman, *Common Whites: Class and Culture in Antebellum North Carolina* (Lexington: University Press of Kentucky, 1992); Robert C. Kenzer, *Kinship and Neighborhood in a Southern Community: Orange County, North Carolina, 1849–1881* (Knoxville: University of Tennessee Press, 1987); Morris, *Becoming Southern,* pp. 56–62; Stevenson, *Life in Black and White,* pp. 31–32, 140–56; Wyatt-Brown, *Southern Honor.*

27. Both legal practice and the willingness of domestic dependents, particularly those in the white working class, to use the courts were similar in Baltimore; see Cole, "Keeping the Peace." Manuals for justices of the peace dating from the early part of the century clearly stated that wives could swear out peace warrants against their husbands. In law, the offense acquired the status of a "public" crime, because it was a breach of the public peace. There was no clear legal line between peace warrants and other crimes involving violence. By this logic, local officials could charge abusive husbands with the crime of assault either in addition to or as a component of the peace warrant. Yet offense prosecuted was against the body public, not the body of the wife. See Haywood, *The Duty and Office of Justices of the Peace,* pp. 6–7, 15–16, 28–32, 191; Grimké, *The South Carolina Justice of the Peace,* pp. 7–9, 23–32, 450–68. For a discussion of peace bonds, see note 19.

28. For the use of peace warrants in fights involving free white men, see Criminal Action Papers, Granville County, NCDAH; Anderson County, Court of General Sessions, Peace Bonds, 1828–1905, SCDAH.

29. Edwards, "Law, Domestic Violence, and the Limits of Patriarchal Authority in the Antebellum South," elaborates on this idea. Also see Morris, *Becoming Southern*, pp. 84–102.

30. *State* v. *Violet*, 1854, case #160, 2921; Trial Records, Magistrates and Freeholders Court, Spartanburg District, SCDAH.

31. *State* v. *Thomas Chandler*, 1825, Criminal Action Papers, Granville County, North Carolina Department of Archives and History (NCDAH). *Sarah Chandler* v. *Thomas Chandler*, 1826, Divorce Papers, Granville County, NCDAH.

32. Ibid.

33. These patterns emerge from the cases in Trial Records, Magistrates and Freeholders Court, Spartanburg District, and Trial Records, Magistrates and Freeholders Court, Anderson and Pendleton District; both in SCDAH. In addition to the works cited in note 5, see also Lawrence W. Levine, *Black Culture and Consciousness: Afro-American Folk Thought from Slavery to Freedom* (New York: Oxford University Press, 1977); Joseph P. Reidy, *From Slavery to Agrarian Capitalism in the Cotton Plantation South: Central Georgia, 1800–1880* (Chapel Hill: University of North Carolina Press, 1992); Julie Saville, *The Work of Reconstruction: From Slave to Wage Laborer in South Carolina, 1860–1870* (New York: Cambridge University Press, 1994); Leslie A. Schwalm, *A Hard Fight for We: Women's Transition from Slavery to Freedom in South Carolina* (Urbana: University of Illinois Press, 1997); Betty Wood, *Women's Work, Men's Work: The Informal Slave Economies of Lowcountry Georgia* (Athens: University of Georgia Press, 1995).

34. *State* v. *Violet*, 1854, case #160, 2921; Trial Records, Magistrates and Freeholders Court, Spartanburg District, SCDAH.

35. *State* v. *Thomas Chandler*, 1825, Criminal Action Papers, Granville County, NCDAH. *Sarah Chandler* v. *Thomas Chandler*, 1826, Divorce Papers, Granville County, NCDAH.

36. *State* v. *Violet*, 1854, case #160, 2921; Trial Records, Magistrates and Freeholders Court, Spartanburg District, SCDAH.

37. *State* v. *Thomas Chandler*, 1825, Criminal Action Papers, Granville County, NCDAH. *Sarah Chandler* v. *Thomas Chandler*, 1826, Divorce Papers, Granville County, NCDAH.

38. *State* v. *Violet*, 1854, case #160, 2921; Trial Records, Magistrates and Freeholders Court, Spartanburg District, SCDAH.

39. Ibid. *State* v. *Thomas Chandler*, 1825, Criminal Action Papers, Granville County, NCDAH. *Sarah Chandler* v. *Thomas Chandler*, 1826, Divorce Papers, Granville County, NCDAH. For an expanded discussion of these issues, see Edwards, "Women and Domestic Violence," and Edwards, "Law, Domestic Violence, and the Limits of Patriarchal Authority in the Antebellum South."

CHAPTER 2

Muerto por Unos Desconocidos
(Killed by Persons Unknown)

Mob Violence against Blacks
and Mexicans

WILLIAM D. CARRIGAN AND CLIVE WEBB

> Whatever faults and failings other nations may have in their dealings
> with their own subjects or with other people, no other civilized nation
> stands condemned before the world with a series of crimes so
> peculiarly national. . . . [A] large portion of the American people avow
> anarchy, condone murder and defy the contempt of civilization.
>
> —Ida B. Wells, from "A Red Record: Lynchings in the United States" in
> *Southern Horrors and Other Writings: The Anti-Lynching Campaign of
> Ida B. Wells, 1892–1900*

> Thus it is that justice is executed in this country, where they pretend
> there are laws, and rights and liberty. They lie! Here when they pretend
> to punish a crime, they commit another still greater.
>
> —Francisco P. Ramírez, from an editorial in *Alta California,* June 14,
> 1858

On November 2, 1910, a twenty-three-year-old laborer was arrested
for the murder of a white woman in Rock Springs, Texas. The next
day an angry mob broke into the jail, smothered his body with oil and
burned him at the stake. According to local residents, the mob's actions
were justified by the threat to white womanhood. Newspaper reports
nonetheless revealed no evidence that connected the laborer with any
crime.[1]

This scene is sadly all too familiar to students of American history. What
one might not have predicted, however, is that the victim of this brutal act of
mob violence was not an African American but rather a Mexican named

Antonio Rodriguez. Scholars of racial violence have inevitably focused much of their attention on the impact of white mob law on blacks. While the significance of these studies is unquestioned, they have unwittingly obscured the reality of white violence against other racial and ethnic minorities. During the nineteenth and early twentieth centuries, white mobs exacted deadly vengeance against American Indians, Chinese, Sicilians, and others not considered fully "white" by the Anglo majority. Second to blacks, no minority suffered more at the hands of white mobs than did Mexicans. This chapter seeks to draw explicit comparisons between the lynching of blacks and Mexicans. In doing so, it attempts to provide not only an original treatment of the little-studied subject of Mexican lynching but also endeavors to provide a new perspective on what was unique about the lynching of African Americans.[2]

Although scholars have long been aware of mob violence against Mexicans, there is no systematic study of this subject. The literature on lynching in particular is blinded by a black-white dichotomy that precludes any substantial analysis of mob violence against nonblack minorities. A comparative analysis of the lynching of African Americans and Mexicans also reveals the degree to which the black-white dichotomy has shaped racial and ethnic relations in the United States. African Americans asserted that their rights to protection under the law were greater than the rights of immigrants. By contrast, Mexicans protested mob violence by emphasizing their legal status as "white." These different protest strategies limited opportunities for collaboration.

Although they shared a common oppressor, African Americans and Mexicans did not die in similar numbers at the hands of white mobs. In terms of sheer numbers, the hundreds of Mexicans lynched in the United States do not compare with the thousands of African Americans murdered by mob violence. Scholars have confirmed that between 1882 and 1930, at least 3,346 blacks were lynched in the United States. By contrast, our research has verified the lynching of some 597 Mexicans between 1848 and 1928.[3]

As with the total for African Americans, this is a confirmed count of actual victims compiled from extensive archival research rather than an estimate. The 597 victims named in our database and analyzed in the tables below represent years of archival research. We have consulted dozens of English- and Spanish-language newspapers; scores of diaries, journals, and memoirs; the organizational files of civil rights organizations; oral history sources; government reports; local court records; and the diplomatic correspondence between the Mexican Embassy and the U.S. State Department. Despite the extent of this research, certainly many more than 597 Mexicans died at the hands of lynch mobs. As with African Americans, the names of all the Mexican victims will never be known.

Table 2.1. Mexican and African American Victims of Lynching per 100,000 of Population

Time Period	Mexican Lynching Victims per 100,000	African American Lynching Victims per 100,000
1880–1930	27.4	37.1

The greater number of confirmed African American lynching victims has led many scholars to concentrate on white mob action against blacks. Our research reveals, however, that Mexicans were as likely to be lynched as were African Americans. Because of the smaller size of the Spanish-speaking population, the chance of being murdered by an extralegal mob was roughly equal for both Mexicans and blacks (see table 2.1).[4]

Statistics alone can never explain lynching in the United States. A lynching victim's fate was sealed by the actions of vengeful mobs that often cared little for the individual's guilt or innocence. Such statistics, however, do establish the validity of a comparison between the lynching of Mexicans and African Americans. More than other Americans, blacks and Mexicans lived with the threat of lynching throughout the second half of the nineteenth and the first half of the twentieth century.

The media and historians have virtually ignored the lynching of Mexicans. One of the reasons that the lynching of Mexicans has remained so poorly investigated can be traced to the history of the word "lynching" itself. Although the term arose in the late eighteenth century, it did not come to mean an act of mob violence leading to the death of an individual until the 1830s. Even then, "lynching" was fairly restricted in the minds of many Americans. Especially in the North—where the abolitionists frequently used the term when reporting incidents of racial violence—the word came to be associated with the murder of a black man by a white Southern mob. This connection grew only stronger during the late nineteenth and early twentieth centuries. At that time, newspapers, colleges, and civil rights organizations began to compile statistics on lynching. They noted that mobs were murdering dozens and dozens of Americans each year. Most of these crimes occurred in the South. Most of the victims, the sources reported, were black. The connection of lynching with Southern white mobs and alleged black criminals now stood on verifiable, quantifiable ground.[5]

Yet, something was amiss with these statistics.[6] The way in which the principal groups collected their data failed to represent the complexity of the subject. Most of the organizations that compiled lynching data—Tuskegee

University, the Association of Southern Women for the Prevention of Lynching, and the National Association for the Advancement of Colored People—were primarily interested in the lynching of African Americans in the South. Although these organizations claimed to cover all lynchings in the United States, the collection of data was clearly biased regionally and racially.

The principal collectors of lynching data in the United States significantly undercounted lynching in the American Southwest in general and the lynching of Mexicans in particular. The undercount is obvious when one compares our data on Mexican lynching with that compiled by Tuskegee University. According to Tuskegee's archival records, the states of Texas, New Mexico, Arizona, and California played host to fifty lynchings involving Mexican victims. Yet our research has turned up more than two hundred Mexican lynching victims during that period. In other words, Tuskegee University failed to include in their statistics more than three-quarters of the Mexicans lynched during the period that they claimed to be systematically covering the crime of lynching. Similar undercounting errors plague the data compiled by the NAACP, the ASWPL, and the *Chicago Tribune.*

In addition to undercounting lynching victims, the primary lynching data sets conceal the multiethnic character of lynching. When Tuskegee researchers released their data on lynching to the public, they divided lynching victims into two racial categories, black and white. A close inspection of the actual lynching files in the archives of Tuskegee University reveals, however, that this division was misleading. In fact, Tuskegee had divided its data set into black victims and nonblack victims. The "white" category actually included Mexicans, Native Americans, Chinese, and a host of other ethnic minorities who were not considered fully "white" by the Anglo mobs that lynched them. For example, Tuskegee reported that mobs lynched thirty-six people in New Mexico between 1882 and 1968. Tuskegee reported that thirty-three of these victims were "white" and that the other three were black. Our investigation of Tuskegee's own records indicates that nine of the thirty-three whites were Mexicans and that one was a Native American. The pattern of ethnic misidentification is prevalent throughout the data on the Southwest and the states of the Far West. This error was in many ways more critical even than the undercount, because it virtually erased ethnicity from the discussion of lynching in the public journals and newspapers of the Northeast, Midwest, and Deep South.[7]

While Tuskegee and the other compilers of lynching data neglected mob violence against Mexicans, their inattention is understandable. They were headquartered east of the Mississippi where few Mexicans were lynched, and they were no doubt influenced by the long-standing cultural disposition to see lynchings as phenomena peculiar to the South and its racial problems. Yet, the tendency to see lynching as a peculiarly "Southern problem" has always competed with another explanation of lynching: one that associated mob law with the frontier and the American West.

Indeed, many Americans from the middle of the nineteenth century to the present—both in scholarly circles and in the public at large—have associated lynching with the image of a posse hanging a horse thief or with a "vigilance committee" executing a murderer. This view of lynching tends to portray the mob's actions as an essential function of the frontier. This argument, it will be clear from later parts of this chapter, is not entirely without merit. The frontier played a significant role in encouraging certain forms of violence. But this interpretation of western violence is too easy and too simple, for it accepts the justifications offered by the lynch mobs and the vigilance committees themselves. Furthermore, those who favor this view almost always assume that racism and ethnic competition played no significant role in western vigilantism. As recently as 1994, one of the most important scholars of violence in the United States gave no attention to race and ethnicity in his exposition of western violence.[8] Our research, however, suggests that race and ethnicity were significant aspects of the history of mob violence in the American West. One of the reasons that the lynching of Mexicans has been ignored by those fascinated with violence in the West is that it undermines the explanation that "inadequate legal institutions" resulted in western violence. If the actions of western mobs were animated by racism, it becomes harder to argue that they were simply taking the place of absent courts. The imperfections of early legal institutions may have encouraged lynching, but most of the mob violence directed at Mexicans was—like that directed at African Americans—designed to circumvent the legal authorities and the legal rights of the victims.

Although the similarities between the lynching of African Americans and Mexicans are revealing, the differences are even more enlightening. Mob violence against blacks and Mexicans followed different time lines. Although no reliable data exists for the period prior to 1880, the lynching of African Americans probably peaked first during the late 1860s and early 1870s. Thousands of blacks met their death at the hands of the Ku Klux Klan and other less-organized mobs during this period. The second peak for African American lynchings occurred during the 1890s and has been much better documented. By contrast, the last decade of the nineteenth century witnessed a relative absence of acts of mob violence against Mexicans. The lynching of Mexicans occurred with greatest frequency during the 1850s, then again in the 1870s, and once again in the second decade of the twentieth century (see table 2.2).

Table 2.2. Lynchings of African Americans and Mexicans by Decade

Decade	African Americans in Ten Southern States	Mexicans
1848–1850	No data	8
1851–1860	No data	160
1861–1870	No data	43
1871–1880	No data	147
1881–1890	445	73
1891–1900	822	24
1901–1910	580	8
1911–1920	431	124
1921–1930	184	10
Total	2,462	597

Source: Statistics for African American lynching victims are from Tolnay and Beck, *A Festival of Violence,* pp. 271–72. Tolnay and Beck did not include Texas or Virginia in their statistics. They also include no data on the period before 1882.

These striking differences suggest the need to rethink the traditional chronology of lynching. For several reasons, including the poor data available prior to 1880, almost all scholarly works on African American lynching hold to the same rough time frame, 1880–1930.[9] Any study of the lynching of Mexicans that confined itself to this framework would miss a significant number of those lynched and a crucial chapter in the overall story. More than half of all Mexicans who were lynched died before 1881. A study of Mexican lynching that began in 1880 would be severely limited by its lack of discussion of the tremendous anti-Mexican violence that arose during the 1850s and 1870s.

The story of African American lynching might be better understood if we had reliable data on mob violence against African Americans prior to 1880. In fact, George C. Wright's 1990 case study of racial violence in Kentucky has already suggested just that. Wright pointed out that many lynchings occurred during the period of Reconstruction in Kentucky. His evidence revealed that the decade after the Civil War—a period given little attention in many lynching studies—saw the most mob violence against African Americans. The history of Mexican lynching suggests even more powerfully the need to expand the traditional framework of lynching studies.[10]

Most lynchings of African Americans occurred in the South, whereas most lynchings of Mexicans occurred in the Southwest. In fact, nearly ninety-seven percent of all Mexican lynching victims met their fate in one of the four states bordering Mexico—Texas, New Mexico, Arizona, and California. These states contained nearly all of the Spanish-speaking population in the United States during the nineteenth and early twentieth centuries. As late as 1930, three-quarters of the Mexican population in the United States lived in just two states, Texas and California. Even within these states, the Mexican population was concentrated in certain regions. Mob violence was most frequent in those areas with dense Mexican populations. Scholars have long noted that the lynching of African Americans varied tremendously within the South depending upon demographic and economic factors. The same is true for Mexicans.[11]

The lynchings of both Mexicans and blacks were most commonly justified on the grounds that the victims had committed murder. Furthermore, Mexicans and African Americans were executed for assault, theft, and robbery—noncapital crimes for which whites seldom, if ever, suffered (see table 2.3).[12]

Yet the mobs that lynched Mexicans had their own defining characteristics. In contrast to mobs that lynched blacks, those executing Mexicans rarely charged their victims with committing sexual offenses. According to Stewart Tolnay and E. M. Beck, one-third of white mobs lynching blacks justified their actions on such a basis.[13] Only eight Mexicans, or less than two percent, were lynched for violations of sexual norms, even when defined broadly to mean any "inappropriate" behavior toward white women. Among these individuals was Juan Castillo, who was given three hundred lashes and confined in a boxcar in Trinidad, Colorado, for allegedly assaulting a young girl in the summer of 1884. When the girl died from her wounds, the mob took Castillo from the train car and hanged him.[14]

Whites generally appear to have believed that Mexicans constituted a different sort of racial menace than African Americans. Contemporary racial discourse portrayed African Americans as dangerous, brutal rapists who threatened the safety of white women. By contrast most whites did not view Mexicans as sexual predators. A white farmwife said, "You are more safe with them than with the Negroes."[15] Mexican control of economic resources, particularly land, constituted the primary threat to Anglo dominance of the West. It is therefore not surprising that struggles over property often triggered anti-Mexican violence. As table 2.3 demonstrates, Mexicans were nearly five times more likely than African Americans to be lynched for theft and robbery. Again, by contrast, African Americans historically had little access to property, but they did possess de jure constitutional rights. The need to maintain strict maintenance of social control

Table 2.3. Alleged Crimes of Lynching Victims

Alleged Crime	African Americans (%)	Mexicans (%)
Murder	37.3	56.8
Violations of Sexual Norms	33.6	1.3
Rape and Murder	1.9	0.2
Non-sexual Assault	9.8	2.5
Theft or Robbery	4.0	19.4
Other	10.3	5.9
Unknown	3.2	13.9

and de facto second-class citizenship consequently underpinned anti-black violence.

Victims of lynch mobs—no matter their race and ethnicity—were usually young men with little connection to the region where they were lynched. Mobs rarely tended to lynch women. When they did, however, they were more likely to lynch African American women than Mexican women. While 3.0 percent of African American victims were female, this was true of only 0.7 percent of Mexican victims.[16]

Although relatively few women were lynched in the United States, the lynching of one Spanish-speaking woman has garnered great attention. On July 5, 1851, a mob of thousands watched the lynching of a Mexican woman—sometimes called Juanita, more often known as Josefa—in Downieville, California. Josefa was convicted before a vigilante court of stabbing and killing Frederick Canon. Canon had attempted to break into Josefa's home. Historian Ralph Mann wrote that any mention of a "Spanish woman" by an Anglo in nineteenth-century California "invariably denoted a prostitute."[17] Canon was turned away, only to return again. Upon his arrival at her door the second time, Josefa stabbed and killed Canon. Until the moment she was hanged, Josefa claimed that her actions were motivated by self-defense.[18] Frederick Douglass, one of the first black leaders to comment on the lynching of a Mexican, wrote that if she had been white she would have been lauded for her deed instead of hanged for it. Douglass concluded that she was executed because of her "caste and Mexican blood."[19]

The attention of Frederick Douglass indicates this episode's notoriety. Indeed, it is probably the most infamous and most studied Mexican lynching. Unlike hundreds of other Mexican lynchings in the United States, Josefa's lynching is remembered today through sketches drawn by contemporary artists and by a historical marker in Downieville (see figure 2.1). The infamy of this episode is due to a number of reasons—the fact that the vic-

Figure 2.1. The hanging of a Mexican woman named Josefa in Downieville, California, on July 5, 1851. Racial stereotypes of Mexican females portrayed them as morally degenerate, far removed from their genteel white counterparts. This illustration appeared in William Downie, *Hunting for Gold* (San Francisco: The California Publishing Co., 1893), p. 151. *Courtesy* The Huntington Library, San Marino, California

tim was a woman, the size of the crowd, and the dignity of Josefa as she faced her impending doom.

Whites certainly viewed Mexican women as their inferiors and were ready to lynch them when they allegedly violated white ideas of acceptable behavior. Anglos, however, did not view Mexican women as murderers and cattle thieves. Only one of the four Mexican women lynched was branded as a bandit. In September, 1853, the woman—described only as a "game little vixen"—was taken from jail along with her six fellow prisoners, all Mexican men, and hanged in San Luis Obispo, California.[20] By contrast, two of the four female victims were lynched for the crime of witchcraft. In May, 1880, Refugio Ramirez, his wife—Silvestre Garcia—and their sixteen- or seventeen-year-old daughter, Maria Ines, were lynched in Collin County, Texas, for allegedly bewitching their fellow townspeople.[21]

Regardless of whether they were male or female, Mexican lynch victims suffered different forms of execution than did African Americans. Although hanging was the most common form of execution for both groups, Mexicans were more often shot by mobs than were African Americans. Conversely, blacks were more commonly burned or tortured.[22]

Mexicans were more commonly the victims of multiple lynchings than were African Americans. According to Stewart Tolnay and E. M. Beck, 2,018 lynchings involving African Americans occurred in ten Southern states between 1882 and 1930. Of these, only 286, or approximately 1 out of every 7, was a lynching that involved more than one victim. Our own data suggests that the proportion of Mexicans who were lynched in groups of two or more was markedly higher. Indeed, 2 out of every 5 cases involving Mexicans were multiple lynchings (see table 2.4).[23]

These figures include some of the largest lynchings ever to have occurred in the United States. Eleven Mexicans were hanged along the banks of the Nueces River in 1855.[24] In February, 1876, another eight were hanged for murder and robbery in Edinburg, Texas. Most startling of all was the July, 1877, mob killing of at least forty Mexicans in Nueces County, Texas. In an act of vengeance for the murder of Lee Rabb, Anglos rampaged through the county, indiscriminately murdering any Mexican who crossed their path.[25]

Mexicans were more likely to be lynched in groups of two or more for several reasons. First, most Mexicans lived and worked with other Mexicans. Whether in the gold mines of California or on the cattle ranches of Texas, Mexican labor often involved a dozen or more people. By contrast, African Americans in the late nineteenth and early twentieth centuries were primarily sharecroppers who worked in single-family units. Lynch mobs seeking victims were thus likely to find several Mexican men at the same time but might come across black men one at a time. A second factor is related to the different racial stereotypes discussed earlier. Sexual assault—a crime with which whites often accused blacks (but rarely Mexicans)—is usually considered the act of a single individual. Theft and robbery, crimes for which Mexicans were often lynched, can be regarded as group crimes.

Finally, the third reason that Mexicans were more likely to be lynched in large groups involves the cultural distance between whites and Mexicans and whites and blacks. A considerable gulf existed between white and black culture in the South. Racism led many whites to confuse or misidentify blacks. The record of African American lynching is replete with the murder of innocent victims. Such tragedies occurred despite the fact that whites and blacks shared the same language, the same religion, and a history of close contact for more than two centuries. It is not difficult to imagine the even greater difficulties that whites had in identifying Mexicans. Not only did they speak a different language and practice a different religion; most whites and Mexicans had little contact until the middle of the nineteenth century. The unfamiliarity with Mexican culture, especially the Spanish language, made it difficult for Anglo mobs to conduct investigations and determine who among a group of Mexicans was guilty of the alleged transgression. Unable to decide who was "guilty" and who was not, white mobs indiscriminately lynched whole groups of Mexicans.[26]

One tragic example of the mob's lack of discrimination when pursuing Mexican criminals occurred in 1857 after the murder of a sheriff near Los

Table 2.4. Multiple-Victim Lynchings

Number of Victims	African Americans (%)	Mexicans (%)
1	85.8	60.8
2	9.4	17.9
3	2.8	10.3
4	1.3	3.3
5	0.4	2.2
More than 5	0.3	5.5

Angeles, California.[27] A Southern Californian named Bill Rubottom recalled: "It has been estimated that one hundred and fifty-eight persons were killed to avenge the death of Sheriff Barton and his posse, and not one of his murderers was of this number. No, not one! They escaped and innocent men were slaughtered. It makes my blood boil to think of it." During this violent period, Rubottom was living at El Monte. Unaware of the dangerous white mobs about, he sent his servant, a Mexican named Joe, to facilitate the sale of some corn with a neighbor. When Joe did not return on time, Rubottom went to investigate. One Anglo told him that a mob had killed one of Barton's murderers over at the mission. They were certain because the Mexican had possessed Barton's saddle, bridle, and spurs. Arriving at San Gabriel, he met an Anglo who told him, "Well, we got him!" Upon further inquiry, Rubottom was told that the victim was one "of them greasers that killed Barton and the boys." When shown the corpse, Rubottom saw "a headless, bloody corpse on the floor. So horribly was the body mutilated with knives that it was unrecognizable, nor could the identity be established by clothes for most of them were gone." The head had been cut off by a doctor and sent to Los Angeles. Rubottom found the saddle, bridle, and spurs that had belonged to Joe and had never belonged to Barton. "For a moment I felt paralyzed, the world seemed to have slid from under my feet, I gasped for breath. There was a great roaring in my head." Rubottom later recovered the head and gave Joe a Christian burial. While not technically a multiple lynching, this episode reveals all too well the lack of careful investigation that led to the deaths of large numbers of Mexicans. In the final analysis, the number of multiple lynchings suggests that Mexicans, even more than blacks, may have been the victims of random and indiscriminate mob violence.[28]

Historians of racial violence in the South have debated the underlying causes of African American lynching for decades. W. Fitzhugh Brundage wrote that "the pathology of lynchings was neither random nor irrational. A brutal logic underlay the violence."[29] Indeed, few scholars or members of the media question the fact that underlying socioeconomic and cultural factors shaped the lynching of African Americans. Rampant black criminal behavior, the cause attributed by the mob and its defenders, has been rightfully dismissed as a sufficient explanation.

Historians have also debated the origins of violence in the American West. Traditionally, they have been far more sympathetic to the justifications offered by the lynch mobs and the vigilante courts, noting that the economic and demographic development of the frontier rapidly outpaced the growth of legal and governmental institutions. Faced with the absence or impotence of proper legal authorities, historians have suggested that the frontiersmen were forced to take the law into their own hands. As Wayne Gard observed over half a century ago: "Sometimes they imposed overly severe penalties, or executed wrong men; but usually they were fair, and their activities discouraged crime. The work of the vigilance committees was a form of social action against bad men and a step toward the setting up of statutory courts."[30] Although the New Western History challenges these traditional notions, historians such as Gard still influence popular theories of frontier violence. Even the recent work of Richard Maxwell Brown, one of the most sophisticated scholars of western violence, minimizes the role of racism.[31]

Much evidence exists to support the traditional view of mob violence in the West. The diaries, journals, and letters of western settlers are filled with references to the instability of society and the weakness of the judicial system. One Californian wrote in 1853: "I am opposed to Capital Punishment in communities when they have prisons to keep murderers secure for life, but in new settlements, and new countries, like California where there is little or no protection from the hands of such monsters in human shape, it becomes necessary to dispose of them by the shortest mode, for the safety of the community."[32] This defense of mob law was not limited to California or to the gold rush period. In the early 1880s, citizens in Socorro, New Mexico, formed a vigilance committee out of frustration with the local judicial system. Claude D. Potter remembered that the committee "had the tacit endorsement of the highest territorial official, was composed of the reputable Americans of the town including in its membership, bankers, clergymen, merchants, ranchmen, miners, lawyers, doctors, and all others interested in the enforcement of law and order."[33] In 1920, a Texan cited the weakness of the government as a justification for vigilante action. Mexican "raiding parties began to come over and wantonly destroy ranches, murder, and rob until it got to be unbearable, and the people, the citizens themselves rose, en masse."[34]

Although the instability of legal institutions certainly contributed to violence in the West, this explanation is lacking. Most Mexican victims of lynching were not executed by vigilante courts that followed the spirit of the laws. Vigilance committees were responsible for relatively few lynchings involving Mexicans. Mexicans were much more likely to be lynched on the spot after being captured by a "posse" or hanged quickly after being forcefully taken from the judicial authorities by a "terrorist" mob.[35]

Even those lynchings involving vigilance committees sometimes exhibited a lack of respect for the rights of the accused. For example, in the early 1850s, a mob apprehended a Mexican whom it accused of horse theft. Although some members of the mob were in favor of shooting the victim immediately, one mob member proclaimed, "to shoot those Greasers ain't the best way. Give 'em a fair jury trial, and rope 'em up with all the majesty of the law." Persuaded by this eloquence, the mob elected a vigilance committee that retired to a room to debate the case. When they emerged with a verdict of "not guilty," a mob leader told them that the decision was "wrong" and asked them to reconsider. After resuming discussion for a half-hour, the vigilance committee emerged with a guilty verdict. The mob leader proclaimed the decision "right" . . . and revealed that the Mexican had already been hanged an hour earlier.[36]

Such an incident reveals that Anglo mobs were not primarily interested in administering justice in the absence of formal legal structures. Indeed, a legal system was in place from the very beginning in those territories acquired from Mexico in 1848. Historians Joseph A. Stout, Jr., and Odie B. Faulk note the smooth transition from Mexican law to American law when the United States annexed the Southwest.[37] Most vigilance committees were not created to be substitutes for courts but were instead designed to circumvent them. This was certainly the case in 1880s Socorro, New Mexico, where an all-white vigilance committee arose in opposition to the Mexican American legal authorities.[38] The problem lay not in the lack of a western legal structure but rather in the Anglos' disdain of a judicial system influenced by or controlled by Mexicans. One observer wrote in 1849: "As to government, we would do very well for ourselves if we were not cursed by the interference of Gen. Riley . . . insisting that Mexican law must rule here which every decent white man here is convinced is inapplicable to Americans."[39] In 1859, an officer in the United States Army arrived in Santa Barbara, California, to investigate a recent spate of ethnic conflict that had led to the lynching of an elderly Mexican man and his sixteen-year-old son. In explaining the affair to his superiors, he wrote that Mexicans outnumbered local whites four to one, outvoted them at the polls, and controlled the judicial system. These conditions, he concluded, created a prejudice against Mexicans that was "almost a monomania" and made the whites "morally insane."[40]

Our investigation of Mexican lynching reveals that most mob actions occurred not only in areas with a fully-operating legal system but that many lynchings occurred in the presence of law officers themselves. A United

States senator from California, for instance, remembered observing a lynching in which officials of the law stood by and tacitly approved of the mob's actions.[41] In many cases, law officers played a key role in fomenting anti-Mexican extralegal violence. In 1849, a deputy sheriff in California named Dick Clark decapitated a Mexican with his bowie knife after he refused an arrest warrant.[42] The Spanish-language newspaper of Los Angeles, *El Clamor Público,* reported on February 14, 1857, that a justice of the peace in the vicinity of Mission San Gabriel took out his knife and cut the head off the body of a Mexican, then "rolled it around with his foot as if it were a rock; then he thrust the knife into the chest several times with a brutality rarely seen even amongst these very barbarians."[43]

Texas Rangers were particularly notorious for their use of extralegal violence against Mexicans. Walter Prescott Webb wrote that the border violence of the early twentieth century was an "orgy of bloodshed" in which "the Texas Rangers played a prominent part, and one which many members of the force have been heartily ashamed."[44] Estimates for the number of Mexicans killed by or with the approval of Texas Rangers in the Southwest are in the hundreds, if not the thousands.[45] During the night of September 13, 1915, three alleged Mexican bandits were taken from their jail cells in San Benito, Texas. After they were shot and killed, their corpses were left to rot some five and a half miles from San Benito. Officials claimed that they were shot attempting to escape.[46] January 27, 1918, marked the most infamous incident involving the Texas Rangers: the massacre at Porvenir. The Texas Rangers surrounded the community of Porvenir and questioned its residents about an earlier raid. When the Mexicans were not forthcoming, the Rangers selected fifteen men, marched them to a rock bluff, and shot them dead.[47]

The actions of the Texas Rangers and other western officials suggest that mob attacks on Mexicans were motivated by underlying factors which had little to do with the lack of formal legal institutions in the West. As with the lynching of African Americans, Mexican lynching was often motivated by forces more complicated than the simple desire to punish alleged criminals.

One factor that no doubt played a role in the lynching of Mexicans was that they were often immigrants to the United States and thus strangers to the majority of the resident Anglo population. Roberta Senechal de la Roche has persuasively argued that lynchings more commonly occurred when those accused of transgressions were strangers to the local community. Cultural distance indeed influenced mob violence against Mexicans. However, this is not in itself a sufficient explanation for the disproportionate number of Mexicans lynched in the Southwest. For example, much of the mob violence that occurred during the early years of the gold rush was inflicted by Anglo "immigrants" against the Mexicans and Native Americans who already lived in California.[48]

In addition to cultural distance, scholars of lynching have emphasized the important role that economic conditions played in instigating mob violence against blacks. Arthur Raper's 1933 classic, *The Tragedy of Lynching*, identified this connection, and it has been forcefully reiterated in the recent studies of Stewart Tolnay, E. M. Beck, and W. Fitzhugh Brundage. Tolnay and Beck found that lynchings were almost twice as numerous in the cotton belt of the South. Attacks were most frequent when cotton prices were falling and in counties with large numbers of white tenants. They concluded that white elites, anxious over possible coalitions of black and white workers, combined with the poor white population, themselves anxious over competition with blacks for employment, to make certain regions of the South especially prone to lynching.[49] Brundage also explained regional variation in lynching by noting that mob violence was particularly common in cotton counties dominated by sharecropping.[50]

As with African Americans, economic factors greatly contributed to Anglo–Mexican violence in the Southwest. The California gold rush provides the clearest example of this. According to one estimate, as many as 25,000 Mexicans migrated to the mining regions of California between 1848 and 1852. Few were able to stay long enough to share in the wealth generated by the discovery of gold. White settlers asserted their sovereignty over the mines through discriminatory legislation and mob violence. A typical example of conflict between Anglos and Mexicans was recorded on December 29, 1850, in the diary of Chauncey Caufield. Some miners "found out that the Mexicans had struck the biggest kind of deposit. It made them mad to think that a lot of 'greasers' were getting the benefit of it, so they organized a company and drove them away by threats and force and then worked the grounds themselves."[51] According to numerous sources, mobs murdered at least 163 Mexicans in California during the peak gold rush years of 1848–60. These acts of mob violence also often involved the destruction of property. In an 1853 diary entry, Elias Ketcham recorded the actions of a mob in search of Mexican criminals: the "pursuers are reported to have destroyed all the Mexican tents or dwellings that came in their way . . . the innocens [*sic*] must suffer for the guilty in that case, but many persons who are prejudiced say they are all alike, a set of cut throats [and] should be exterminated, or drove out of the country."[52] These repressive measures forced most Mexicans to abandon both the mines and their prospects.

Although the California gold rush witnessed some of the worst acts of mob violence against Mexicans, whites also resorted to savagery—in order to secure economic supremacy—on other occasions. Actions during the Texas "Cart War" of 1857 exemplify this. During the 1850s, Tejano businessmen developed a freight-hauling service between Indianola and San Antonio. Frustrated at having been beaten out by the lower prices of their Mexican rivals, white competitors resorted to murdering cartmen, driving off their oxen and burning their carts and freight. Economic rivalry with Mexicans continued to inspire retributive action by whites throughout the late nineteenth and early twentieth centuries. In 1898, a group of Gonzales, Texas, men—probably poor white sharecroppers in competition with Mexican immigrants—posted this warning: "Notice to the Mexicans. You have all got ten days to leave in. Mr. May Renfro and brother get your Mexicans all off your place. If not, you will get the same they do. Signed, Whitecaps." In the 1920s, alarm at the increasing number of Mexican laborers who settled in the Rio Grande valley contributed to the growth of the local Ku Klux Klan.[53]

Economic competition, although a significant force, does not sufficiently explain the history of anti-Mexican or anti-black mob violence. If mobs had considered only economics, they would have been just as likely to murder or expel any group standing in their way. But, in fact, mobs specially targeted Mexicans in the southwestern United States. Racism and prejudice, it is clear, played a fundamental role in encouraging mob violence against Mexicans. Mexicans were portrayed as a cruel and treacherous people with a natural proclivity toward criminal behavior. Racist stereotypes abounded in private correspondence, contemporary literature, and the popular media. "The lower class of Mexicans, on the west coast, appear to be a dark, Indian-looking race, with just enough of the Spanish blood, without its appropriate intelligence, to add a look of cunning to their gleaming, treacherous eyes," wrote Theodore T. Johnson in 1849.[54] In April, 1872, the *Weekly Arizona Miner* exclaimed: "Bad Mexicans never tire of cutting throats, and we are sorry to be compelled to say that good Mexicans are rather scarce."[55] These assumptions, legitimated by pseudoscientific research, remained prevalent well into the twentieth century. A track foreman interviewed in the late 1920s in Dimmit County, Texas, observed: "They are an inferior race. I would not think of classing Mexicans as whites."[56]

Although widespread, Anglo racial attitudes toward Spanish-speakers differed depending upon class, national origin, ethnic background, and skin color. The Anglo majority sometimes considered elite Mexicans and Spanish-speakers from other Latin American nations to be "white." At the same time, Anglos likely regarded Mexicans of evident African ancestry as "black." This fluidity illustrates one of the great differences between the Mexican experience and the African American experience. African Americans—like Mexicans—were ethnically diverse. In addition to the significant ethnic diversity among Africans themselves, African Americans have intermarried with Anglos, Mexicans, Asians, Indians, and other groups for centuries. Yet, Anglos carefully separated all those of even the slightest African ancestry into a single group denoted by their "blackness." At the same time, Anglos constructed an identity of "whiteness" to link those with European backgrounds.[57]

"Whiteness" was not, however, automatically bestowed upon all non-blacks in American society. The case of Mexicans shows that an individual's background played a significant role in his or her ability to partake in the benefits of "whiteness." During the gold rush, whites often distinguished among Mexicans. Anglos, in particular, drew clear distinctions between the native Californian elite and the mass of Mexican gold seekers. "The Californians, as a race, are vastly superior to the Mexicans," wrote *New York Times* journalist Bayard Taylor. The "families of pure Castilian blood resemble in features and build the descendants of the Valencians in Chili and Mexico, whose original physical superiority over the natives of the other provinces of Spain has not been obliterated by two hundred years of transplanting."[58]

The fact that the white majority sometimes distinguished elite Mexicans from other Spanish-speakers allowed some Mexicans to escape some of the worst aspects of prejudice in the United States Southwest. For example, wealthy, well-established Mexican leaders were not likely to be lynched by white mobs. In fact, upon occasion, such leaders were actually invited to participate in the deliberations and actions of vigilance committees. These benefits were always contingent, however, upon cooperation with the white majority. Antonio Franco Coronel was appointed to a vigilance committee to decide the fate of three Mexicans alleged to have murdered an Anglo. When Coronel declared that the death penalty was not warranted, his opinion was disregarded, and the three Mexicans were hanged.[59]

No matter how highly regarded Spanish-speakers might be due to their class status or elite background, Anglos reserved the right to deny them citizenship rights. An 1857 incident in Southern California proves illustrative. In June, a gentleman of obvious social standing named Sir Ramon Garcia applied for admittance to the Temperance Society of Green Valley. He was denied, being deemed "too dark skinned" by the society's leaders.[60] It was this fact of life—that one's rights depended upon docile cooperation with the will of a fickle white majority—that forged another parallel between the black experience and the Mexican experience. In the end, the white majority perceived most Spanish-speakers, as they did African Americans, as threats to the stability of the social order. This fear seared white minds and predisposed them to acts of repressive violence against Mexicans. One Anglo wrote in 1850 that the phrase "see the elephant" in California meant "to shoot three Indians, hang two greasers (Mexicans), kill a grisly bear, and dig a seven pound lump of gold."[61] The *Austin Statesman* described the killing on May 27, 1893, of a Mexican in Cleburne, Texas, as advantageous, because it left the world "one greaser less."[62] Mary J. Jaques commented in her account of Texas ranch life that "it is difficult to convince these people that a Mexican is a human being. He seems to be the Texan's natural enemy; he is treated like a dog, or, perhaps not so well."[63]

The actions of mobs in both Mexican and African American lynchings frequently contained acts of ritualized torture and sadism, something that rarely happened to white victims of mob law. The most common forms of mutilation included the burning and shooting of bodies after they had been hanged, although more extreme examples occurred. The beheading of a Mexican accused of the murder of Sheriff Barton was discussed earlier. Another case of bodily torture took place in January, 1896, when Aureliano Castellón was lynched in Senior, Texas, for allegedly making sexual advances toward a white teenage girl. Shot repeatedly by his assailants, his body was then covered with oil and set alight until it had been "burned almost beyond recognition." Similar acts of brutality against Mexicans continued into the twentieth century.[64] By turning the lynching of Mexicans into a public spectacle, whites sent a powerful warning that they would not tolerate any challenge to their political hegemony.

Although white racism and economic competition both helped foment mob violence against blacks and Mexicans, the lynching of Mexicans was often tied to a third factor for which there is no direct comparison with African American lynching—border conflict and diplomatic tensions with Mexico. The three greatest periods of mob violence against Mexicans occurred during the 1850s, the 1870s, and 1910s, decades when ethnic tension along the border reached its most dangerous peaks. Conflicts between Americans and Mexicans did not conclude with the signing in 1848 of the Treaty of Guadalupe Hidalgo. In fact, the next decade was rife with anti-Mexican violence, especially along the newly established border. After a brief period of stability during the American Civil War, the border had by the 1870s again become engulfed in intense and continuous conflict that reached to the highest levels of government in both nations. During this period of diplomatic tension, at least 131 Mexicans were murdered by lynch mobs. A similar situation arose during the Mexican Revolution, when thousands of Mexicans crossed and recrossed the U.S.-Mexican border. The first decade of the twentieth century witnessed a sharp decline in the lynching of Mexicans; the figure fell below one per year for the first time since the U.S.-Mexican War. This downward trend was dramatically reversed during the decade of the Mexican Revolution. Between 1911 and 1920, at least 123 Mexicans were lynched the largest number in a single decade since the disturbances of the 1870s.

At times of heightened diplomatic tensions between Mexico and the United States, the lynching of Mexicans occurred with the greatest ferocity. The dramatic increase in mob violence led to the rapid deterioration of diplomatic relations. This in turn intensified negative stereotypes of Mexicans, stirring yet further brutalities. As Secretary of State Hamilton Fish observed in January, 1873, of Anglo reaction to Mexican cattle raiders: "The exasperation of the immediate sufferers will inevitably extend to the rest of their countrymen, and retaliation will be demanded in a tone which it may be difficult to resist."[65]

Although diplomatic conflict did not directly cause lynching, it was a crucial contributory factor. On one hand, instability in the Mexican government undermined appeals for protection of Mexican citizens in the United States. On the other hand, hostilities between the two governments in the international arena filtered down to the local level. Ultimately, the role of international politics represents one of the most defining characteristics of anti-Mexican mob violence.

Both Mexicans and African Americans vigorously protested lynching, but Mexicans possessed opportunities for resistance that were unavailable to most African Americans. Such differences may account for the end of Mexican American lynching decades before the demise of mob violence against African Americans.

Although blacks could and did resist white mob violence by arming and defending themselves, such retaliatory violence was more common among Mexicans in the Southwest because of the ability of Mexicans to retreat from angry mobs by crossing the U.S.-Mexico border. Any African American or Mexican American who could be found after violently assaulting a white man (even in self-defense) was likely to be killed. Only by flight could one realistically hope to commit such an act and live. A hidden base camp in one of the many isolated parts of the American West may have offered viable refuge during the middle of the nineteenth century, but an escape across the border represented the best of all options at any time. As the population density of the West increased, it became the only real possibility.

African Americans themselves occasionally benefited from the Mexican border to escape white brutality. Thousands of enslaved Africans abandoned slavery in Texas to cross into Mexico during the antebellum period.[66] Even in the postbellum period, blacks in Texas escaped across the Mexican border after committing acts of retaliatory violence. On January 4, 1891, three black men in Central Texas assassinated George Taylor, "whom the negroes accused of leading the lynchers" of an African American named Charles Beall two days earlier. The vengeful whites who subsequently set out in search of the three black men never caught them. They presumed that the black men fled to Mexico.[67] Although such incidents may be more common than scholars of African American history have previously appreciated, Mexicans were certainly better able to exploit the advantages of the border than were most blacks.

Most whites in the nineteenth century attributed Mexican violence to the natural criminal proclivities of the Mexican race, whom they often branded as "bandits." Although whites used the term derisively to mean organized bands of murderers and thieves, Mexicans, like the peasants of early modern Europe, attached a different meaning to the word. They perceived "bandits" as heroic figures who defended the Mexican population against Anglo brutality.[68]

Many Mexicans had indeed turned to "banditry" as a result of white mob violence. Ygnacio Villegas recalled that because of rampant mob violence "many Mexicans became desperate and stole and killed to get money and food."[69] The Anglo newspaper *Alta California* observed in a moment of rare introspection that "if a foreign people had subjugated our native land, and had so oppressed its citizens, and trampled upon their individual rights, that we do not know and cannot say, that we could have felt differently towards our oppressors, than do the Spanish population towards us." Paradoxically, the newspaper then went on to urge the formation of vigilance committees to rid the country of Mexican "bandits" and the "vagrant population."[70]

The most famous of the so-called Mexican "bandits" is probably Joaquín Murrieta. According to various accounts, Murrieta was one of the thousands of Mexicans driven from the gold mines of California. Although he attempted to establish an honest trade around the camps as a merchant, he was accused of horse theft and severely whipped. His half brother was hanged for the same offense. Twice a victim of white brutality, Murrieta turned to force and retaliation until his own violent death several years later.[71] Murrieta was not alone. In 1852, Tiburcio Vásquez turned to violence after two of his friends were hanged for their role in a fight with Anglos at a dance in Monterrey, California.[72] After he was caught years later, Vásquez explained his actions. "A spirit of hatred and revenge took possession of me," he said, "I had numerous fights in defense of what I believed to be my rights and those of my countrymen." He concluded: "I believed we were being unjustly deprived of the social rights that belonged to us."[73]

Another Mexican who greatly angered whites was Juan Cortina. Between 1859 and 1873, Cortina and his gang engaged in a series of bitter and bloody confrontations with the U.S. military along the Texas border. Cortina proclaimed to be an instrument of divine retribution sent to avenge those murdered and dispossessed by whites. Cortina reserved particular wrath for the local and state authorities who continued to tolerate the lynching of his people. He once observed: "There are to be found criminals covered with frightful crimes, but they appear to have impunity until opportunity furnish [*sic*] them a victim; to these monsters indulgence is shown, because they are not of our race, which is unworthy, as they say, to belong to the human species."[74] Scholars have described Murrieta, Vásquez, and Cortina as "social bandits" who raided in retaliation against the forces of racism that repressed Mexicans throughout the Southwest.[75]

Mexicans' retaliatory actions often served only to compound racial conflict. Retaliatory raids provoked whites to further reprisals against Mexicans. This in turn strengthened the bitter resolve of the recalcitrant Mexicans. A vicious circle of violence and retribution was therefore created. In October, 1859, Texas Rangers lynched Thomas Cabrera, a leading member of the Cortina gang. An enraged Cortina immediately launched a murderous assault on white settlers near Brownsville, Texas.[76] The persistence of these raids provided whites with an excuse to condemn all Mexicans as a dangerously criminal people whose presence in the Southwest posed a continued threat to white settlement. Francisco P. Ramírez of the Spanish-language newspaper *El Clamor Público* understood the danger of retaliatory action. He wrote on July, 1856, that "the Mexicans are growing tired of being run over and having injustices committed against them; but to take up arms to redress their grievances, this is an act without reason."[77]

Although retaliatory violence provided Mexicans with an additional option for resisting white violence that most African Americans did not have, this resistance carried the very real risk of stirring whites to yet greater brutalities. White mob violence did not end as a result of retaliatory violence by Mexicans. Indeed, much evidence exists that it exacerbated tensions and enflamed white mobs. In the end, another form of resistance proved more effective at curtailing the actions of white mobs. Like retaliatory violence, this mode of resistance was one largely unavailable to African Americans.[78]

Mexicans, especially those born in Mexico, were eventually able to place diplomatic pressure upon the American government to end mob violence against Mexicans in the United States. The Mexican newspaper *El Sonorense* kept its readers abreast of the expulsions and violence in the Southwest, sarcastically concluding: "Such is the behavior of illustrious free men in civilized North America."[79] In 1853, the Mexican government responded to this news by vigorously protesting violence against Mexican citizens who resided in the United States. Mexican Minister Don Manuel Larrainzar complained about the treatment and expulsion of Mexican miners. Later Mexican consuls made repeated complaints to the U.S. State Department regarding "the unjustly depressed and miserable condition in which Mexicans resident in the State of Texas and Territory of New Mexico are held."[80]

Although Mexican officials continued throughout the next twenty years to draw the attention of the Department of State to the suffering of their citizens, U.S. officials effectively ignored their outrage. In 1881, the Mexican ambassador in Washington, Manuel de Zamacona, wrote to Secretary of State James G. Blaine to report a lynching of a Mexican accused of horse theft in Willcox, Arizona. Blaine conceded that the man was hanged illegally, but he also observed that José Ordoña and his accomplice "were probably outlaws" and that he therefore deserved his fate. Blaine based his conclusion entirely on the testimony of the local sheriff, R. H. Paul. Rather than send its own representatives to the scene of a lynching, the State Department relied upon reports written by local officials who condoned the actions of the mob—if indeed they were not actual members of it.[81]

Not until the 1890s did the protests of Mexican officials finally start to receive a positive response from the State Department. On August 26, 1895, a mob stormed the jailhouse at Yreka, California, and seized four men awaiting trial on separate murder charges. The prisoners were hauled into the courthouse square and hanged from an iron rail fastened into the forks of two trees. One of the victims was a Mexican by the name of Luis Moreno.[82]

The Mexican government demanded that those responsible be punished and that a suitable indemnity be paid to the heirs of Luis Moreno. Although a grand jury failed to return any indictments against members of the mob, President William McKinley recommended to Congress the payment of a $2,000 indemnity.[83]

The Moreno case established a precedent for Mexican and U.S. governmental responses to later lynchings. For instance, on October 11, 1895, a small gang of armed men took Florentino Suaste from a prison cell in Cotulla, Texas. The men shot and then hanged him. An investigation by Mexican officials revealed a deliberate attempt by local authorities to conceal the identities of the murderers. The grand jury placed its proceedings under seal after failing to return a single indictment. When the proceedings were eventually ordered opened, no evidence existed that the grand jury had summoned a single witness. The report compiled by the local district attorney was based entirely upon the testimony of a deputy sheriff named Swink. Because Swink and his superior officer, W. L. Hargus, were later sued by the relatives of Suaste for their involvement in the lynching, his word could not be considered reliable. The federal government cited its decision in the Moreno case in awarding the Suaste relatives a $2,000 indemnity.[84]

After years of disregarding Mexican protests, what provoked this change in U.S. policy? By the late nineteenth century, governments throughout the world were criticizing the United States for its inability to protect foreign nationals on its soil. Although the federal government continued to insist that it had no authority to intervene in the affairs of individual states, it did endeavor to resolve any incipient domestic crises by providing financial compensation to the families of lynching victims. This occurred after the 1888 massacre of Chinese miners at Rock Springs, Wyoming, and again in 1891, following the murder of Sicilian immigrants in New Orleans and, in 1895, in Hahnville, Louisiana. The indemnities paid to the families of Luis Moreno and Florentine Suaste must therefore be seen in the context of efforts by the federal government to safeguard the international reputation of the United States.[85]

Mexican protest was also instrumental in the eventual decline and end of the lynching of Mexicans. Antonio Rodriguez's lynching on November 2, 1910, provoked a storm of protest throughout Mexico. Rioting erupted on November 8 in Mexico City as angry demonstrators stoned the windows of American businesses and tore and spat upon the United States flag. Three days later, rioters in Guadalajara wreaked similar damage against American property. In Chihuahua, American citizens were openly mobbed on the streets. Tensions along the Rio Grande were so strained that an estimated two thousand Texans armed themselves in advance of a suspected Mexican invasion. Although the Mexican government denounced the violence, rumors of war grew ever louder. Tensions increased severely as Mexicans announced widespread boycotts of U.S. goods.[86]

The reaction to the lynching of Antonio Rodriguez revealed to the United States that Mexico would not tolerate the continued abuse of its citizens. The nationally circulated news magazine, the *Independent*, asserted that the people of Mexico had believed that Rodriguez was one of their citizens, and this had led them to rise "in righteous wrath" against the United States. According to the *Independent*, diplomatic tensions would deteriorate still further unless the federal government took decisive action to protect the rights of Mexican nationals. Indeed, throughout the following decade Mexico repeatedly raised this issue. Mexican officials carefully prepared for publication an extensive list of violent assaults against Mexican citizens.[87]

The persistence of Mexican protests undoubtedly played a key role in the eventual decline of Mexican lynchings. Acts of racial violence against Mexicans continued sporadically throughout the 1920s. Though the U.S. government had previously failed to secure justice for the families of Mexican lynch victims, it now took tough action. Perhaps the most telling example of the impact of Mexican protest is the case of five Mexicans lynched in September, 1926, in Raymondville, Texas. Initial reports of the lynchings were wildly contradictory. According to Sheriff Raymond Teller, the Mexicans had murdered two of his officers. After their arrest, Teller took the suspects out of jail into the countryside in search of their cache of arms. Teller claimed that they were ambushed and that the prisoners were killed in the cross fire. Yet others testified that Teller himself was responsible for the deaths of the suspects. The crucial breakthrough occurred when the bodies were exhumed. Examiners discovered that the officers had executed and tortured the dead men. One of the suspects, Thomas Nuñez, had even reportedly been beheaded. For decades the State Department had, in its investigations of Mexican lynchings, invariably accepted the reports of local law officers without question. The Nuñez case demonstrated the new determination to avoid diplomatic tensions with Mexico over the lynching of its citizens on American soil. Sheriff Teller and his fellow officers were tried for their involvement in the murder of the five Mexicans. The historical record is unclear as to whether or not Teller and his men were convicted. Nevertheless, the Nuñez case effectively concluded one of the worst chapters in the history of the West.[88]

Although diplomatic protest and retaliatory violence provided Mexicans with options for resistance unavailable to African Americans, the two groups shared other forms of resistance. Journalists and newspaper editors, for example, spoke out for both groups. W. E. B. Du Bois and Ida B. Wells devoted great energy to exposing the brutality of African American lynching in the United States. Francisco P. Ramírez in Los Angeles, California, and Carlos I. Velasco in Tucson, Arizona, protested the mistreatment and lynching of Mexicans. Both Mexicans and blacks eventually organized civil rights groups that protested lynching. In 1909, African Americans and sympathetic Anglos formed the National Association for the Advancement of Colored People, dedicated to the extension of civil rights for blacks in general and the end of mob violence against blacks in particular. On September 14, 1911, four hundred Spanish-speaking delegates gathered at El Primer Congreso Mexicanista in Laredo, Texas, and denounced the brutal oppression of Mexicans that had continued unchecked since the signing of the Treaty of Guadalupe Hidalgo.[89]

Despite the fact that blacks and Mexicans shared the danger of white mob violence and similar forms of protest, they rarely united to protest lynchings. Indeed, each group tended to distance itself from the other during much of the era of mass lynching. Mexicans hoped to make the most of their ambiguous position between blacks and whites by emphasizing their "whiteness." Lieutenant Colonel Cyrus Roberts wrote from the border in 1899 that Mexicans accepted their inferior relationship with local whites but believed themselves superior to the black soldiers stationed on the border. Mexicans, he believed, sought social mobility by assuming the racial views of the Anglo majority who reinforced this strategy by openly siding with the Mexicans against the blacks whenever a dispute occurred.[90] The League of United Latin American Citizens formally sanctioned Mexican prejudice against African Americans. The organization urged the Anglo majority to recognize that Mexicans were "white" and to treat them as such. To help foster this process, LULAC leaders urged their membership not to associate with African Americans, reinforcing the color line separating black from white.[91]

The lack of coalition-building between Mexicans and blacks is exemplified in the absence of each group in the other's civil rights organizations. Whereas LULAC actively urged members to distance themselves from African Americans, the NAACP had no such policy. In practice, however, Mexicans were involved in neither the organization's leadership nor in its local branches. The membership rolls of the NAACP reveal that local branches throughout New Mexico—in such cities as Albuquerque, Las Cruces, Gallup, and Raton—had no Mexican members. Membership lists from Texas cities with large Mexican populations, such as El Paso and Corpus Christi, indicate not one person with a Mexican surname.[92]

Although African Americans never defended the lynching of Mexicans, they tended to resent the greater attention given to Mexican victims of mob violence by the State Department. If Secretary of State "Hughes can ask Governor Neff [of Texas] about a lynched Mexican why shouldn't" the Department of Justice "ask about a lynched AMERICAN?" lamented the *Chicago Defender,* one of the nation's leading black newspapers.[93] African Americans charged the American government with a double standard—that federal officials urged state and local authorities to track down those responsible for lynching Mexicans while ignoring the more frequent murders of blacks by white mobs.[94]

Such attitudes prevented African Americans and Mexicans from fully uniting against the Anglo American majority's discriminatory policies. As time progressed, however, the two groups came to recognize their shared interests. In 1911, the organ of the NAACP, the *Crisis,* printed an article on the Mexican Revolution that argued that Anglo citizens of the United States "lack consideration for all dark-skinned races."[95] Roy Nash of the NAACP wrote in 1919 that many "Texans look upon Mexicans as they look upon Negroes, that is, as not entitled to the rights of citizens, with the result that lynching them has been condoned."[96] In 1920, black newspaper editor Cyril V. Briggs of the *Crusader* issued one of the strongest calls for blacks to unite with other minority groups: "The Negro who fights against either Japan or Mexico is fighting for the white man against himself, for the white race against the darker races and for the perpetuation of white domination of the colored races with its vicious practice of lynching, jimcrowism, segregation, and other forms of oppression."[97]

A small group of Mexicans went even further in the quest for unifying the nation's minority groups. In January, 1915, a band of Mexicans signed the Plan of San Diego. This revolutionary manifesto called upon the racial minorities of the southwestern states to overthrow white rule in the region violently. In the revolution's wake the insurrectionists sought to establish separate borderland republics for Mexicans, Indians, and African Americans. "Yankee arrogance has reached its limit," asserted the authors of the plan; "it is not content with the daily lynching of men, it now seeks to lynch an entire people, a whole race, an entire continent. And it is against this arrogance that we must unite." Under the leadership of Aniceto Pizaña and Luis de la Rosa the insurrectionists undertook a series of bloody raids. These raids failed miserably. Not only did the minorities of the American Southwest fail to rise up in revolt, the Anglo authorities responded by indiscriminately slaughtering unknown numbers of innocent Mexicans. As one scholar has suggested, many whites declared "open season on any Mexican caught in the open armed or without a verifiable excuse for his activities."[98]

Although the Plan of San Diego did not resonate widely in either black or Mexican communities, both groups became marginally more open to practical forms of cooperation in the early twentieth century. One incident in particular provided the opportunity to forge such an alliance. On November 11, 1922, a mob of fifteen men took Elias Zarate from a jail in Weslaco, Texas, and shot him dead. Mexican authorities demanded an immediate response from Washington. Within hours a second telegram had been sent to the State Department, stating that the entire Mexican communities of Weslaco and Breckenridge, Texas, were exposed to "intolerable" mistreatment. As if to prove the Mexican government correct, on November 16, three hundred whites marched through the streets in Breckenridge, ordering both Mexicans and blacks to leave before nightfall. The NAACP responded with a telegram to President Warren G. Harding, calling "attention to [the] international situation created by the lynching of Mexicans and Negroes" and urging the passage of the Dyer Anti-lynching Bill.[99] The Mexican government also responded, demanding that the U.S. authorities provide immediate security for its citizens. These joint protests proved effective. Ironically, authorities ordered a detachment of Texas Rangers—the same force that had been so instrumental in terrorizing Mexicans in the past—to Breckenridge to protect the citizenry.[100]

The positive results from this case led to continued cooperation between blacks and Mexicans. In 1923, the NAACP requested information from the Mexican Embassy in Washington about Mexicans murdered in the past twelve months. In 1926, the NAACP also conducted its own investigation into the murder of Mexican nationals in Willacy County, Texas.[101] Despite such positive steps, relations between African Americans and Mexicans remained tenuous for decades. In the final analysis, the two peoples employed different definitions of what made someone American. Blacks emphasized their constitutional and legal rights as native-born citizens. Mexicans, in contrast, based their claims to Americanness upon the fact that they were "white." As Neil Foley will show in chapter five of this volume, these conflicting interpretations of American identity remained a serious obstacle to the development of a multicultural alliance, and a powerful legacy of America's historic black-white dichotomy.

Appendix A

Essay on Sources

The database upon which this chapter is based has been created from examining several sets of primary sources. In sifting those primary sources for cases of lynching, the authors were forced to confront the problem of defining what is and what is not a lynching. Aware that multiple and contrasting definitions of lynching have existed over the last two hundred years, the authors composed their own definition of lynching and applied it rigorously throughout the period of their study. Lynching, for the authors, is the premeditated, extralegal murder of one or more individuals by a group of persons for an alleged affront to perceived social norms. The perceived transgressors may be either individuals or groups of individuals. For example, a singular individual may be identified for lynching for being a horse thief or a rapist. A group, however, may also be singled out for mob violence, such as when several "foreign" miners are targeted for refusing to abandon their claims to the "American" gold fields. In many cases, the difference between "riot" and "lynching" is narrow. The authors maintain that a lynching involves considerable premeditation whereas a riot is relatively unplanned.

In creating the database, the lynching inventories compiled by newspapers and civil rights organizations beginning in the late nineteenth century were useful. These include the files of the Association of Southern Women for the Prevention of Lynching; the *Chicago Tribune*; the National Association for the Advancement of Colored People; and Tuskegee University.

Although such inventories were quite helpful, they are not a substitute for personal testimonies that must be consulted to obtain a crucial first-person perspective on mob violence. These testimonies come in numerous forms, including diaries, journals, memoirs, private correspondence, and oral interviews. Pertinent personal testimonies are housed at the following: the Bancroft Library of the University of California; the Center for American

History of the University of Texas; the Huntington Library in San Marino, California; the Library of Congress; the Center for Southwest Studies of the University of New Mexico; the Texas State Archives; and the UCLA Research Library.

Mob violence against Mexican nationals provoked a regular exchange of correspondence between the Mexican Embassy in Washington and the U.S. State Department. Some of this correspondence was published in the *Papers Relating to the Foreign Relations of the United States*. Other critical materials must be located in the "Notes from the Mexican Legation in the United States" to the Department of State, housed at the National Archives.

The governments of both the United States and Mexico launched a series of investigations into disturbances along their mutual border. Most of the reports resulting from the investigations conducted by the United States have been published in the annual reports of the House of Representatives and Senate. Mexican reports are housed at the Biblioteca Nacional de Mexico.

Local court records are a largely underutilized resource for the study of Mexican American history. We employed local court records to illuminate the connections between the legal system and extralegal mob violence against Mexicans. We have examined more than five hundred court cases in early Los Angeles.

English- and Spanish-language newspapers are an essential source of information for the project. Among the most important Spanish-language titles are *El Clamor Público* (Los Angeles, California), *El Excelsior* (Mexico City); *El Fronterizo* (Tucson, Arizona), *El Nuevo Mexicano* (Santa Fe, New Mexico), and *La Prensa* (San Antonio, Texas). Significant English-language titles include *Alta California* (San Francisco), *Arizona Weekly Miner, Brownsville Herald, Albuquerque Evening Democrat, Daily New Mexican* (Santa Fe), *Los Angeles Star, Sacramento Union, San Antonio Express, San Francisco Examiner,* and the *Sonoma County Journal.*

Additional Tables

Table 1. Lynchings of Mexicans by State

State	*Number of Lynchings*
Texas	282
California	188
Arizona	59
New Mexico	49
Colorado	6
Nevada	3
Nebraska	2
Oklahoma	2
Oregon	2
Kentucky	1
Louisiana	1
Montana	1
Wyoming	1
Total	**597**

Table 2. Alleged Crimes of Mexican Lynching Victims

Murder	301
Theft or Robbery	116
Murder and Robbery	38
Being of Mexican Descent	10
Attempted Murder	9
Cheating at Cards	7
Rape or Sexual Assault	5
Assault	5
Witchcraft	3
Kidnapping	3
Courting a White Woman	2
Taking Away Jobs	2
Rape and Murder	1
Attempted Murder and Robbery	1
Refusing to Join Mob	1
Threatening White Men	1
Being a "Bad" Character	1
Killing a Cow	1
Being a Successful Cartman	1
Miscegenation	1
Refusing to Play Fiddle for Americans	1
Taking White Man to Court	1
Protesting Texas Rangers	1
Serving as a Bill Collector	1
Giving Refuge to Bandits	1
Unknown	83
Total	**597**

Note on Comparitive Statistics

Although it is impossible to determine a precise "lynching rate" for either blacks or Mexicans, we can get a better sense of the hazard faced by both blacks and Mexicans by comparing numbers of lynchings with the total population at risk. Unfortunately, the number of Spanish-speakers living in the United States is difficult to determine. One rough way to approximate the Mexican population during the period of 1848–1930, is to average the number of Mexican-born people residing in the United States in 1850 (13,317) with the number of Mexican and Mexican Americans living in the United States in 1930 (1,422,533). This number equals 717,925 and is, if anything, a high estimate for average population during the period because all observers concede that the Mexican population of the United States increased sharply during the early twentieth century. Dividing this number by the 597 Mexican American and Mexican national lynching victims gives you a figure of 83.2 Mexican lynching victims per 100,000 of population.

This number, however, is only really useful as a comparison with black lynching victims. Unfortunately, such statistics are only available for the period of 1880–1930. Figures for African Americans have been compiled in Stewart E. Tolnay and E. M. Beck, *A Festival of Violence: An Analysis of Southern Lynchings, 1882–1930* (Urbana: University of Illinois Press, 1995), p. 38. Tolnay and Beck followed the same mathematical strategy adopted above. They averaged the African American population of ten southern states and divided that number by the number of lynching victims. Tolnay and Beck's statistics are restricted to only ten southern states. For a national black "lynching rate," we divided the number of African American lynching victims reported by Tuskegee between 1880 and 1930 by the average black population of the United States between 1880 and 1930. Specific details can be found below.

Because the data from Tolnay and Beck only cover the period of 1880–1930, we found it necessary to construct data for that time period for Mexican victims. United States census figures for 1880 only include persons born in Mexico, so we had to estimate the population born in the United States, but of Mexican descent. We did this by using the percentage of U.S.-born persons of Mexican descent living in 1930 (55 percent) to estimate the "missing" Mexicans in 1880. We then averaged the new 1880 estimate with the 1930 figures to arrive at the best possible average population for this time period. It should be noted that we have always chosen to calculate our statistics conservatively, in a way that would go against our hypothesis that Mexicans suffered great danger from lynch mobs. For example, we feel certain that the percentage of Mexicans born in Mexico was declining between 1880 and 1930 relative to the percentage of persons born in the United States but of Mexican descent. Yet, we used the percentage from 1930 to calculate our 1880 estimate. In any case, the population data that we used and our estimates are included below for future discussion and criticism.

Mexican "Lynching Rate"

1850 population of U.S.-born in Mexico: 13,317

1880 population of U.S.-born in Mexico: 68,399

1880 population of U.S.-born in United States but of Mexican descent (estimated): 83,599

1880 population of U.S.-born in Mexico or of Mexican descent (estimated): 151,998

1930 population of U.S.-born in Mexico or of Mexican descent: 1,422,533

1930 population of U.S.-born in Mexico: 641,462

1930 population of U.S.-born in United States but of Mexican descent: 781,071

Percentage of Mexican population not born in Mexico in 1930: 55%

Estimated average Mexican population, 1850–80: 82,658

Estimated average Mexican population, 1880–1930: 787,266

Estimated average Mexican population, 1850–1930: 717,925

Estimated number of Mexicans lynched in United States, 1882–1930: 216

"Lynching rate" for Mexicans in United States: 27.4

Black "Lynching Rate"

1880 population of African Americans: 6,518,372
1930 population of African Americans: 11,759,075
Estimated average black population, 1880–1930: 9,138,723.5
Tuskagee estimate of blacks lynched in United States, 1882–1930: 3,386
"Lynching rate" for blacks in United States, 1880–1930: 37.1

Population statistics taken from United States Bureau of the Census, *Seventh Census of the United States: 1850 Population,* (Washington: Government Printing Office, 1853); United States Bureau of the Census, *Statistics of the Population of the United States at the Tenth Census (June 1, 1880),* (Washington: D.C.: Government Printing Press, 1883); United States Bureau of the Census, *A Compendium of the Eleventh Census, 1890 Population* (Washington, D.C.: Government Printing Press, 1892); and United States Bureau of the Census, *Fifteenth Census of the United States: 1930 Population,* 3 vols., (Washington: Government Printing Office, 1932).

Notes

1. *New York Times,* Nov. 11, 1910, p. 2; "Anti-American Riots in Mexico," *The Independent,* Nov. 17, 1910, pp. 1061–62; Harvey F. Rice, "The Lynching of Antonio Rodriguez" (Master's thesis, University of Texas at Austin, 1990), pp. 26–30.

2. The authors use the term "Mexican" to refer to all persons of Mexican descent residing in the United States, regardless of their nationality. This decision has been made for the sake of clarification and simplicity.

3. The statistics on African American lynching are taken from W. Fitzhugh Brundage, ed., *Under Sentence of Death: Lynching in the South* (Chapel Hill: University of North Carolina Press, 1997), p. 4. As with all other tables in this chapter, statistics involving Mexican lynching victims are from our own research. See appendix A for a full discussion of the archival sources upon which we based our research. See appendix B for additional statistical information.

4. See appendix C for a detailed discussion of how these figures were calculated.

5. For a discussion of the history of lynching and lynching rhetoric, see Christopher Waldrep, *The Many Faces of Judge Lynch: Extralegal Violence and Punishment in America* (New York: Palgrave, 2002).

6. We will not dwell in this chapter on the frequent, factual errors in these data sets. The limitations of these sources and the need to confirm the veracity of each case with primary source evidence has been well made in Stewart E. Tolnay and E. M. Beck, *A Festival of Violence: An Analysis of Southern Lynchings, 1882–1930* (Urbana: University of Illinois Press, 1995), pp. 265–68.

7. Scholars of lynching, like those who collected and compiled lynching data at the turn of the century, have paid little attention to the ethnicity of lynching victims. Most of those who have studied lynching have maintained the false division of white and black. One notable but flawed attempt to discuss ethnicity and lynching in Texas is David L. Chapman, "Lynching in Texas" (Master's thesis, Texas Tech University, 1973). Chapman uses the Tuskegee figures and thus seriously undercounts the number of Mexicans lynched in Texas. See Brundage, *Under Sentence of Death,* p. 4; Tolnay and Beck, *A Festival of Violence;* Robert L. Zangrando, *The NACCP Crusade Against Lynching, 1909–1950* (Philadelphia: Temple University Press, 1980), pp. 3–4; Arthur F. Raper, *The Tragedy of Lynching* (Chapel Hill: University of North Carolina Press, 1933); Walter White, *Rope & Faggot: A Biography of Judge Lynch* (New York: Alfred A. Knopf, 1929); and James Elbert Cutler, *Lynch Law: An Investigation into the History of Lynching in the United States* (New York: Longman, Green, & Co., 1905). We recognize that Tuskegee's records also pay little attention to ethnicity among African Americans. Although significant ethnic diversity certainly existed among African Americans, such differences seemed to matter little to lynch mobs in the United States who categorized all those with some African ancestry into one group. By contrast, we argue that ethnic differences between those lumped together in Tuskegee's "white" category mattered greatly to lynch mobs throughout the American Southwest.

8. Richard Maxwell Brown, "Violence," in *The Oxford History of The American West* (New York: Oxford University Press, 1994). Another important account of mob violence in the West is David A. Johnson, "Vigilance and the Law: The Moral Authority of Popular Justice in the Far West," *American Quarterly* 33 (winter, 1981): 558–86. Johnson recognizes that racism was the one unchanging factor in the history of mob violence in California but goes on to offer an analysis of mob violence in which race plays almost no role. Two caveats. First, we are certainly not alone in calling for greater attention to race as an analytical category in western history. A similar appeal was made recently by Arnoldo De León in *A New Significance: Re-Envisioning the History of the American West,* ed. by Clyde A. Milner II (New York and Oxford: Oxford University Press, 1996), pp. 90–96. Second, there are many, many important works that acknowledge and emphasize race

and ethnicity in the American West. One of the most recent is Susan Lee Johnson, *Roaring Camp: The Social World of the California Gold Rush* (New York: W. W. Norton & Company, 2000).

9. See, for example, W. Fitzhugh Brundage, *Lynching in the New South: Georgia and Virginia, 1880–1930* (Urbana: University of Illinois Press, 1993); Tolnay and Beck, *A Festival of Violence;* Edward L. Ayers, *Vengeance and Justice: Crime and Punishment in the 19th Century American South* (New York: Oxford University Press, 1984); Terence Finnegan, "At the Hands of Parties Unknown: Lynching in Mississippi and South Carolina, 1881–1940" (Ph.D. dissertation, University of Illinois, 1993), and Michael J. Pfeifer, "Lynching and Criminal Justice in Regional Context: Iowa, Wyoming, and Louisiana, 1878–1946" (Ph.D. dissertation, University of Iowa, 1998).

10. George C. Wright, *Racial Violence in Kentucky, 1865–1940: Lynchings, Mob Rule, and "Legal Lynchings"* (Baton Rouge: Louisiana State University Press, 1990), p. 71; Winthrop Jordan, *Tumult and Silence at Second Creek, An Inquiry into a Civil War Slave Conspiracy,* revised edition (Baton Rouge: Louisiana State University Press, 1995), p. 6.

11. See table 1 in appendix B for specific data. For a detailed discussion of the Mexican population in 1930, see Elizabeth Broadbent, "The Distribution of the Mexican Population in the United States" (Ph.D. dissertation, University of Chicago, 1941), pp. 60–117. Broadbent's analysis is based on United States Bureau of the Census, *Fifteenth Census of the United States: 1930. Population,* 3 vols. (Washington: Government Printing Office, 1932). Michael Pfeifer's dissertation helps explain the relationship between regions and mob violence. See Pfeifer, "Lynching and Criminal Justice."

12. Statistics for African Americans cover period 1882–1930 and are from Tolnay and Beck, *A Festival of Violence,* p. 48.

13. Tolnay and Beck, *A Festival of Violence,* p. 92.

14. *San Antonio Express,* Jan. 31, 1896; *Albuquerque Evening Democrat,* Aug. 4, 1884.

15. As quoted in Paul Schuster Taylor, *An American-Mexican Frontier: Nueces County, Texas* (New York: Russell & Russell, 1934), p. 274.

16. Statistics for African Americans cover period 1882–1930 and are from Tolnay and Beck, *A Festival of Violence,* p. 269.

17. Ralph Mann, *After the Gold Rush: Society in Grass Valley and Nevada City, California, 1849–1870* (Stanford: Stanford University Press, 1982), p. 50.

18. Among the multitude of sources to consult on the lynching of Josefa, see *Alta California,* July 9 and 14, 1851; John R. McFarlan Journal, July 7, 1851, The Huntington Library, San Marino, Calif. (hereafter HEH); Stanton A. Coblentz, *Villains and Vigilantes: The Story of James King of William and Pioneer Justice in California* (New York: A. S. Barnes & Company, 1961 [1935]), p. 64; Leonard Pitt, *The Decline of the Californios: A Social History of the Spanish-Speaking Californians, 1846–1890* (Berkeley and Los Angeles: University of California Press, 1966), pp. 73–74; Hubert Howe Bancroft, *Popular Tribunals—Volume I* (San Francisco: The History Company, Publisher, 1887), pp. 577–87.

19. Oct. 16, 1851, Item # 26171, Frederick Douglass Papers, Rochester, N.Y.

20. Horace Bell, *Reminiscences of a Ranger or Early Times in Southern California* (Santa Barbara: Wallace Hebberd, 1927), p. 150.

21. Manuel Maria de Zamacona to James G. Blaine, Oct. 30, 1880; Reel 18, Notes from the Mexican Legation in the United States to the Department of State, 1821–1906, National Archives at College Park, Maryland; Zamacona to Blaine, Apr. 7, 1881, Reel 19, Notes from the Mexican Legation.

22. Statistics for mobs lynching African Americans are unavailable, but a reading of the relevant literature suggests the majority of lynchings resulted in hanging. However, it is equally obvious that a significant percentage of African Americans were burned, certainly more than the 0.8 percent of Mexican victims. See Tolnay and Beck, *A Festival of Violence;* Brundage, *Lynching*

in the New South; and especially Leon F. Litwack, *Trouble in Mind: Black Southerners in the Age of Jim Crow* (Knopf: New York, 1998), pp. 280–325.

23. Statistics on African American multiple lynchings are from period 1882–1930 and are taken from Tolnay and Beck, *A Festival of Violence,* p. 274.

24. Rodolfo Acuña, *Occupied America: A History of Chicanos,* third edition (New York: Harper Collins, 1988), p. 28.

25. "Testimony taken by the Committee on Military Affairs in Relation to The Texas Border Troubles," House Reports, Misc. Doc. 64, 45th Cong., 2nd sess., 1878 (1820), p. 51; Taylor, *An American-Mexican Frontier,* p. 54; J. Frank Dobie, *A Vaquero of the Brush Country* (Boston: Little, Brown, and Co., 1929), pp. 118–19.

26. For an important theoretical work on collective violence which emphasizes cultural distance, see Roberta Senechal de la Roche, "The Sociogenesis of Lynching" in *Under Sentence of Death,* ed. by Brundage, pp. 48–76.

27. *Los Angeles Star,* Feb. 7, 1857; *Sonoma County Journal,* Feb. 20, 1857; *New York Times,* Mar. 17, 1857.

28. Bill Rubottom quoted in *On the Old West Coast: Being further Reminiscences of a Ranger, Major Horace Bell,* ed. by Lanier Bartlett (New York: William Morrow & Co., 1930), p. 100.

29. Brundage, *Lynching in the New South,* p. 49.

30. Wayne Gard, *Frontier Justice* (Norman: University of Oklahoma Press, 1949), pp. v, 167. Scholars of mob violence in the West who have emphasized the impotence of the legal system include Hubert Howe Bancroft, *Popular Tribunals,* 2 vols. (San Francisco: History Company, 1887), Charles Howard Shinn, *Mining Camps: A Study in American Frontier Government* (New York: Charles Scribner's Sons, 1885), Theodore H. Hittell, *History of California,* 4 vols. (San Francisco: N.J. Stone & Company, 1897), and John Walton Caughey, *Their Majesties, the Mob* (Chicago: University of Chicago Press, 1960).

31. Richard Maxwell Brown, *No Duty to Retreat: Violence and Values in American History and Society* (New York: Oxford University Press, 1991).

32. John Eagle to his wife Margaret, Gold Hill, Calif., Sept. 12, 1853, HEH.

33. Claude D. Potter, "Reminiscences of the Socorro Vigilantes," ed. Paige W. Christiansen, *New Mexico Historical Review* 40 (1965): 23–54.

34. "Investigation of Mexican Affairs," Senate Documents, 66th Cong., 2nd sess., Vols. 9–10, Serial Set #: 7665–66, (Washington: Government Printing Office, 1920), p. 1893.

35. The mob types are taken from Brundage, *Lynching in the New South.* We consciously followed Brundage's mob type categorization as closely as possible so that a comparison would be possible. However, our research forced us to add an additional category—vigilance committee— that Brundage did not include in his statistics. We are convinced that this type of mob was peculiar to the American West and did not exist (or was at least exceedingly rare) in the late– nineteenth-century and early-twentieth-century South.

36. Clarence King, *Mountaineering in the Sierra Nevada* (Boston: J. R. Osgood and Company, 1872), pp. 283–87.

37. Joseph A. Stout and Odie B. Faulk, *A Short History of the American West* (New York: Harper & Row, 1974), pp. 250–51.

38. Erna Ferguson, *Murder and Mystery in New Mexico,* pp. 21–32.

39. C. V. Gillespie to A. H. Gillespie, July 30, 1849, Gillespie Papers, UCLA Library, Department of Special Collections, Manuscripts Division, Los Angeles, Calif.

40. Charles Fernald, *A County Judge in Arcady: Selected Private Papers* (Glendale, Calif.: Arthur H. Clark Co., 1954), p. 115.

41. Cornelius Cole, *Memoirs of Cornelius Cole* (New York: McLoughlin Brothers, 1908), pp. 85–91.

42. Benjamin Butler Harris, *The Gila Trail: The Texas Argonauts and the California Gold Rush* (Norman: University of Oklahoma Press, 1960), p. 133.

43. Quoted in Douglas Monroy, *Thrown Among Strangers: The Making of Mexican Culture in Frontier California* (Berkeley: University of California Press, 1990).

44. Walter Prescott Webb, *The Texas Rangers: A Century of Frontier Defense* (Austin: University of Texas Press, 1935), p. 478.

45. Robert J. Rosenbaum, *Mexicano Resistance in the Southwest: "The Sacred Right of Self-Preservation"* (Austin: University of Texas Press, 1981), p. 51; Don M. Coerver and Linda M. Hall, *Texas and the Mexican Revolution: A Study in State and National Border Policy, 1910–1920* (San Antonio: Trinity University Press, 1984), p. 107.

46. *Brownsville Herald,* Sept. 15, 1915.

47. Glenn Justice, *Revolution on the Rio Grande: Mexican Raids and Army Pursuits, 1916–1919* (El Paso: Texas Western Press, 1992), pp. 37–40. For further examples of Texas Ranger brutality toward Mexicans, see unpublished manuscript, Alfred B. Anzaluda Papers, Box 3B36, Center for American History, University of Texas at Austin, and Reed Dean, Tape #132, Reel #2, Pioneer Foundations Oral History Collection, Center for Southwest Studies, University of New Mexico, Albuquerque.

48. Senechal de la Roche, "The Sociogenesis of Lynching."

49. Tolnay and Beck, *A Festival of Violence,* pp. 119–65.

50. Brundage notes that "the heart of race relations throughout much of the rural South was agriculture and the role that blacks played in it." He then goes on to describe the key role of agriculture in shaping the geography of racial violence. Brundage, *Lynching in the New South,* pp. 103–60 (p. 103, quote).

51. Chauncey L. Caufield, *The Diary of a Forty-Niner* (New York and San Francisco: Morgan Shepard Company, 1906), p. 40.

52. Jan. 24, 1853, Elias S. Ketcham Diary, HEH.

53. *Waco Times-Herald,* Feb. 17, 1898; David J. Weber, ed., *Foreigners in Their Native Land: Historical Roots of the Mexicans* (Albuquerque: University of New Mexico Press, 1973), p. 153; George P. Garrison, *Texas: A Contest of Civilizations* (Boston: Houghton Mifflin Co., 1973), p. 274; Frank W. Johnson, *A History of Texas and Texans* (Chicago: American Historical Society, 1914), vol. 1, pp. 515–16; J. Fred Rippy, *The United States and Mexico* (New York: F. S. Crofts & Co., 1931), pp. 179–80; Charles C. Alexander, *The Ku Klux Klan in the Southwest* (Lexington: University of Kentucky Press, 1965), p. 24. For further evidence of economic competition precipitating mob violence, see Mary Romero, "El Paso Salt War: Mob Action or Political Struggle?" *Aztlán* 16, nos. 1–2 (1985): 119–38.

54. Theodore T. Johnson, *Sights in the Gold Region and Scenes by the Way* (New York: Baker and Scribner, 1849), p. 240. Another early example of Anglo prejudice against Mexicans can be found in T. J. Farham, *Life, Travels, and Adventures in California and Scenes in the Pacific Ocean* (New York: William H. Graham, 1846), pp. 356–57.

55. *Weekly Arizona Miner,* Apr. 26, 1872.

56. Paul S. Taylor, *Mexican Labor in the United States: Dimmit County, Winter Garden District, South Texas* (Berkeley: University of California Press, 1980), p. 446 (quote). For additional accounts of prejudicial views toward Mexicans, see Robert Lee Maril, *Poorest of Americans: The Mexican Americans of the Lower Rio Grande Valley of Texas* (Notre Dame, Ind.: University of Notre Dame Press, 1989), pp. 10–11, 30, 33, 41–47, 49, 51–54, 79, 81, 151–55; Américo Paredes, "With His Pistol in His Hand," in *Chicano: The Evolution of a People,* ed. by Renato Rosaldo, Robert A. Calvert, and Gustav L. Seligmann, Jr. (Malabar, Fla.: Robert E. Krieger Publishing Company, 1982), p. 101; Richard Griswold del Castillo and Arnoldo De León, *North to Aztlán: A History of Mexican Americans in the United States* (New York: Twayne Publishers, 1996), p. 30; Frank W.

Johnson, *A History of Texas and Texans* (Chicago: American Historical Society, 1914), vol. 1, p. 516; Mark Reisler, "Always the Laborer, Never the Citizen: Anglo Perceptions of the Mexican Immigrant during the 1920s," in *Between Two Worlds: Mexican Immigrants in the United States,* ed. by David G. Gutierrez (Wilmington, Del.: Scholarly Resources Inc., 1996), pp. 25–29.

57. For discussion of "whiteness," see George Lipsitz, "The Possessive Investment in Whiteness: Racialized Social Democracy and the 'White' Problem in American Studies," *American Quarterly* 47, no. 3 (Sept., 1995): 369–87; Neil Foley, *The White Scourge: Mexicans, Blacks, and Poor Whites in Texas Cotton Culture* (Berkeley: University of California Press, 1998).

58. Bayard Taylor, *Eldorado, or Adventures in the Path of Empire* (New York: Alfred A. Knopf, 1949), p. 109. See also Edwin Bryant, *What I Saw in California* (Palo Alto, Calif.: Lewis Osborne, 1967), p. 446, and R. N. Wilcox, *Reminiscences of California Life* (Avery, Ohio: Wilcox Print, 1897), p. 293.

59. Antonio Franco Coronel, *Tales of Mexican California: Cosas de California,* trans. by Diane de Aualle-Arce (Santa Barbara, Calif.: Bellerophon Books, 1994), p. 70.

60. *Sonoma County Journal,* June 12, 1857.

61. Charles Daniell to his mother, July 29, 1850, Charles Daniell Papers, HEH.

62. *Austin Statesman,* May 28, 1893.

63. Mary J. Jaques, *Texan Ranch Life* (London: Horace Cox, 1894), p. 361.

64. Monroy, *Thrown Among Strangers,* pp. 209–10; Arnoldo De León, *They Called Them Greasers: Anglo Attitudes Towards Mexicans in Texas, 1821–1900* (Austin: University of Texas at Austin, 1983), p. 90; Howard R. Lamar, *Texas Crossings: The Lone Star State and the American Far West, 1836–1986* (Austin: University of Texas Press, 1991), p. 34; *San Antonio Express,* Jan. 31, 1896, p. 8. For further evidence of bodily mutilation, see *San Antonio Express,* Oct. 13, 1895, and Wayne Gard, *Frontier Justice,* pp. 179–80.

65. *House Reports,* Doc. No. 701, 45th Cong., 2nd sess., 1877–78 (1824), p. 95.

66. William Dean Carrigan, "Slavery on the Frontier: The Peculiar Institution in Central Texas," *Slavery & Abolition* 20, no. 2 (Aug., 1999): 63–96.

67. *Waco Daily News,* Jan. 5, 1891.

68. European scholarship on social banditry is useful for understanding the violent actions of many Mexicans during the nineteenth and early twentieth centuries. Among the most important of the early works is George Rudé, *The Crowd in History: A Study of Popular Disturbances in France and England, 1730–1848* (New York and London: J. Wiley, 1964); Edward P. Thompson, "The Moral Economy of the English Crowd in the Eighteenth Century" first published in *Past and Present* 50 (1971): 76–136; and Eric Hobsbawm, *Bandits* (London: Weidenfeld & Nicolson, 1969). More recent works on popular and collective violence in Europe include Stephen Wilson, *Feuding, Conflict and Banditry in Nineteenth-Century Corsica* (Cambridge and New York: Cambridge University Press, 1988); Ian Gilmour, *Riot, Risings and Revolution: Governance and Violence in Eighteenth-Century England* (London: Hutchinson, 1992); Edward Muir, *Mad Blood Stirring: Vendetta and Factions in Friuli during the Renaissance* (Baltimore: Johns Hopkins University Press, 1993); Eric A. Johnson and Eric H. Monkkonen, eds., *The Civilization of Crime: Violence in Town and Country Since the Middle Ages* (Urbana: University of Illinois Press, 1996); Peter Spierenburg, ed., *Men and Violence: Gender, Honor, and Rituals in Modern Europe and America* (Columbus: Ohio State University Press, 1998); and John Walter, *Understanding Popular Violence in the English Revolution: The Colchesster Plunderers* (Cambridge and New York: Cambridge University Press, 1999).

69. Albert Schumate, *Boyhood Days: Ygnacio Villegas' Reminiscences of California in the 1850s* (San Francisco: California Historical Society, 1983), pp. 44–45.

70. *Alta California,* Oct. 2, 1853.

71. Coblentz, *Villains and Vigilantes,* p. 27; Lee Shippey, *It's an Old California Custom* (New

York: Vanguard Press, 1948), pp. 136–40. For accounts of Murrieta, see Johnson, *Roaring Camp*; James F. Varley, *The Legend of Joaquín Murrieta* (Twin Falls, Idaho: Big Lost River Press, 1995); Frank F. Latta, *Joaquín Murrieta and His Horse Gangs* (Santa Cruz, Calif.: Bear State Books, 1980); John Rollin Ridge [Yellow Bird], *The Life and Adventures of Joaquín Murrieta* (Norman: University of Oklahoma Press, 1953); Walter Noble Burns, *The Robin Hood of El Dorado* (New York: Coward-McCann, Inc., 1932); and Ireneo Paz, *Life and Adventures of the Celebrated Bandit Joaquín Murrieta,* trans. by Frances B. Belles (Chicago: Regan Publishing Corp., 1925). In addition to these books, dozens and dozens of additional accounts of Murrieta exist. A lengthy bibliography can be found in Margaret Walker, "Joaquin Murrieta," unpublished typescript, HEH.

72. Eugene T. Sawyer, *Life and Career of Tiburcio Vásquez: The Bandit and Murderer* (Washington, D.C.: Office of the Librarian of Congress, 1875), p. 4.

73. Quoted in Pedro Castillo and Albert Camarillo, eds., *Furia y Muerte: Los Bandidos Chicanos* (Los Angeles: Aztlán Publications, 1973), p. vi.

74. S. Dale McLemore, *Racial and Ethnic Violence in America,* second edition (Newton, Mass.: Allyn and Bacon, Inc., 1983), pp. 219–21; Jerry D. Thompson, ed., *Juan Cortina and the Texas-Mexico Frontier 1859–1877* (El Paso: University of Texas at El Paso Press, 1994), p. 6; Jerry D. Thompson, "The Many Faces of Juan Nepomuceno Cortina." *South Texas Studies* 2 (1991): 88, 92; Webb, *Texas Rangers,* p. 176.

75. Social banditry and Mexican outlaws are discussed in Pedro Castillo and Albert Camarillo, eds., *Furia y Muerte.* John Boessenecker believes that most Mexican bandits were not social bandits. See John Boessenecker, "Pio Linares: Californio Bandido," *The Californians* 5, no. 6 (Nov.–Dec., 1987): 34–44.

76. Matt S. Meier and Feliciano Rivera, *The Chicanos: A History of Mexican Americans* (New York: Hill and Wang, 1972), pp. 101–102; Thompson, "Many Faces," p. 89; Thompson, *Juan Cortina,* p. 102, notes 1 and 3; Lyman L. Woodman, *Cortina: Rogue of the Rio Grande* (San Antonio, Tex.: Naylor, n.d.), pp. 21–22; "Report on the Accompanying Documents of the Committee on Foreign Affairs on the Relations of the U.S. with Mexico," U.S. House, No. 701, 45th Cong., 2nd sess., Serial Set 1824, pp. 75–76.

77. *El Clamor Público,* July 26, 1856. English translation from Zaragosa Vargas, ed., *Major Problems in Mexican American History* (Boston and New York: Houghton Mifflin Company, 1999), p. 147.

78. Susan Lee Johnson explores the costs of retaliatory violence by Mexicans during the California gold rush in her recent book, *Roaring Camp,* especially pp. 36–37 and chapter 4.

79. Quoted in James E. Officer, *Hispanic Arizona, 1536–1856* (Tucson: University of Arizona Press, 1987), p. 247.

80. William R. Manning, *Diplomatic Correspondence of the United States: Inter-American Affairs, 1831–1860* (Washington: Carnegie Endowment for International Peace, 1937), vol. 9, pp. 129–30, 133–34, 568–70; *Papers Relating to the Foreign Relations of the United States 1863,* vol. 2, pp. 114–41; "The Condition of Affairs in Mexico," U.S. Congress, *House Executive Documents,* No. 73, 39th Cong., 1st sess. 1865–66 (1262), vol. 2, pp. 208–10.

81. Zamacona to Blaine, Oct. 30, 1880, Reel 18; Apr. 7, 1881. Roll 19, Notes from the Mexican Legation in the United States to the Department of State, 1821–1906, National Archives; Zamacona to Blaine, June 30, 1881, and Aug. 8, 1881, *Papers Relating to the Foreign Relations of the United States,* 1881, pp. 840–44, and 1882, 407–408; Garcia, "Porfirian Diplomacy," pp. 5–8.

82. *New York Times,* Aug. 27, 1895; *San Francisco Examiner,* Aug. 27, 1895, p. 1; Aug. 28, 1895, p. 3; Nov. 29, 1895, p. 8.

83. "Indemnity to Relatives of Luis Moreno," House of Representatives, Document No. 237, 55th Cong., 2nd sess. (3679), Vol. 51, pp. 1–3; *New York Times,* Jan. 19, 1898.

84. *Senate Report* 1832, 56th Cong., 2nd sess. (4064), pp. 1–14, 28–30.

85. On the continued complaints made by Mexican officials during the twentieth century, see J. Fred Rippy, "The United States and Mexico, 1910–1927," in *American Policies Abroad: Mexico* (University of Chicago Press, 1928), p. 29.

86. *New York Times,* Nov. 10, 1910, p. 1; Nov. 11, 1910, p. 2; Nov. 12, 1910, p. 5; Nov. 13, 1910, part 3, p. 4; Nov. 15, 1910, p. 1; Nov. 16, 1910, p. 1; Nov. 17, 1910, p. 1; Nov. 18, 1910, p. 10; "Anti-American Riots in Mexico," *The Independent,* Nov. 17, 1910, pp. 1061–62; "The Situation in Mexico," *The Independent,* Nov. 24, 1910, pp. 1120–21; *Papers Relating to the Foreign Relations of the United States, 1911* (Washington: Government Printing Office, 1918), pp. 355–57; Rice, "The Lynching of Antonio Rodriguez," pp. 31–39, 49–51, 79.

87. "A Mexican Boycott," *The Independent,* Nov. 17, 1910, pp. 1111–12; *New York Times,* Sept. 2, 1919, p. 1; Jan. 10, 1920, p. 3; Aug. 4, 1921, p. 10.

88. *Montgomery Advertiser,* Sept. 19, 1926; *Atlanta Constitution,* Oct. 24, 1926, Jan. 8, 1927.

89. *El Clamor Público; El Frontierzo;* Zangrando, *The NAACP Crusade Against Lynching;* Manuel G. Gonzalez, "Carlos I. Velasco," *Journal of Arizona History* 25, no. 3 (autumn, 1984): 265–84.

90. Garna L. Christian, *Black Soldiers in Jim Crow Texas, 1899–1917* (College Station: Texas A&M University Press, 1995), p. 42. See also Garna L. Christian, "Rio Grande City: Prelude to Brownsville Raid," *West Texas Historical Association Year Book* 57 (1981): 120.

91. Benjamin Márquez, *LULAC: The Evolution of a Mexican American Political Organization* (Austin: University of Texas at Austin Press, 1993), pp. 32–34; Foley, *The White Scourge,* 209–10.

92. Membership Records, Boxes G-128, G-201, G-202, Branch Files, National Association for the Advancement of Colored People Papers, Library of Congress, Washington, D.C. (hereafter NAACP Papers).

93. *Chicago Defender,* Nov. 25, 1922.

94. Arnold Shankman, *Ambivalent Friends: Afro-Americans View the Immigrant* (Westport, Conn.: Greenwood Press, 1982), p. 75.

95. *The Crisis,* July, 1911, p. 106.

96. Roy Nash to editor of the *Gazette* (Northampton, Mass.), Nov. 18, 1929, Administrative Files, Box C-338, Subject File: Lynching—General, NAACP Papers.

97. *The Crusader,* Dec., 1920, p. 12.

98. James A. Sandos, "The Plan of San Diego: War and Diplomacy on the Texas Border, 1915–1916," *Arizona and the West* 14, no. 1 (1972): 5–24; James A. Sandos, *Rebellion in the Borderlands: Anarchism and the Plan of San Diego, 1904–1923* (Norman and London: University of Oklahoma Press, 1992); Emilio Zamora, *World of the Mexican Worker in Texas,* p. 83; Alfred Arteaga, "The Chicano-Mexican Corrido," *Journal of Ethnic Studies* 13, no. 2 (summer, 1985): 83–84; James L. Haley, *Texas: From Spindletop through World War II* (New York: St. Martin's Press, 1993), pp. 94, 121; Foley, *White Scourge,* p. 56.

99. James Weldon Johnson to President Harding, Nov. 17, 1922, Administrative Files, Box C-338, NAACP Papers.

100. *Houston Post,* Nov. 16, 1922; *New York American,* Nov. 17, 1922; *New York News,* Nov. 25, 1922; *New York Tribune,* Nov. 17, 18, and 21, 1922; *New York Times,* Nov. 16, 17, 18, and 23, 1922; *Excelsior* (Mexico City), Nov. 16, 18, 19, and 20, 1922.

101. Assistant Secretary to Don Manuel C. Teller, Jan. 5, 1923; James Weldon Johnson to Mexican Embassy, Dec. 9, 1926, Administrative Files, Box C-339, NAACP Papers.

CHAPTER 3

Finding Race in Turn-of-the-Century Dallas

STEPHANIE COLE

In the summer of 1900, twenty-five enumerators for the twelfth federal census walked the streets of Dallas, ready to count and categorize its residents. Enumerators were instructed to record—along with names, occupations, and places of birth for all residents—a racial identity. For this census, as in virtually every preceding one, the government had once again decided upon a new way to capture the country's racial makeup. Yet bureaucratic instructions remained sketchy at best. Ten years before (that is, for the eleventh census), Congress had insisted that enumerators mark not only white, black, Chinese, Japanese, and Indian, but also mulatto, quadroon, and octoroon—a task that required an attention to details and inside information past the ken of most enumerators, according to an analyst of the twelfth census. In 1900, having apparently thought better of the need to record shades of blackness, the Census Bureau merely told its workers to record each resident as a member of one of four racial categories: White, Negro, Mongolian (actually Chinese and Japanese, but all aggregate statistics collapsed these two), or Indian. How to assess that membership fell to individual enumerators. An early census director seemed to realize (without using this language, of course), that the circumstances fit well with the idea from our own turn of the century—that race is socially constructed. In his 1906 analysis of the eleventh census, Director S. N. D. North noted with chagrin, "their answers [to racial identification] reflect local opinion, and that opinion probably is based more upon social position and manner of life than upon the relative amounts of blood."[1]

Armed, or rather unarmed, to this extent, the enumerators' decisions demonstrated that "finding race" in turn-of-the-twentieth-century Dallas was no easy chore. Confusion reigned, particularly when enumerators came across nonblack persons of color, or those outside the categories of "White" and "Negro." They sporadically employed unauthorized categories such as "Russian Jew" or "Mexican." Asian residents proved especially baffling. Hop Lee, born in California of Chinese parents and able to speak but not write English, was listed as "white," while two blocks down (and met by a different enumerator), Hop See, born in China but actually literate in English, was "Chinese." Their Japanese neighbors, dressmakers Emma Sek and Annie Yashikara, were both listed as white. Documents originally recorded two other households of Chinese men as "white," but overmarkings, perhaps supplied by a more savvy supervisor, apparently noted their "Mongolian" or "Chinese" heritage.[2]

Children of marriages between different nonwhite groups perplexed enumerators further still. Ostensibly, virtually any amount of nonwhite blood "trumped" white ancestry, and southern custom long mandated that a black mother could only have a black child, regardless of the degree of non-black blood in her or the child's father. Lupe Tarrico provided an example. Though the father of her two children was from Mexico, the children were both listed as "black," as was she. But interracial children of Chinese parentage were apparently more complicated, as the cases of John Dodge and Sing Wing attest. Dodge's father was from New York, his wife and stepson were "whites" from Kentucky, and he owned his own home (a rarity in Dallas in 1900). Because he carried his mother's taint of nonwhite blood, he was labeled "Chinese." Sing Wing's father was Jim Wing, a restaurateur who had been born in China in 1872, although he had lived in the United States long enough to learn to speak, read, and write English. Her mother was Henrietta Wing, nee Johnson, a literate African American. In a stunning reflection of the potential power of "Chinese blood" in a southern setting, Sing was listed not as "black" as her mother was listed, but as "Chinese."[3]

Two things seem immediately important when trying to make sense of so many contradictions. First, confusion reigned because turn-of-the-century Dallas, like most U.S. cities of this era, was experiencing rapid demographic and social change. The entrance of large numbers of immigrants, mainly from Europe but also from Asia and Latin America, presented a challenge to native-born white Americans who (to put it bluntly) saw racial, or blood, differences where we might see ethnic, or cultural, differences. Second, our own ability to stand back and marvel at their misplaced certainty about racial identity stems from recent developments within scholarship on the history of race, and on the construction of white racial identity in particular. Current historical scholarship on the making of whiteness highlights the connections between rising immigration, the justification of American imperialism, and the building of the segregated South at the turn of the twentieth century.

When seen through the lens of this literature, Dallas reveals the inconsistencies of the making (or "finding") of race in a New South city. On the one hand, Dallasites firmly identified with their southern neighbors about the necessity of subordinating the rights of African Americans. That obsession with blackness created interstices for other nonblack people of color—Mexican Americans, Asian immigrants, Russian Jews, and others—to claim privileges not offered in other locales. On the other hand, southern-born white Dallasites' interest in protecting the entitlements accruing to whiteness (without seeming to do so), left those same nonblack groups tainted with a sense of "otherness" quite similar to that attributed to African Americans. In other words, the flexibility of white racial identity worked both for and against them. When we look at the practical application of racialized thinking at this unique place—where the South meets the Southwest—we come face to face with the complicated and perhaps even improbable history of the making of white privilege. Moreover, by expanding our investigation of this process outside the Deep South and by paying attention to a broad spectrum of ethnic groups, we have the means to uncover just how fragile Americans' compromises were as they faced the demographic and political shifts brought by the twentieth century. At the local level and especially in a city with a growing economy and a diverse population, we can see the complex negotiations and reconceptions necessary to support what might otherwise often seem to be a self-evident and natural racial dynamic for the new social order.

Indeed, recent scholarship about this era illustrates that what had once seemed a southern story—the creation of separate worlds for whites and blacks—was really a national project. Northerners concerned with controlling immigrants and rationalizing "the white man's imperial burden" accepted and furthered southerners' rewriting of their own racial history. That rewriting made slavery into a benign institution, repainted the Civil War as a glorious Lost Cause, and thereby rationalized legislation and lynchings that limited African Americans' postbellum autonomy. One measure of nationwide commitment to the southern Jim Crow agenda can be located in national advertisers' success in marketing shared whiteness. By including some and excluding others, segregation had made that sense of shared whiteness possible; those looking to boost consumption discovered its appeal across the United States.[4] Yet if white racial identity was the goal, recent studies of attitudes about immigrants tell us that southern and central European immigrants as well as Mexican immigrants faced significant barriers to that goal. Prior to the widespread acceptance of the category of "Caucasian" to encompass "whites" from across Europe and Latin America (an acceptance that occurred mainly in the 1920s), most native-born Americans with native-born parents ascribed cultural differences between themselves and foreign-born Americans to physical, racialized distinctiveness. Increasingly after the logic of the "four great races" of Negroid, Mongoloid, Indian, and Caucasian spread, the lines between Italians and native-born whites or between Jewish and non-Jewish whites became lines of ethnicity rather than race.[5]

In the intermediate period—after heavy immigration began but before notions of the unity of a Caucasian race were widely accepted—immigrants soon learned that the key to avoiding the taint of racial inferiority was distancing themselves from those further down the racial hierarchy that damned them. To borrow an example from outside the South, Irish Americans were disparaged as savage "Celts" in New York but found themselves labeled "white" in San Francisco when they protested Chinese immigration. Within the South, Sicilian immigrants to Louisiana discovered the transitional difficulties when they accepted field work. In 1906, an Italian official describing their plight contended that "a majority of the plantation owners cannot comprehend that . . . Italians are white" and instead considered them "white-skinned negroes" because they, like African Americans, engaged in farm labor.[6] A similar association with agricultural work influenced Anglo Texans' views of Mexican Americans, as Neil Foley has argued in his study of the cotton-producing areas of Central Texas. Though Tejanos and Mexican immigrants were not of African descent, they seemed to share many of the same characteristics as the "colored" population. The limited degree to which a few enjoyed privileges of whiteness during the first part of the twentieth century depended upon their own wealth and, at least in part, upon how much the local African American population threatened native-born whites.[7]

Given the current status of the scholarly discussion of race then, "finding race in Dallas" requires substantial attention not only to groups other than those identified as African Americans, a group long assumed to be the only ones having "race." Such a discussion also necessitates recognizing when turn-of-the-century Dallasites were struggling to characterize social differences as ones inhering in physical, or blood (that is, *racial*) terms, and when they sought some other explanatory factor. One key moment—the spring of 1891—and one key group—Chinese immigrants—together offer a starting point to see how racial lines in Dallas emerged. That spring, the Texas legislature passed the first Jim Crow law requiring separate cars for whites and African Americans on railroads. For a decade on either side of that important milestone, Chinese workers in Dallas complicated, some times more obviously than others, how "white" Dallasites thought about race. Though those two elements provide the backbone for the discussion that follows, all sorts of other groups, including Mexican American railroad workers and wealthy Jews, must be included in the story. It makes for a messy analysis, but then, the creation of white supremacy in Dallas relied upon contingencies and manipulations that somehow came together to make the accident of white skin seem like an inevitable reason to rule. It is incumbent upon us to try to pull that process apart and figure out how it happened.

In the spring of 1891, one of the bloodiest lynchings in American history—as measured by the number of victims at one time—involved not African Americans, but Italian immigrants in the city of New Orleans. Under the guise of saving the city from a "flourishing" Mafia, a local lawyer known for his interest in reform, S. W. Parkerson, led a noontime attack on the local "parish prison" where eleven defendants were held during their trial for the murder of the police chief, David C. Hennessy. The day before, the first of the defendants had been acquitted, and charges of jury tampering followed quickly behind. To rectify a perceived miscarriage of justice, the mob "battered down the jail doors," chased the "miserable Sicilians" from their hiding places, and shot them, mostly in the back. In the public spectacle phase of the lynching, two of the eleven were later hung in the courtyard "in order to satisfy" the huge mob remaining outside. Commentary following the lynching predictably lauded the "righteous authority" of the "solemn" mob to correct the failure of the justice system, but the commentary also carried sinister racial overtones.[8] In the views of a local judge, the "Italian colony" was too clannish; a merchant noted their "treacherous ways." Perhaps the most overtly racialized depiction of the Sicilian victims appeared in a fictionalized version of the story, which was published in periodical form just a few weeks later, entitled "The New Orleans Mafia: or, Chief of Police Hennessy Avenged." Here, the Sicilians were "the most bloody-minded and revengeful of the Mediterranean races. . . . Owing to their Saracen origin, murder and intrigue [are] natural with them."[9] Clearly, in this commentary, Italians were not truly white.

Definite regional patterns affected the degree to which editors blamed these Italians' lynching on racial inferiority. "The New Orleans Mafia" tract was published not in New Orleans but in New York. A depiction of Italian pre-lynching behavior as "an explosion of cheap Latin fury and braggadocio" appeared even further away, in Portland, Oregon.[10] In Dallas, neither major newspaper made any such comment. The tragic lynching in New Orleans resulted from a jury system gone bad and "outraged justice assert[ing] itself," according to the *Dallas Times Herald*.[11] Though it would have been unlikely for the Dallas newspapers to attack the New Orleans crowd as racist and "blood thirsty" in light of the general acceptability of lynching at this point, their restraint from justifying the mob's action as based upon white Anglo superiority was noteworthy. Instead, editorialists bemoaned a legal procedure that gave juries such power and even warned that in light of a string of recent "mistrials, hung juries and acquittals" in Dallas, "one of these days our people will be confronted with just such a condition as that which prevailed in the Crescent City."[12] The *Morning News*, which tended to take a strong stand against lynching, went so far as to object to the lynchings on the grounds that the victims were "defenseless outcasts" selected over "prominent murderers [who] are escaping every day" through courts in New Orleans and elsewhere.[13] Americans must, the editors insisted, "maintain safeguards for foreigners as for themselves."[14] Indeed, the *Morning News,* in a rather surprising critique of racial and nativist leanings, asked and answered what might happen if "eleven Americans had been lynched by an openly organized band of Mexicans after the victims had been acquitted by a Mexican court and jury." "The furious indignation of the average American can hardly be imagined," the editorial posited.[15]

None of this righteousness should be taken at face value, surely. Dallas publishers were not immune to contemporary assessments of problematic Sicilian culture. Both newspapers dutifully carried the wire copy that reported the violent initiations of the Mafia—where, with "a skull in the left hand" and a "dirk in the right hand," initiates led "innocent dinner guests" to their demise. Such tales undoubtedly helped to explain why most whites believed that "the sovereign mob" should take action.[16] Even so, in Dallas newspapers, beyond the single wire copy reprint, no further comment on Mafiosos, or "treacherous dagos," was forthcoming.

What the local papers did cover was a positively breathless account of the mob's effort to locate the Irish private detective, Dominick O'Malley. The crowd had identified O'Malley as the chief culprit in the false exoneration of the prisoners; he allegedly had facilitated the jury bribes that led to their acquittal. Prior to the lynching, the mob leadership claimed that their actions were about bringing surer justice to the guilty, and, in their last act of whipping up the crowd, they "denounced O'Malley." Most witnesses to the lynching agreed that had O'Malley not vanished in a timely fashion, one Irish body would have swung alongside those eleven Italians.[17] In the days after the lynching, the *News* falsely reported several "O'Malley sightings" across the nation, perhaps anticipating what might still lie in store for the accused detective.[18] The preoccupation with O'Malley is important because O'Malley, like the murdered police chief avenged by this lynching, was Irish. As the appointment of one of their own to so high a position implies, the Irish in New Orleans were almost "honorary Anglo Saxons," according to one scholar.[19] But for quick thinking and even quicker feet on one Irishman's part, however, an "honorary Anglo-Saxon" might well have been included with the "bloody-minded Saracens." In a context where the Irish were so accepted, a lynching of O'Malley would have complicated our ability to cast this as an obvious racial attack.

The lack of attention to Italians' racial characteristics within Dallas papers seems related to the lack of familiarity or at least fear of this group of immigrants. In both 1890 and 1900 just over 160 Italians lived in the city, and they were a relatively acculturated lot. Most had lived first in New York or New Orleans and, once settled in Dallas, held occupations that marked them as respectable. Most owned their own businesses, working as grocers, confectioners, or shoemakers, and perhaps less than six percent were laborers.[20] They seemed to blend in, becoming a source of benign local color, much like the Irish in Dallas. The activities of Dallas' Irish community indicate the benign nature of these differences. That same March of 1891, Irish citizens in Dallas were planning and carrying out their first large-scale celebration of St. Patrick's Day. So unconcerned were they about calling attention to their differences from white Anglo-Saxon Protestants that organizers seriously entertained the possibility of making their celebration "an Irish affair exclusively" and denying entry to any who were not themselves of Irish lineage. Calmer and more ecumenical heads prevailed, and the group eventually issued invitations to decidedly non-Irish dignitaries such as Governor Hogg and Bishop Garrett, in their effort to "give as good a celebration as any other nationality on the face of God's green earth."[21]

Returning to the question of measuring the extent of racialist thinking (Italian or otherwise), it seems that Dallas commentaries on the New Orleans victims took the form of objections to "the jury problem" rather than "the Italian problem" or even the "immigrant problem," because, at this point, in the spring of 1891, Dallasites and Texans did not see Italians as much more of a threat than the Dallas citizens who were full of Irish national pride. They *were,* however, concerned about limiting the freedom of movement—and the concomitant freedom of attitude—of which African Americans were taking greater and greater advantage. Having made the separation of the races in trains a voluntary right of railway companies in 1890, the Twenty-second Texas legislature heard few, if any, complaints when it made segregation mandatory. In what southern historians have recognized as the first step toward a new organization of white power based upon Jim Crow, or segregation, laws, Texans of white southern extraction focused on the need for "wise legislation" to separate white and "colored" passengers to avoid "regretful" disorder. Governor James S. Hogg, who had previously been "a paternalist moderate in matters of race," feared losing support for other more important concerns if he did not back the implementation of segregation laws. The legislation was one of six actions the governor called for at the opening of the legislature in January of 1891, and it was never seriously contested.[22] Nevertheless, a closer look at the language and reception of the "separate cars" law indicates that it caused a bit more racial reflection on the part of the legislature than such easy passage might suggest.

Following the governor's request for such a measure, no less than seven versions of a bill that would require railroads to provide separate and well-labeled accommodations for "white" and "colored" passengers were read on either the floor of the House or the Senate. All used that nomenclature—indicating the need for the "races" to be segregated as "white and colored." In the House, most of the bills were referred to the Internal Improvements committee. The committe considered five bills and submitted a new version, based on the stipulations included in those five, but using new terms. In this new version, the segregation was intended for "white" and "Negro" passengers, wherein "Negro" was carefully defined as "every person of African descent."[23] When the Senate bill arrived in the House for consideration—the Senate had worked more quickly and had passed a "separate cars" bill first—the House, led by Representative W. L. Adkins, an attorney from Columbus, Texas, "scalped" the Senate's bill, and inserted its own white-Negro language. State representatives even voted affirmatively to change the caption of the bill to reflect the corrected terminology.[24] After a joint conference convened to rectify the differences between the House and Senate versions, both houses passed essentially that piece of legislation.

This review charts a remarkable attention to the language of blackness, which would not have been expected until a few years later. By 1896, Homer Plessy had unsuccessfully challenged the state of Louisiana's definition of him as "colored," claiming that as an "octoroon," or mostly white, he could not be subjected to laws pertaining to "coloreds." Indeed, Plessy's questioning of racial definitions rather than the legality of the act of racial segregation per se formed part of his charge against segregation in *Plessy* v. *Ferguson*. But Texas legislators expressed their concern about the fuzziness of the term "colored" several months before the group of African Americans who supported Plessy even met.[25] Moreover, the Texas legislators' choice of the word "Negro" (and a carefully crafted definition of "Negro") in this instance contrasts with the 1876 Texas Constitution, which used the term "colored" with ease.[26] That document mandated separate public schools for white and "colored" students; widespread opinion held that "colored" referred only to those of African heritage. (Those who supported segregated schools for Mexicans seldom, if ever, argued that the Texas Constitution's call for the separation of "colored" students mandated Mexicans' separation but instead justified Mexican Americans' exclusion on other, usually pedagogical, grounds.[27]) Yet by the time legislators were writing the 1891 act segregating railroad cars, they had decided upon the need for more precision, perhaps because they did not intend for Tejano constituents to be included in its scope. Though in some communities Mexican Americans would be restricted by custom from riding with whites, the state clearly wanted to avoid a law that might conceivably *mandate* their exclusion.[28]

Having defined "Negro" so carefully, the legislators left "white" unclear, which prompted a telling critique of the logic behind Jim Crow legislation. Perhaps the law implied that "white" meant by default *everyone* without

African blood. In other southern contexts that had been so.[29] It seemed unlikely, though, in turn-of-the-century Dallas, as at least one African American activist knew. In March of 1891—at the same time that the Italians were under attack in New Orleans, and the Irish were loudly celebrating their non-Anglo-Saxon heritage in Dallas—this activist, the Reverend A. Stokes, asked a remarkably acute question. What "the Negro" wanted to know, he revealed, was where the "Chinamen, Mexicans and the Indians are to ride" in the new railway system. Would they ride "with us" or with "the whites"? In pointing out that these groups were not easily categorized as either black or white, he highlighted the inconsistencies of the entire racial system that Anglo Texans were creating.[30]

Stokes only had to read the local papers or take a stroll downtown to know that whites in the city characterized the small Chinese minority as nonwhite. A heated mayoral race was underway in Dallas that spring, and a split within the Democratic Party had significantly complicated the political debate. A reporter from the *Dallas Times-Herald* noted that politics was consuming the male population. A new newspaper had been started by the "prince of Bohemians, Col. Mose Harris, known in journalistic circles as 'Rabbi.'" The effort to convince African American voters to side with the Democratic Party had brought the "colored man . . . cheek by jowl with the gentlemen of Caucasian blood." The reporter asked a "humble man of Confucius" whom he preferred in the next election as the man dashed through a crowded street corner. The reporter determined that "John Chinaman is the only man in the city who is not interested in politics." The Chinese man had merely responded that he was for (according to the reporter's racist idiom) "Dlam Melican [the American] man. Me no votee; me washee." Since the expansion of suffrage during the Jacksonian era, manhood had been closely allied with citizenship. As a nonvoter, John Chinaman was no man, let alone white. Bohemians and blacks had a say, but the Chinese did not.[31]

From this perspective, Stokes recognized that the racial hierarchy implied in the separate cars bill was inconsistent. Why, he asked, if whites wanted to rank the races, would they ignore what their history together told them of black character? Negroes had long proven their closeness to whites, he averred, protecting their homes during the war in ways that recent history suggested they could never have expected if Mexicans, Chinese, or Indians had been the slaves. Stokes even implied that former slaves were continuing to serve as protectors of whites. "We feel that we do not want them to ride with us," he noted, "but if the whites are satisfied with them it is all right with the negroes."[32] This African American was not questioning the reality of race, or even the inferiority of certain races, but simply the debased position of his own. However, the suggestion that men could make mistakes in their understanding of race may have opened the door to the implication that men, rather than God or nature, created the most important racial lines.

During the spring of 1891, the contradictions among what newspaper reporters and editors wrote, the observations of local black leaders, and the actions of legislators illustrated the instability of the terms "white" and "black" at the moment that they became essential to the order of southern society. The fact that few of the Reverend Stokes's contemporaries seemed even to take notice of his point about the lack of clarity concerning the place of other nonwhite groups testifies to just how invisible those "white" contemporaries' actions were to themselves. The pressing question of where exactly Mexicans and Indians would ride was never settled in law, let alone answered regarding the even more problematic Chinese—who in very few contexts within the United States ever became "white."[33] That Texas legislators were content to pass a law that left unclear the status of three to five percent of the state's population (Mexican immigrants, as well as others not listed by census enumerators as "Negro" or "White") calls attention to one of the central misrepresentations of the Jim Crow South.[34] Governor Hogg may have claimed that this "wise legislation" would bring order to a chaotic society, but by failing to clarify where nearly 75,000 Texans (a low estimate) belonged, the separate cars bill could not be expected to bring that order.

That an African American invoked Chinese residents in his questioning of the political and social order gets to the heart of the problem of assuming that we can see a southern city in black and white. Native-born Dallasites were overwhelmingly southerners, but they lived in a state that simultaneously bordered a Latin American nation and considered itself the gateway to the western United States.[35] They also claimed status as "Americans" as well as clearly identifying themselves as products of the progress of western (that is, European) civilization. Each of these identities necessitated a different vocabulary of race. These different vocabularies presented inconsistencies and contradictions, of which most "white" Americans were apparently blithely unaware. Nevertheless, those contradictions exposed the "constructedness" of the racial lines that they contended were "natural" and God-given.

White Dallasites continually altered the "Other" against whom they identified themselves. The Chinese were meaningless in these first three identities: for white southerners the only "race problem" was one associated with blacks; as Texans they were holding the line against Mexicans; and (in the Texas-version, at least) cowboy westerners worried about Indians and water rights. As Americans they did indeed fret about the "yellow peril." But, at the same time, as benefactors of Occidental civilization, they were fascinated by "Oriental" civilization.[36]

It was, perhaps, as members of this last category that Dallas socialites became infatuated with Eastern societies and frequently designed social functions around Far and Middle Eastern themes. Dallas' turn-of-the-century society magazine, the *Beau Monde,* frequently described posh parties centered on what could only be labeled as an "Oriental" fad. Fashionable though the elites who threw the parties might be, they had only a limited grasp of the other world that so fascinated them. *Beau Monde's* editor, the inimitable Mrs. Hugh Fitzgerald, declared the room decorated for a "Japanese Tea Party," given by the Trezvants as a fund-raiser for the St. Matthew's Home for Children, "very Japanesey." "The entire suite was a vista of handsome draperies, dado, lights, flowers and porcelains suggestive of the land of the Mikado. And the women! Well they were too bewitchingly oriental for anything. Several of the costumes worn came from the 'Flowery Kingdom' and others from that high priest in this country, Vantine." If dresses by Vantine hinted that interest in all things "Japanesey" grew out of trendiness rather than true interest in the Far East, then the mixed-up decor confirmed it. The women in kimonos sat in front of "Bagdad [*sic*] curtains [hung from] crossed Damascus blades," "chinese lilies [wafting] their fragrance" adorned the tables, alongside "ruby lights . . . over a dainty Teakwood smoker, upon which was a slender vase of Beauty roses." Those roses, Fitzgerald remarked, were "just a gentle reminder that these fair Orientals were very loyal Americans."[37] (See figure 3.1.) For those so unfortunate as to have lost in the mail their invitations to the Trezvants' bash, Mme. Blanther's "oriental toilet suite" in the Middleton building offered a similar experience. The general public in pursuit of manicures could luxuriate in the evocative (and decidedly inauthentic) décor of her suite. She too included "Bagdad draperies" as a part of a "Far Eastern" influence, which she placed alongside a "Sultan's couch and canopy piled with great silken cushions," "a Japanese tea table and service," "graceful bronzes," "crimson walls" and "a rich Persian rug."[38]

What is particularly curious about this otherwise mundane effort to appropriate and possess the "Other" is that it coincided with the United States' embarkation on its most substantial and controversial effort at colonizing the Far East to date—the war in the Philippines. That expansionist project met the distinct disapproval of the editor's husband, Mr. Hugh Fitzgerald, who wrote a breezy editorial commenting on local, national, and international politics at the start of each issue of *Beau Monde.* In the very same issue in which Mrs. Fitzgerald glowed with enthusiasm for "Bagdad draperies" and the "luxuriant" East, Mr. Fitzgerald derided attacks on the Filipino insurrectionary leader Aguilnaldo who, he claimed, merely wanted to "set up a republican form of government." Unfortunately for those who truly identified with "the Nazarene" (Jesus) and thus had trouble recognizing the new state of affairs, civilization now came with a Gatling gun, he asserted, tongue in cheek.[39] Thus at the same time that Mrs. Fitzgerald promoted stereotypes of "Orientals" and exaggerated their differences from

Figure 3.1. The setting for a Japanese tea party in Dallas, January, 1899: This illustration and a gushing description of the "very Japanesey" event appeared in the society magazine *Beau Monde*. While *Beau Monde*'s readership seemed fascinated with Oriental décor and fashion, they ignored Dallas' Chinese residents, whose uncertain racial identity presented problems for those whites engaged in drawing simple black and white racial boundaries. *Courtesy* Texas/Dallas History and Archives of the Dallas Public Library

Americans, Mr. Fitzgerald accepted the ability of a Far Easterner (Aguilnaldo) to understand the benefits of republican government and the right of Filipinos to question the motives of Christian missionaries. Even if the Fitzgeralds managed this cultural and political chasm in their marriage, they (along with other Democrats who used language like Fitzgerald's in protesting imperialism) were sending their readership mixed messages about the extent and relevance of Asian racial difference.[40]

This disjuncture, however, did not trouble Dallasites. Perhaps the most popular fraternal organization open to the elite at the turn of the century was a group of Dallas boosters who called themselves "the Grand Order of the Kaliph." In September of 1899, the Kaliphs spent thousands of dollars in a showy cross-country journey to Dallas, in which they assumed the identities of "Mustapha Ben Selim, the Kaliph; Ali Ben Tabourak, First Vizier; Abdul Hassen, First Courier," etc. Once in Dallas, they led a grand parade and sponsored a lavish ball for seven thousand with the theme of "A Night in Bagdad." According to the gushing *Beau Monde,* the Kaliph (actually a millionaire railroad baron by the name of E. H. R. Green but never identified in this article) was "the first potentate to tread the soil of Texas, the first mighty monarch to break bread with Occidentals—in these climes at least." Never one to miss an opportunity to describe what people were wearing, Mrs. Fitzgerald noted that he and his court "wore magnificent costumes of royal silk and velvet. The Kaliph's cost $600 alone."[41] The Kaliphs' objective, wholeheartedly supported by the Fitzgeralds and apparently the rest of Dallas society, was to bring publicity to the burgeoning New South city, and signal to the nation and potential investors that Dallas was as wealthy and sophisticated as any town of its size in the Northeast. How ironic that, to do so, the Dallas elite turned to celebrate (after a fashion) the culture of dark-skinned, if exotic, racial inferiors. The message seems to be that in refuting the image of backward southern barbarians, Dallasites had to prove themselves capable of a more cosmopolitan, indeed globalized, scale of racial appropriation. So comfortable did they become in this mode, moreover, that the Grand Order of the Kaliph was the center of attention at the quintessential southern gathering held for the first time in Dallas in 1902, the Confederate Reunion.[42]

Their claims of knowledge of "the Oriental other" notwithstanding, non-Asian "white" Dallas residents were often unsettled by the presence of actual Asians among them, as their confusions about the racial identity of Chinese immigrants in the 1900 census so aptly illustrates. Not only were Chinese immigrants improperly identified according to the enumerators' instructions, they were also seriously undercounted, as a quick comparison of city directory and census statistics indicates.[43] But more than suggestive of the invisibility of Asians in Dallas at the turn of the century, contradictions in their racial identity illustrate how an obsession with blackness shaped Texans' ability to define race across the board. On one hand, Jim Wing's Chinese blood "trumped" his wife's black blood and made their infant daughter Sing "Chinese." But on the other, Chinese heritage was escapable in a way that African blood was not. For this Jim Wing may well have been the owner of a very successful Dallas restaurant, known between 1898 and 1900 as the Jim Wing Restaurant, and which by 1901 had changed its name to the Star Restaurant, with Jim Wing still functioning as sole proprietor. Whether or not he was the same Jim Wing, the successful entrepreneur demonstrates that in Dallas, it was, at least partly, possible to shed one's "Chinese" identity. In the city directory, at least between 1891 and 1910, two racial groups were regularly marked as different: African Americans appeared with a "(c)" beside their names, and Chinese residents were labeled "(Chinese)." Jim Wing was so labeled in each appearance at the turn of the century until 1901, when his restaurant was so successful as to merit advertising on the back cover of the directory, one of only four businesses so advertised. In that year, Jim Wing was no longer listed as "(Chinese)" in the listings, though apparently all of his compatriots still were. His wealth and success had evidently "whitened" him.[44]

George Sekiya offers another example of the flexible status of so-called "Orientals." Sekiya opened a restaurant in 1901, known as "The Japanese Restaurant," which served both "ladies and gentlemen," with private boxes available for the former. Most Japanese restaurants of this era were named after their decor rather than their cuisine, however, and Sekiya was probably not introducing Dallasites to sushi and tempura vegetables. But his success does indicate that the fascination with "Orientals" was not pursued solely by the rich. Sekiya claimed the best twenty-five-cent meal in the city, a rather low price, and his restaurant never garnered the attention of the snobbish Mrs. Fitzgerald, who undoubtedly would have described the restaurant in the pages of Beau Monde with relish had it devoted itself to a more exclusive clientele. To whatever group of whites Sekiya appealed, they certainly outnumbered by far any Asian customers he might have served. Like Wing, he undoubtedly relied on the Anglo majority, and somehow found himself counted among them. He was never listed as "(Japanese)" in the city directory.[45]

As wealthy and successful African Americans who never escaped the "(c)[olored]" marker knew, the "whitening" of Chinese residents in turn-of-the-century Dallas almost certainly would not have occurred if they had lived in large and therefore threatening numbers in the city. Consider, for example, the experience of an African American physician, Dr. Benjamin R. Bluitt. By 1909, Bluitt was successful enough to have opened a sanitorium in the city for "the benefit of the general public where all the most scientific operations are being successfully made," and purchased a half-page ad in the city directory that marked his success and was undoubtedly intended to garner him more. Yet Bluitt was always marked with a "(c)" (to mark his "colored" status).[46] Nor should the early history of Chinese in Dallas be interpreted as a significant model, exceptional or otherwise, of Asian immigrant experience. Rather, the idiosyncrasies of Chinese life in Dallas reflect that the templates forming to govern African American life could apply to other persons of color but did not always do so. At this point at least, the presence of Chinese residents could still raise questions about racial hierarchy. Their place was unclear. Whites often portrayed them as the lowest of the races—shamefully disengaged from politics and manly citizenship—yet, at other times, whites viewed them as distinctly better than African Americans. Chinese Dallasites could potentially transcend racial markings.

Having raised the specter of class in its relation to race, it seems worthwhile to examine briefly the ability of other not-truly-white groups to cross into white privilege, after attaining wealth. In Dallas, of course, the most prominent group within the "Other" white category comprised Mexican immigrants. Though Mexicans did not move into North Texas in large numbers until after 1910, preliminary evidence suggests that they, like the Chinese, were undercounted in Dallas in 1900. They may well have lived in marginal places (e.g., railroad boxcars or tents north of town), and there were certainly enclaves of Mexican immigrants like the one south of Houston Street, in which eleven of forty residences were filled by Mexican immigrants who worked at the railroads, sold tamales, or made candy.[47] That their "Mexican" lineage worked against their efforts to gain greater acceptance in the city is supported by the telling correlation between successful businessmen in Dallas who had last names like Gonzales and Martinez and a claim to "Spanish" parentage. A quick consultation of the Soundex listings for Texas in 1900 indicates that although virtually every other Gonzales or Martinez in the state identified family origins in Mexico, established residents of that name in Dallas did not. Even Pedro Martinez, the well-to-do tobacco manufacturer who successfully marketed the "Mexican Commerce" cigar, had apparently come to Dallas from Spain, via New Orleans.[48]

Eastern European immigrants had an easier time than Mexicans in blending into whiteness in Dallas, not surprisingly. Though residents might label new arrivals racially as "Russian Jews," long-term Jewish immigrants, such as those from the Sanger and Kahn families became influential among the Dallas elite. Yet, in 1900, even successful Jews met limits to their inclusion in the realm of white privilege. "Hebrew" organizations were listed separately in the city directory's compilation of local voluntary societies, apart from all other church-related groups, which appeared together under another heading. In the pages of *Beau Monde,* Jewish society received extensive coverage of debuts and other fashionable affairs—but, similarly, the articles were always treated distinctively. References to Jewish belles and matrons always marked them as part of "the Phoenix set" (after the social club patronized by Jews in the city), and in discussions of elaborate Jewish weddings, Mrs. Fitzgerald seldom failed to highlight the expense and taste of wedding presents, which she apparently expected to outshine the prosaic gifts wealthy Protestant couples received.[49] Social interactions between "the Phoenix set" and the rest of the "beautiful world" were rare indeed. Jewish women only appeared at galas with non-Jewish women if the cause was charitable, and then at mostly women-only affairs held before 6 P.M.[50] Though some of the most important leaders in politics and business in the city of Dallas were Jewish, the existence of a "6 P.M. curtain" that separated Jews and non-Jews at night but not during business hours testifies to a lingering sense of racial, that is, permanent, separateness that no amount of wealth or political success could erase.

Considering that even the wealthiest members of the city could be the objects of racial prejudice, who was behind the establishment of the sharp line between black and white? Many sorts of people wrote for newspapers, counted citizens, created law, or undertook other enterprises that helped to substantiate ideas about race. But none were among the poor or even the working class. Census enumerators—those perhaps less-than-earnest civil servants struggling to squeeze residents belonging to many ethnic groups into constricted racial categories—were not the "movers and shakers" of the city. As a group nationally, they were professionals, clerks, and skilled artisans; in 1900 Dallas enumerators included several carpenters and plumbers, a jeweler, agents of various sorts, along with an attorney, a few teachers, a preacher, and an aspiring police officer, all of whom were apparently white.[51] In terms of wealth they were quite distant from another group, the society mavens who engaged in the subtle racism of the *Beau Monde*. The eminently middle-class Mrs. Fitzgerald stood at the helm of a clearly elitist publication that lauded Filipinos' republicanism, silently excluded Jews, and objectified and significantly discounted "Orientals."[52]

A third group that played a role in the making of race took a more public part—the Texas legislators who passed the first Jim Crow legislation. Of the eighteen members of the Internal Improvements committee who wrote the law, eleven were farmers, all but one were white men born in the South (the eighteenth was born in Ireland), and thirteen were from counties in which African Americans represented a significant minority group.[53] In C. Vann Woodward's words, these were men who knew well the value of "ritual and Jim Crow to bolster the creed of white supremacy in the bosom of a white man working for a black man's wages."[54] It is perhaps notable that not all of the whites discussed here even explicitly supported the Jim Crow regime; E. H. R. Green, (the "Kaliph of Bagdad") was a Republican who offered support to a prominent African American Republican, W. M. "Gooseneck" McDonald, who wanted to maintain black power within the party in Texas.[55] All the same, Green's actions were part and parcel of the larger cultural project whereby the differences of darker-skin peoples from "civilized" white society were highlighted.

From this list then, it may appear that all whites—from plumbers to powerful merchants, farmers, lawyers, teachers, and capitalists, members of both the Democratic and Republican parties—played a role, however subtle, in helping to bolster the status of the white race in this place and time. But at least one group of whites seemed not to have taken part. Those "white men working for black men's wages" apparently did not participate in any way that made the public record. Their silence seems remarkable, particularly as contrasted with the broad social representation among those in occupations above the laboring classes. Part of this apparent silence undoubtedly emerges from the sources, which, apart from the census, favor the more highly literate newspaper editors and elected officials. Still, biases within the sources notwithstanding, this close look at Dallas racial politics illustrates how the "creation of whiteness" maintained economic and political advantage to some "whites" at the cost of the promise of those advantages to other "whites." Acceptance of this inviolable line between black and white separated poor whites from nonwhites, most of whom shared their economic and political disempowerment.

All sorts of "better off" Texans participated in the cultural exchanges that defined white privilege, and that process gradually solidified their political and/or economic position. Laboring whites, however, who benefited socially but not materially from this racial construction, were of consequence only in the abstract.

When Dallas is examined in this way, with attention to racial nuances that have often seemed invisible, the ironies of the Jim Crow period stand out conspicuously. The outcome that we know is coming—the creation of a "lily white Texas"—seems strangely ungrounded or destabilized. Whites united in the New South, but a precise definition and method of identifying "white" people was under negotiation in many places within the region. To wit, what it meant to be white was not clear in turn-of-the-century Dallas, despite the fact that "whites" of that city seemed firmly committed to the separation of "white" and "black" races.

Segregation was indeed built on many lies. Among them was the notion that even with Jim Crow "white" and "black" worlds were in fact separate (and thus more orderly than they would have been without Jim Crow laws).[56] More essential was the lie that "white" and "black" were actually meaningful ways to differentiate Americans. As most everyone in Dallas must certainly have been aware—by experience or by the reminders issued by African Americans such as the Reverend Stokes—Dallasites existed along a wider racial spectrum than Jim Crow allowed. Though they operated in a culture that focused with a "black and white" lens, they did so in a city more multicultural than we might have expected, and while maintaining vocabularies of race with intrinsic (though not always apparent) contradictions. That the black-white segregationist logic triumphed for so much of the century to follow should tell us that the framework had powerful appeal, but we should not assume that its victory was inevitable. At the turn of the century in Dallas, a clear sense of race—and especially who was white—was difficult to find.

Notes

1. From this bureaucrat's perspective such looseness was a mistake, and in his discussion racial breakdowns took the opportunity to advocate a slightly more "scientific" definition for future censuses. If S. N. D. North (the census director) had his way, all whites listed in the next censuses would have seven-eighths white or Caucasian blood and be regarded in the community as white. Standards for racial minorities were, not surprisingly, lower: Negroes would have to have one-eighth Negro, or African blood, have more Negro than Indian or Mongolian blood, and be regarded in the community as Negro, while similar rules of having at least one-eighth of Indian or Mongolian blood, less of any other racial minority's blood, and community regard as such would count one as either Indian or Mongolian, respectively. Department of Commerce and Labor, Bureau of the Census, S. N. D. North, director, *Special Reports: Supplementary Analysis and Derivative Tables, Twelfth Census of the United States: 1900* (Washington: Government Printing Office, 1906).

2. United States Census for 1900, manuscript schedule for Dallas County, Vol. 26.

3. U.S. Census 1900, manuscript schedule for Dallas County. See Lucy M. Cohen, *Chinese in the Post-Civil War South: A People without a History* (Baton Rouge: Louisiana State University Press, 1984), pp. 154–68, for evidence of similar confusions about the racial identity of the children of Chinese fathers and mothers of African, Creole, or Mexican descent. Moreover, having tracked the same Chinese-black families in several censuses, Cohen found that the same children labeled "Chinese" in 1880 became "black" in 1900. As an indicator of the cultural arbitrariness of these determinations, Cohen points to rules for keeping track of Chinese racial blood in the Philippines in this era that were quite different from Louisiana's rules.

4. Grace Elizabeth Hale, *Making Whiteness: The Culture of Segregation in the South, 1880–1940* (New York: Pantheon, 1998).

5. Gail Bederman, *Manliness & Civilization: A Cultural History of Gender and Race in the United States, 1880–1917* (Chicago: University of Chicago Press, 1995), p. 29; Matthew Frye Jacobson, *Whiteness of a Different Color: European Immigrants and the Alchemy of Race* (Cambridge: Harvard University Press, 1999). The category of "Caucasian" certainly did not spare from racist treatment all foreign-born Americans who might have qualified for the label. A significant body of literature illustrates that racism still touched Mexican Americans long after the 1920s, despite their ostensible qualifications as "Caucasians."

6. James R. Barrett and David Roediger, "Inbetween Peoples: Race, Nationality, and the 'New Immigrant' Working Class," *Journal of Ethnic History* 16 (Spring, 1997): 32.

7. Neil Foley, *The White Scourge: Mexicans, Blacks, and Poor Whites in Texas Cotton Culture* (Berkeley: University of California Press, 1997), pp. 40–44. Foley argues, moreover, that the decline of the profitability of cotton farming in Central Texas, along with the prevalence of Mexican American and African American laborers and small tenant farmers in the cotton economy, led to the "darkening" of native-born white tenant farmers who did not succeed. Though they grasped at vestiges of the privileges that were to accompany their white skin, and attempted to restrict nonwhites' access to unions and perks, they soon found their own racial integrity and, as a correlate, their manhood, questioned.

8. *Dallas Morning News,* Mar. 15, 1891; *Dallas Times Herald,* Mar. 16, 1891; Jacobson, *Whiteness of a Different Color,* pp. 56–60.

9. Jacobson, *Whiteness of a Different Color,* p. 58; quotations from "The New Orleans Mafia: or, Chief of Police Hennessey Avenged" (*New York Detective Library,* April 25, 1891, vol. 1, no. 439, from Jacobson, pp. 60–61.

10. Jacobson, *Whiteness of a Different Color,* p. 58.

11. *Dallas Times Herald,* Mar. 16, 1891. *Dallas Morning News,* Mar. 15, 1891, noted that "a determined body of citizens who took into their own hands what justice had ignominiously failed to do." See that issue of the *News* also for the resolution passed by Dallas' local Cotton Exchange in support of the actions in New Orleans because of "the deplorable administration of criminal justice."

12. *Dallas Times Herald,* Mar. 16, 1891. A similar editorial, assaulting lawyers for being too clever, appeared in the *Dallas Morning News,* Mar. 15, 1891.

13. *Dallas Morning News,* Mar. 23, 1891.

14. Ibid., Mar. 22, 1891.

15. Ibid., Mar. 18, 1891.

16. Ibid., Mar. 17, 1891.

17. "O'Malley the detective would have shared the same fate of the assassins had he been caught." *Dallas Morning News,* Mar. 15, 1891.

18. *Dallas Morning News,* Mar. 15, 16, and 17, 1891; *Dallas Times Herald,* Mar. 18, 22, and 23, 1891. According to the *Dallas Times Herald,* Apr. 4, 1891, O'Malley eventually turned himself into the New Orleans police, claiming he had been in the city the whole time.

19. Jacobson, *Whiteness of a Different Color,* p. 59.

20. Cavaliere Valentine Belfiglio, *The Italian Experience in Texas* (Austin, Tex.: Eakin Press, 1983), pp. 52–61. Belfiglio's statistics are for a slightly later year. According to a rough estimate gleaned checking the occupation of Dallas residents with Italian names in *Morrison & Forney's General Directory of the City of Dallas* (Galveston: Morrison & Fourney Compilers and Publishers, 1891), less than ten percent of Italians in the city worked as laborers or in menial capacities. The largest occupation by far involved selling fruit, confections, and/or tobacco from a cart or in a store, as almost a third of all Italians were listed as peddlers or owners of stores or stands offering these goods.

21. *Dallas Morning News,* Mar. 9 and 12, 1891.

22. Governor James S. Hogg's "State of the State" message, House Journal, 22nd Leg., p. 111; Alwyn Barr, *Reconstruction to Reform: Texas Politics, 1876–1906* (Austin: University of Texas Press, 1971), p. 108. For two of the best overviews of the creation of Jim Crow legislation, see Edward L. Ayers, *The Promise of the New South: Life After Reconstruction* (New York: Oxford University Press, 1992); and C. Vann Woodward, *Origins of the New South, 1877–1913* (1951; reprint, Baton Rouge: Louisiana State University Press, 1971).

23. House Journal, p. 600.

24. *Austin Statesman,* Feb. 26, 1891.

25. Brook Thomas, ed., *Plessy v. Ferguson: A Brief History with Documents* (Boston: Bedford Books, 1997), pp. 186–89. As Hale, *Making Whiteness,* p. 23, notes, Plessy based his challenge not on the concept that barring "colored" passengers from white compartments was wrong per se, but that *he,* as an octoroon, was not "colored." His challenge forced the court to insist that "racial differences lay outside the law, beyond or before any act of human agency," and deny that he, or anyone, could be biracial and then "set this lie at the very center of modern society."

26. Note that as part of its definition of who would be deemed "Negro" the House version used a more customary reference to "every person of African blood as the term is generally understood"; the final law used the stricter terminology of "every person of African blood as defined by the statutes of this state." See House Journal, p. 420, and *General Laws of Texas,* 22nd Leg., 1891, pp. 46–47.

27. Hershel T. Manuel, *The Education of Mexican and Spanish-Speaking Children in Texas* (Austin: The Fund for Research in Social Sciences, University of Texas, Austin, 1930), p. 57, notes in evaluating the 1876 Texas Constitution's impact on separate schools for Mexican children that "white classification includes children of all races except those who have descended in whole or

part from negro ancestry. The Mexican of Indian descent as well as the Mexican of Spanish descent is regarded as white;" and Guadalupe San Miguel, Jr., *"Let All of Them Take Heed": Mexican Americans and the Campaign for Educational Equality in Texas, 1910–1981* (Austin: University of Texas Press, 1987), pp. 74–82, indicates that in their public reasoning, officials who supported segregation of Mexican students did so by claiming the need on pedagogical, language, or sometimes hygiene reasons, rather than explicit legal justification. In 1931, the case of *Amada Vela* v. *Board of Trustees of Charlotte ISD* successfully proved the point that a Mexican child could not be segregated merely on racial basis in Texas. See Manuel, *Education of Mexican and Spanish-Speaking Children,* p. 83, and San Miguel, *"Let All of Them Take Heed,"* pp. 76–77.

28. For evidence of the customary exclusion of Mexican immigrants and Tejanos, see Miguel, *"Let All of Them Take Heed,"* pp. 91–94; Arnoldo De León, *They Called Them Greasers* (Austin: University of Texas Press, 1983).

29. Note "Mexican Jim's" claim to whiteness in nineteenth-century Georgia, because he was "free from negro blood" as cited in Foley, *The White Scourge,* p. 23. The 1907 Oklahoma Constitution defined "white children" to mean all other children other than those of "African descent." *States' Laws on Race and Color in Appendices Containing International Documents, Federal Laws and Regulations, Local Ordinances and Charts,* compiled and edited by Pauli Murray (Cincinnati: Women's Division of Christian Service, 1950), and *General Statutes of Oklahoma* compiled by Benedict Elder (Kansas City, Mo.: Pipes & Reed, 1908).

30. *Dallas Morning News,* Mar. 17, 1891.

31. *Dallas Times Herald,* Mar. 27, 1891.

32. *Dallas Morning News,* Mar. 18, 1891.

33. See Roger Daniels, *Asian America: Chinese and Japanese in the United States since 1850* (Seattle: University of Washington Press, 1988); K. Scott Wong and Sucheng Chang, eds., *Claiming America: Constructing Chinese American Identities during the Exclusion Era* (Philadelphia: Temple University Press, 1998); Ronald T. Takaki, *Iron Cages: Race and Culture in Nineteenth-Century America* (New York: Alfred A. Knopf, 1979), pp. 215–40.

34. These statistics are based on the 1900 census and Arnoldo De León, *Mexican Americans in Texas: A Brief History* (Wheeling, Ill.: Harlan Davidson, Inc., 1999), p. 68. Out of 3,048,710 (the total population of Texas) there were 470 Indians, 849 Mongolians, and 71,062 Mexicans. For more on the undercounting of Mexican American residents, see Arnoldo De León and Kenneth L. Stewart, *Tejanos and the Numbers Game: A Socio-Historical Interpretation from Federal Censuses, 1850–1900* (Albuquerque: University of New Mexico Press, 1989).

35. According to the 1900 census, seventy-five percent (25,348/33,611) of white Dallasites were born in the South. *Census Reports, Twelfth Census of the United States, Volume 1: Population, Part 1* (Washington: United States Census Office, 1901). Terry Jordan, "A Century and a Half of Ethnic Change in Texas, 1836–1986," *Southwestern Historical Quarterly* 89 (Apr., 1986): 421, maintains that, across the state, whites were eighty-four percent southern in 1887 and still seventy-four percent southern in 1930.

36. The literature on "Orientalism" is vast, but the place to start is Edward Said, *Orientalism* (New York: Vintage Books, 1979).

37. *Beau Monde* (Dallas), Jan. 14, 1899.

38. Ibid. Mme. Blanther offered manicures and possibly massages in her "toilet suite." As her advertising copy noted, "Having learned her art in the land of the luxurian, the Far East," Mme. Blanther was well-placed to offer the "authentic" Oriental experience.

39. Mr. Fitzgerald mockingly claimed that "we paid $20,000,000 for the Philippines and their 10,000,000 souls. They are our chattels. . . . Expansion and termination go hand in hand." *Beau Monde,* Jan. 14 and Apr. 15, 1899.

40. It is only fair to note that Mr. Fitzgerald's stance on imperialism was not always clear. In

October, 1899, he seemed to disagree with William Jennings Bryan's speech at a recent local fund-raiser, in which Bryan apparently painted the English assault on the Boers with the same imperialistic brush as Americans' conquest of the Filipinos. "The Boers are Caucasians—Christian men fighting for their rights," he claimed, while "the Tagals are semi-savages . . . fighting their liberators" and "the blessing of civilization." *Beau Monde,* Oct. 14, 1899.

41. *Beau Monde,* Sept. 30 and Oct. 7, 1899.

42. Michael V. Hazel, "A Salute to the Past: The Confederate Veterans Reunion of 1901," in *Dallas Reconsidered: Essays in Local History,* ed. by Michael V. Hazel (Dallas: Three Forks Press, 1995), pp. 290–91.

43. Even a quick survey comparing names in the turn-of-the-century city directories with the 1900 manuscript census schedule for Dallas turns up evidence that Chinese residents were undercounted. Along with the miscategorization (by census rules) of some Chinese residents as "white," these census discrepancies should caution scholars from accepting the totals of 27 Mongolians in Dallas (out of total population of more than 30,000) as accurate. There are no census listings, for example, for Ah Hing, Sam Choi, Sam Gee, Sing Charley, Sing Kee and several others who were established enough to make the city directory for that year.

44. John F. Worley & Co., *Worley's Directory for the City of Dallas, 1891; John F. Worley & Co.'s Dallas Directory for 1900; John F. Worley & Co.'s Dallas Directory for 1901.* By 1910, none of the few Chinese remaining in Dallas, Jim Wing among them, was listed as "(Chinese)." Perhaps Jim Wing had forged a path that others were able to follow.

45. Donna R. Gabaccia, *We Are What We Eat: Ethnic Food and the Making of Americans* (Cambridge: Harvard University Press, 1998), pp. 100–101, discusses the popularity of "Japanese" restaurants. See also the City Directories for 1891, 1900, and 1901.

46. City Directory for 1909.

47. For examples of "hidden" Mexicans, see the manuscript census schedule that shows enumerators clearly missed certain alleys and buildings that may well have had Mexican residents; also, the city directories for several years at the turn of the century indicate that a large number of noted Mexican residents were tamale vendors who may well have served a Mexican clientele larger than indicated by census or city directory counts. *Dallas Times Herald,* Mar. 20, 1891, in an article on a rape of a non-Mexican tamale vendor's wife, revealed the presence of a large community living in tents north of the city; residents of the tent city may have been Mexican immigrants. For evidence that Mexican "section hands" lived in boxcars by the railroad tracks, which were not visited by census enumerators, see Ethelyn C. Davis, "Little Mexico: A Study of Horizontal and Vertical Mobility," (Master's thesis, Southern Methodist University, 1935), p. 19; Gilbert Baillon, "Little Mexico: An Enduring Hub of Mexican Culture in Dallas," (Unpublished seminar paper, University of Texas-Arlington, 1991); Jane Brock Guzman, "Dallas Barrio Women of Power," (Master's thesis, University of North Texas, 1992), pp. 14–16.

48. Manuscript schedule for Dallas County; Soundex for 1900. Fidel J. Gonzales, Jr., ed., *P. P. Martinez, Texas Pioneer, Civic Leader, Philanthropist, Real Estate Tycoon, and Tobacco Manufacturer, Dallas, Texas, 1880–1935* (Dallas: self-published, 1980).

49. See, for example, *Beau Monde,* Nov. 19, 1898 ("Phoenix events are known for their elegant dressing," and a long wedding description); Dec. 31, 1899 (a special issue on Texas belles, in which every Jewish debutante was consistently distinguished as a member of the "Phoenix set.")

50. For single-sex events with Jewish and Protestant women, see *Beau Monde,* Dec. 3, 1898; and Apr. 15, 1899.

51. Descriptions of Enumeration Districts, Sixth Supervisor's District of Texas for the 12th Census, Microcopy T 1210, Roll No. 9; and Wharton's City Directory, 1899–1900 (Dallas, Tex., 1900).

52. According to the 1900 census, the Fitzgeralds lived in their own home on Main Street,

though it is not clear whether they owned or rented the home. They had three teenage children, none of whom worked and two of whom were still in school; both parents were identified with the professional occupation of "editor" (or in the case of Mrs. Fitzgerald, "editoress"). Twelfth United States Census, manuscript schedule for Dallas, Tex., Volume 26, E. D. 101.

53. Of the eighteen members of the committee, thirteen came from counties in which African Americans amounted to larger than ten percent of the total county population. Ten came from counties in which the African American proportion of the population was greater than eighteen percent. Mr. Adkins, who had led the fight for the word "Negro" rather than "colored" came from Colorado County, where African Americans were forty-three percent of the population, and there were only five people who were "colored" but not "Negro."

54. C. Vann Woodward, *Origins of the New South, 1877–1913* (1971 reprint; Baton Rouge: Louisiana State University Press, 1951), p. 211.

55. Paul Casdorph, *History of the Republican Party in Texas* (Austin: Pemberton Press, 1965).

56. Hale, *Making Whiteness,* p. 83.

CHAPTER 4

Being American in Boley, Oklahoma

SARAH DEUTSCH

This chapter is part of a larger project, a survey of the history of the United States West from 1900 to 1940. That project has forced me to think about where I would begin the twentieth-century West, both physically, on a map of the region, and temporally.

Boley, Oklahoma, a black town founded in 1903 on a railroad line in eastern central Oklahoma, may seem to belong more to the nineteenth century than the twentieth—part of the history of the Exodusters Nell Painter told, those who headed west in the years just after Reconstruction, and part of the history of the rise of transcontinental railroads in all their power. It may seem to partake of the history of Gilded Age speculation that filled the region with often ephemeral, mirage-like communities. In its violent confrontations with local Creek Indians, too, Boley may seem a nineteenth-century story of displacement and frontier settlement.

Yet, instead, I see it as a foundational story of the twentieth-century West, and, inescapably, of the twentieth-century nation. Boley's story allows me to discuss not only speculation and political and capital formation—standard facets of most twentieth-century West histories—but the racial/ethnic formations, slippages, and reformations that undergirded them and the related notions of manhood and citizenship. The dramatic and sometimes convoluted history of this early-twentieth-century town illuminates the complexities of the construction of race in the United States. These themes interweave around two primary nodes. One is Booker T. Washington's 1908 article on Boley, and the other is the 1909 so-called "Snake Uprising." Before getting to Boley, I will provide some background as to how I am dividing and not dividing the nineteenth- from the twentieth-century West.

What Makes a Twentieth-Century West?

When I was an undergraduate in the mid-1970s, the nickname of the first half of the survey of the American West was "Cowboys and Indians." The second half was called "Reds and Feds." In many ways, those titles still typify the ways in which we view the nineteenth- and twentieth-century Wests. The break came around 1890, the year that the census, according to Frederick Jackson Turner, declared the line of the frontier dissipated. After that date, scholars dealt with regional history, no longer the history of the frontier. Before the break, what whites had developed on the frontier could be seen as prototypically American. After 1890, the area seemed more often to produce dangerous disruptions, products of a decaying frontier, often labeled "imports": Big Bill Haywood instead of Davy Crockett, the Industrial Workers of the World instead of the lone mountain man. The twentieth century became the time when the East disciplined the West, when consolidation ruled the land, and the federal government, with freer hand than in older states, more effectively imposed its will and shaped the landscape.

Although I would agree with those who argue that the federal government exerted massive power west of the Mississippi in the twentieth century, that was also true in the nineteenth century. Built with heavy federal subsidies in the nineteenth century, even the railroads remained powerful well into the twentieth century, though surpassed in some ways by the highways when the federal government shifted its beneficence. Anyone who has driven through remote parts of Arizona and New Mexico, only to see a train snake through the dramatic and seemingly deserted landscape, realizes that railroads are still a power today.

I would place the distinctiveness of the twentieth-century West elsewhere. It resides, at least in part, in Peter Iverson's description of Indians becoming cowboys, in the adaptive Native American participation in capitalism rather than in the disappearance of Indians and the end of the "frontier." Identities, as in "Indians" *versus* "Cowboys," were unchanging only in Wild West shows and the popular imagination. In the non-Indian imagination, those imagined Indians could stand in for and even block the view of the Indians who actually lived and ranched in Oklahoma, attended its schools, and ran many of its businesses. Indeed, the federal government found it so unimaginable that Indians could become savvy capitalists, that it labeled "mixed blood" those whom it believed could manage the market economy; it labeled "full blood" those it saw as "real" Indians and "protected" them from the land sharks eager to purchase their allotments. It did so despite plentiful testimony that blood quantum was not at all the most accurate way to judge a person's market savvy.[1]

Ironically, some Indians helped prolong the fantasy, not least by continuing to play "Indians" in Wild West shows, as not only Sitting Bull did in the nineteenth century, but the Winnebago Crashing Thunder did in the twentieth. What separated Crashing Thunder from Sitting Bull—the twentieth from the nineteenth century in this realm—besides leadership skills and discipline, was that Crashing Thunder had never lived the part he played. Although Indians were continuous actors in the American West, their parts were not only the ones in which we cast them in our imaginations and our standard histories.

Indians became cattle ranchers, and "Indians" were relegated to Wild West shows, to performances that commodified their identity. That set of transformations, that putative end to the western frontier, did not stop dreams and myths about the West as a limitless land of opportunity for those who did not already live there. And dreams of inclusion based on participating in that mythical western experience also continued to thrive and to structure the way that western newcomers created their expectations and understood their experiences. African American Era Bell Thompson, for example, titled her autobiography of homesteading in the Dakotas, *American Daughter,* as though that frontier experience itself legitimated her claims to Americanness. To lay claim to the West remained, in the most profound sense, as Era Bell Thompson found, to claim to be "American." However, such claims flourished in the twentieth century within a new set of paradigms of race and citizenship that emerged not from the Mexican War but from the Spanish-American War.

Setting the start of the twentieth century at the 1890 census has relieved us of the need to recognize the ways in which the Spanish-American War was crucial to western history. In the standard view, à la Turner, the Spanish-American War stands more as a marker of the West's inability still to serve as the place of boundless opportunity, forcing the seeking of newer frontiers of trade and commerce overseas.

Crucial differences disrupted the seeming continuity of expansionism. The Spanish-American War's proponents succeeded in re-envisioning the American polity. With the war, the United States shifted from a formal philosophy and policy of democratic incorporation of new territories and peoples (however imperfectly practiced) to an imperial philosophy of official colonization. The policies and discourses that supported this shift both emerged from and affected relations on the mainland. Contestants in the twentieth-century West could take their cues from the new imperial culture.

No one could better join the symbolic content of the West and the empire than Teddy Roosevelt, making his reputation by writing up his dude ranch experience out west in the 1880s and then by leading the charge on San Juan Hill during the war. It was no accident that Roosevelt vocally supported the theory of race suicide. Several recent scholars have affirmed that, to Roosevelt and others, taking our rightful place in the "family" of nations as an imperial power and accepting our permanent responsibility for "lesser" races would reinvigorate American manhood and save the republic from decline. The Spanish-American War marked a crucial point in western history, in other words, not just because the United States gained the Philippines, Hawaii, and Guam, but because it redefined "frontier," "race," "citizenship," "manhood," "opportunity," and nationhood.[2]

People referred to the Spanish-American War to make sense of what was going on in Oklahoma and the rest of the West. As Robert Rydell has shown, American international expositions at the turn of the century explicitly linked nineteenth-century westward expansion, Anglo-Saxon racial development, and the new imperial policies. At Omaha in 1898, 2.5 million people visited an exposition that featured mock battles between "Indians" and whites, always ending with the Indians' surrender and promise to learn "civilized" behavior. The exposition also featured a Philippine village with sixteen "Manila warriors" who, the promoter told the *World Herald,* had cannibalistic tendencies. The Filipinos and Indians were joined by an African American village dubbed the "Old Plantation," and a post-emancipation exhibit that featured Aunt Jemimah serving pancakes. Each of these peoples was placed in a subordinate, tutelary relationship to white Americans.[3]

Visiting the fair, President William McKinley insisted that America's continued grace and progress required assuming such tutelary "international responsibilities." At the St. Louis Louisiana Purchase Exposition in 1904, the federal government and St. Louis civic leaders similarly collaborated in juxtaposing an exhibit of just fewer than a thousand Filipinos (including one man labeled the "missing link") with a living ethnology exhibit of Native Americans. "White and Strong are synonymous terms" declared the fair's anthropological organizer, previously at the Bureau of American Ethnology. Such exhibits taught United States viewers that they already had successful experience ruling colonized peoples and cemented the presumptive eternal difference between white Americans and others. In these expositions and in countless historical pageants across the country, our new empire became the logical next chapter in a story of inevitable white progress.[4]

In short, the Spanish-American War could provide a framework for western racial struggles and relegitimize both white supremacy and the concept of whiteness, so that the United States—not in its identity as an experimental republic but in its identity as a "white" people—could assume its "rightful" place among the ruling, not the dependent, nations.[5] As the United States enacted that "white" and "other" dichotomy at home, too, it dispossessed Creeks, disenfranchised blacks, created a sympathetic audience for the white disenfranchised populists in Indian Territory, and created one particular version of the West for the twentieth century among the many possibilities available in 1900.

Such categories as "race" and "citizenship" had long proved particularly unstable in the West. Who would be incorporated, who would be excluded, and who would participate in the civilizing project of the "lesser races"? How would racial categories be defined? How would such categories then be inscribed on this landscape of enclaves? Oklahoma, on the border between South and West, provided a salient location to answer those questions. Historian Jacquelyn Dowd Hall recently noted of Oklahoma, "No Southern state had more homegrown socialists, more crosscutting mixtures of red, black, and white, a more violent heritage of appropriation, or a more multicultural, multiracial past than Oklahoma. But," she continued, "I learned nothing about that history in the public schools of the state. The story we were taught had been radically abridged. Purged of everything of interest and value, it was a triumphalist narrative centering on the land rush that opened the state to white settlement in 1889." Essayist Michelle Wallace, complaining of "the unwillingness of 'American History' to include Oklahoma in its big picture," wrote, "It's like one of those nuclear dump sites . . . some place nobody wants to know anything about."[6]

To begin putting the true Oklahoma back into United States history—thereby gaining a better understanding of the complexities of twentieth-century racial frameworks—we should examine Boley. The town resulted principally from a shift in U.S. relations with the Creeks—a change made official in the same year as the Spanish-American War, 1898. Twelve years earlier, Congress had exempted the Five Civilized Tribes, including the Creeks, from the Dawes Severalty Act, which had promoted the allotment of Indian tribal lands in fixed acreages to individual Indians and opened the "surplus" Indian lands to other settlers. By 1893, decent "surplus" lands were scarce, and the Indian Territory of the Five Civilized Tribes, which adjoined Oklahoma Territory, was full of whites who leased Indian lands and fiercely resented their lack of political and economic rights. It was also full of black and white town site developers who harbored similar resentment.[7] Congress conceded to intense pressure by creating the Dawes Commission to negotiate with the Five Civilized Tribes for allotment. The Creeks, however, having witnessed how allotment had affected other Indian nations, determined allotment a total failure and rejected U.S. attempts to negotiate a new treaty. When the Creeks and other tribes refused, Congress provided for surveying the lands anyway, a clear sign that they intended to move ahead with or without tribal consent. Then in 1896, Congress authorized the Dawes Commission to make an official roll of the members of each tribe; such a role would determine eligibility for alloted land. Those two federal moves alarmed the Creeks, among others, into opening negotiations. When the Creeks nonetheless rejected the ensuing agreement at a special election, Congress in 1898 passed the Curtis Act, unilaterally dissolving the Creek, Chickasaw, Choctaw, and Cherokee Nations, converting the former Indian citizens into U.S. citizens and mandating the allotment of their lands. Trying to salvage what they could, some Creeks ratified an agreement with the U.S. government in 1901, only two years before the founding of Boley.[8] The process of allotment began with Creek land allotted to Creeks and to Creek freedmen, those of African descent who before the Civil War had been enslaved by the Creeks.

The allotment that formed the town site of Boley belonged to a child of Creek freedmen, Abigail Barnett. Her legal guardian, "full-blood" Josiah Looney, arranged the sale with developers working with the Fort Smith and Western Railroad. Ironically, Looney would not have been able to sell his own land to developers. In keeping with racialized notions of market savvy or maturity and competency, only certain allottees were entitled to sell their lands immediately. "Full-blood" Creeks could not sell their allotments for twenty-five years, while Creek freedmen and women and "mixed-bloods" could sell their allotments at will. Other Creek freedmen and women also participated in the founding of Boley. Even though they often identified themselves as "Creek," only spoke Creek, and had no market experience, their government designation as freedmen—not Indians—allowed them to sell their lands.[9] More Creek land became available to the new settlement when other black migrants, such as the Turner brothers, obtained allotments by marrying Indian women.[10] In turn, Boley's new black entrepreneurs from the states (as opposed to blacks from Indian or Oklahoma *Territory*) founded the Creek-Seminole College.[11]

In Boley, Oklahoma, Creeks who had been forced west more than sixty years earlier, dispossessing Comanches, now found themselves being dispossessed in part by Boley's black settlers. The historical record does not specifically illustrate the Creeks' fate, but they did not disappear onto remote reservations or even into Wild West shows. Instead they disappeared into a set of competing racial dualisms central to the twentieth-century West and revealed in the way various players narrated early conflicts in and around Boley.

Black Boley

The seeming black-Creek alliance was more complicated than the founding picture of harmony would imply. To Booker T. Washington, Boley was about blacks, not about Creeks. "Boley," wrote Booker T. Washington in a 1908 *Outlook* article, "represents a dawning race consciousness, a wholesome desire to do something to make the race respected; something which shall demonstrate the right of the negro, not merely as an individual, but as a race to have a worthy and permanent place in the civilization that the American people are building."[12] Boley would, then, cement black claims to be "American."

Washington differentiated between the early Exodusters of the nineteenth century and the twentieth-century Boley migrants from the South and Midwest. These twentieth-century black *civilized* settlers differed from earlier migrants, whom he described as a "helpless and ignorant horde of black people." The new arrivals included "land-seekers and home-builders, men [note only men] who have come prepared to build up the country."[13] These black migrants were "enterprising," had "learned to build schools, to establish banks and conduct newspapers." This was not Turner's rough democracy on the frontier. Indeed, Washington gave his speech at Boley's new $35,000 Masonic Temple.[14] Education, commerce, and communication marked Boley's settlers as worthy of being colonizers rather than colonized.

At the same time Washington claimed for them an "American" identity, he posed them as distinctively African, having "recovered something," Washington wrote, "of the knack for trade that their foreparents in Africa were famous for."[15] Theirs was a uniquely African American civilizing mission.

The civilizing mission would apply, uniquely, to blacks as subjects and not just civilizers. Washington claimed to have achieved a "high respect" for Indians' "character and intelligence" during the last years of his stay at Hampton Institute when, he wrote, "I had charge of the Indian students."[16] By including that backdrop, he established a racial hierarchy that placed African Americans in custodial authority over Indians and simultaneously separated the two as distinct races, a project he was at pains to solidify elsewhere in the article, despite the presence of freedmen among the Creeks who identified themselves as Creeks and the presence of many Creeks, not freedmen, who had some African descent. Washington added, as evidence that Boley stood "on the edge of civilization," "You can still hear on summer nights, I am told, the wild notes of the Indian drums, and the shrill cries of the Indian dancers among the hills beyond the settlement." Indians, as Washington portrayed them, were permanently beyond settlement, signifiers of the frontier.

To Washington, only blacks could be brought into the fold of American civilization. He had been, he wrote, "particularly interested to see [Indians] in their own country [Oklahoma], where they still preserve to some extent their native institutions." However, he claimed that he rarely could catch sight of what he termed "a genuine native Indian." "When I inquired," he confessed, "as I frequently did, for the 'natives,' it almost invariably happened that I was introduced not to an Indian, but to a Negro." Stopping "at the home of one of the prominent 'natives' of the Creek Nation," the superintendent of the Tullahasse Mission, Washington pronounced, "But he is a negro. The negroes who are known in that locality as 'natives' are the descendants of slaves that the Indians brought with them from Alabama and Mississippi, when they migrated to this Territory." Other "natives" he met, he claimed, "as far as my observation went . . . were, on the contrary, white men." When he finally asked, "where . . . are the Indians?" he repeatedly got the reply, "they have gone . . . they have gone back."[17]

Despite the presence of the Creek-Seminole College and Agricultural Institute in Boley, here Washington participated in the classic dominant Anglo American narrative of the disappearing Indian, ever retreating before the advance of civilization. "The Indians," he explained, "who own practically all the lands, and until recently had the local government largely in their own hands, are to a very large extent regarded by the white settlers, who are rapidly filling up the country, as almost a negligible quantity," a view further evidenced by the new state of Oklahoma's constitution's taking "no account of the Indians in drawing its distinctions among the races. For the constitution," he claimed, "there exist only the negro and the white man. The reason seems to be that the Indians have either receded—'gone back,' as the saying in that region is—on the advance of the white race," or have intermarried with whites and been absorbed by that race.[18] Either case foreclosed any distinct Indian presence.

In Washington's schema, blacks formed part of this civilized advance rather than part of the retreat. "The negroes," he insisted, "immigrants to Indian Territory, have not, however 'gone back,'" but instead were working alongside whites, with their banks, businesses, schools, and churches. Moreover, demonstrating the essentially progressive nature of the race, part of the future, not the past of the nation, he claimed that even those blacks labeled "natives" "do not shun the white man and his civilization, but, on the contrary, rather seek it, and enter, with the negro immigrants, into competition with the white man for its benefits." Indeed, in contrast to those Washington labeled as "genuine" Indians, "native negroes" he found, had been helpfully influenced by the black southern migrants, not absorbed by whites, and not defeated. As black troops of the U.S. Army had served in the Philippines during the Spanish-American War, here on the domestic frontier the blacks formed part of the advance guard of "civilization." They were going forward, not back, not as a blended, but as an alternative, future. Indeed, Washington focused attention on Boley, rather than the myriad other black-founded towns, because of its exclusion of whites. Whites could come to trade but could not stay, even overnight. Oklahoma was full of white-only towns, white-dominated towns, and black-founded towns, but Boley stood as the single exclusively black town. "In short," Washington concluded, "Boley is another chapter in the long struggle of the negro for moral, industrial, and political freedom."[19]

Mixing It Up

Washington was correct in noting that the Oklahoma Constitution delineated only two categories: "Wherever in this Constitution and laws of this state the word or words, 'colored' or 'colored race,' 'negro' or 'negro race,' are used, the same shall be construed to mean or apply to all persons of African descent. The term 'white race' shall include all other persons." There was no room for an independent racial category "Indian" here. Was it because Indians had ceased to be a factor? The definitions emerged as part of the constitution's mandate for segregated schools but also would apply to prohibitions on intermarriage. After the Spanish-American War, the world of bipolarities—"white" and "other"—defining who got to be white could be tricky. If the Oklahoma Constitution categorized Indians with blacks, then the means by which Boley was created could be perpetually replicated, and the rapidly growing number of black landholders in Oklahoma, already the majority in some districts, would increase.[20] Black-Creek alliances, marital and otherwise, would be fostered. Unlike the southeastern states, Oklahoma housed Indians with significant landholdings. By such a definition whites could not only alienate large groups of Indian voters who knew quite well the status blacks held in white eyes, but whites could also shoot themselves in the foot in terms of access to land through marriage. This dynamic was acknowledged on a symbolic level at the inauguration of the first governor of the state of Oklahoma. A mock wedding followed the ceremony, in which the white governor, Charles N. Haskell, dressed in formal trousers and a black suit coat, took as his "bride" Anna Trainor Bennett from Muskogee, a woman of Cherokee descent, in a floor-length satin dress. Cowboy married Indian, Oklahoma Territory married Indian Territory.[21]

What, though, did it mean to categorize the Creeks as "white"? Both contemporaries and historians have failed or refused to read the racial lines in these stories. In Washington's record, no people of African descent could be "genuine" Indians. In historians' recent writings, similarly, twentieth-century Afro-Creeks, or free Creeks of African descent, tend to disappear in a historical record that mentions only Creek "full bloods," white Creek "mixed-bloods," and Creek freedmen.[22] Apparently the Creeks themselves understood things differently, at least through the late nineteenth century. After all, Creeks and Cherokees would joke with each other before the Civil War: "You Cherokees are so mixed with whites we cannot tell you from whites," to which Cherokees would reply, "You Creeks are so mixed with Negroes we cannot tell you from Negroes."[23] To those Creeks, "mixed blood" could include African as well as European ancestry. No lines prevented people of joint Indian and African descent from acceptance as "Creek." According to historian Joel Martin, Afro-Creeks had long held important leadership positions as "the most respected 'old beloved woman' or even chief." At the turn of the century Creeks with some African ancestors still held leadership positions, including the elected office of chief.[24] Photographs of Creek leaders at the time bear out the wide range of Creek heritage (see figure 4.1). The official Oklahoma designations, however, led to the spectacle of courts invalidating a marriage between two Creeks, each three-quarters Creek, but the husband a quarter black and the wife, according to her testimony, a quarter "white, I guess."[25] The law brought color and not just cultural lines to the Creek nation.

Yet even before Oklahoma statehood and despite the relatively full acceptance among Creeks of persons of mixed African and Creek descent, Creek relations with freedmen were complicated and contradictory. Freedmen, whether previously enslaved by Creeks or by others, usually had no Creek lineage. After the Civil War and under pressure from the U.S. government, Creeks had granted citizenship to Creek freedmen. In testimony before a Senate investigating committee, freedmen disagreed among themselves as to how eagerly the Creeks had extended citizenship.[26] Testimony before the Senate Investigating Committee elicited that the extension of civil rights to freedmen had been a political maneuver of the Union Creeks hoping that freedmen would help them outvote the Confederate Creeks.[27]

Creek non-freedmen who heavily identified with southern white culture and owned numerous enslaved people tended to have more hostile views about freedmen than did those whose ancestors had intermarried with blacks. Even the latter, however, occasionally resented the increasing black presence and voting power in Creek Territory, as blacks from the southeastern United States fled post–Civil War racial violence and were welcomed into Creek freedmen towns where the elected Creek freedmen chief facilitated their acceptance as Creek citizens.[28] With allotment, they, too, became eligible for the dwindling Creek lands. Criminal codes exacted harsher penalties for freedmen than for Creeks, and civil laws taxed freedmen, but only those who were not tribal members. Moreover, it was unlawful for Creek men to marry black women. These were clear signals that the acceptance of freedmen among Creeks was not universal.

Unquestionably, however, the Creeks had continued their greater openness to blacks than had other groups. As among the Cherokees, the U.S. Civil War split the Creek nation. Among the Creeks, however, the largest group joined the Union. After the war, unlike the Choctaws and the Chickasaws, the Creeks did not delay in granting citizenship to their freedmen.[29] Unlike the Cherokees, they also granted the freedmen property rights in the nation.[30] Although Creek men could not marry black women, Creek women could marry black men. All children of Creek women and black men, when the issue was not more than half black, were counted as Creek citizens (re-

Figure 4.1. The Creek Delegation: This photograph of a Creek delegation demonstrates the diversity of Creek heritage, even among the leadership, and the ability of Creeks to destabilize binary racial systems. *Courtesy* National Anthropological Archives

taining the matrilineal character of tribal identity).[31] Relations between freedmen and Creeks, in short, may have been more about tribal identity than about color hostility. There were, after all, also laws that governed the terms of incorporating whites.

Indeed, terminology regarding race may obscure more than it reveals. Whites had adopted something they thought of as blood quantum as a way of judging racial and ethnic identity, particularly in the South before the Civil War. Indians had not. Many Indians who dealt with whites demonstrated that they had become adept at manipulating the whites' language regarding such matters. Others demonstrated clearly that such criteria were meaningless to them. A man named Redbird Smith testified before the 1905–1906 Senate Committee investigating the chaos in Indian Territory resulting from the 1901 settlement. The committee asked, "Are you a full-blood Indian?" "I am a Cherokee," Smith responded. The senators repeated and, they thought, clarified, "Are you a full blood or part blood?" The question stumped the witness. The interpreter interjected, "From my experience he must be a full blood." The witness chimed in, "I think I must be a full blood; I don't know, but I think I am." At this point even the senators clearly became confused, agreeing with the interpreter that blood quantum was a matter of experience, not biology, "From your experience you must be a full-blood Cherokee Indian?" Answer: "Yes, sir." The senators were in good company. By 1900 the U.S. Census Bureau defined "full-blood," when referring to Creeks, as one-quarter Creek Indian.[32]

Rivalries

Despite Washington's dismissal of Indians as significant actors in Oklahoma's future, Boley's own settlers knew better. Black newcomers deplored the failure of the native population to see the benefit of an alliance by which "negroes and Indians would have the political balance of power in the future state of Oklahoma."[33] At the same time, Boley's booster paper, the *Boley Progress,* repeatedly advertised 20,000 acres "of the finest land in the Creek Nation surrounding Boley to be leased and bought by Negroes." The Boley southern migrant town fathers were chagrined to find that even Creek freedmen, the "native negroes," were often less than welcoming. Washington admitted that, in the first years of the settlement, native negroes had occasionally come in to "shoot up" the town.[34] He framed it as a case of savage drunken revelry. Native negroes reasoned differently, however. "I was eating out the same pot with the Indians . . . while they was still licking the master's boots in Texas," claimed one, signifying the higher status and inclusion granted even enslaved blacks among the Creeks than among southern whites.[35] The dissidents' shooting frequently broke up church services and other public gatherings and shot out windows late at night. According to Norman Crockett, whose otherwise fine study unfortunately makes no distinction between Afro-Creeks and Creek freedmen, Creek freedmen labeled the newcomers "state negroes," saw them as inferior, and recognized a threat to their own tribal position. Their suspicions were born out when, in 1904, only a year after Boley's founding, the Creek Nation's school board introduced segregation, stipulating separate schools for all blacks—whether tribal members or new arrivals—and Creek students. Crockett concluded, unlike Washington, that the violence ultimately subsided into voluntary and complete social separation between Creek freedmen and southern black migrants.[36]

But strictly racial terms may not be the best way to understand even that segregation. In his testimony before the Senate Committee, Creek witness Eufala Harjo complained, "There has always been lots of schools among the Indians ever since we came here, and we were proud of our schools, and our children went to them until the white men came in and crowded us out and took our schools away from us, and it seems to me that the little white children and the little negro children should not be made to go to the Indian schools that the Indians made with their own money. As long as the Indian had his own schools they were good schools and they were proud of them; but they can't say that any more." This mystified the senators. Trying to explain, Harjo offered this analogy: "I came in here a good while ago, and I was sitting back there a long time, but I couldn't understand what was going on only from what my interpreter would tell me. You saw me sitting back there, and I don't like to come forward. Now, when I take a little Indian child to school the white man and the negroes will go before me to school with their children and they will put their children first and they will push mine out of school, and that is the way it will go."[37] The issue in the schools was cultural behavior. In Creek eyes, white and black interlopers shared an aggression that pushed Indians aside. Similarly, to Creek freedmen, the southern migrants, black or white, represented just another set of dispossessors. Boley figured as the literal enactment of the provisions of the Curtis Act: it erased the tribe and replaced it with non-Creek settlers.

Toward a White Oklahoma

Even before the much-resisted 1901 agreement allowing for the allotment of Creek lands, the Snakes, a Creek society, had been meeting at their traditional gathering spot, Hickory Ground. In 1900, in protest against the negotiations delegates of the tribal council had begun with the federal government, the Snakes created an alternative Creek government. Although some contemporaries and historians have labeled that government a restoration of traditional Creek systems and the Snakes as "full-bloods," those terms are misleading. The Snakes included some Afro-Creeks, and the racial makeup becomes crucial later in the story. Also, "traditional" clearly did not mean a pre-contact version of Creek identity. Chitto Harjo, the group's leader, wore Euro-American dress, adhered to syncretic forms of government, and demanded adherence to mid-nineteenth century treaties (see figure 4.2). The Snakes defined "traditional" by refusing to divide up Creek land into individual allotments and refusing to abandon Creek nationhood.

In 1901, the new dissident Creek government—a principal chief, Chitto Harjo, a second chief, and a two-house legislature—reenacted the Creek laws suspended by the Curtis Act and formed a police force to enforce them. They sent an ultimatum to President McKinley and roamed the countryside confiscating allotment certificates from Creeks; they whipped Creeks who took allotments, employed whites (note, not blacks), or rented lands to non-Creek citizens. Local white authorities soon called out the Eighth Cavalry, and federal marshals arrested nearly one hundred Indians.[38]

Two years later, in 1903, southern black migrants and Creek freedmen together founded Boley, a founding in part made possible by allotment and

Figure 4.2. Chitto Harjo, leader of the dissident Creeks, was labeled a "traditionalist." Given his clothing and his politics, "traditional" meant not a pre-contact version of Creek identity but a demand to uphold mid-nineteenth-century treaties, and a refusal to divide up Creek land into individual allotments or to abandon Creek nationhood. *Courtesy* National Anthropological Archives

the destruction of Creek sovereignty in exchange for Creek citizenship in the United States. Incoming African Americans valued U.S. citizenship more highly than Creek citizenship. To the Creeks, becoming U.S. citizens signified the annihilation of the Creek Nation and autonomous Creek citizenship. Conversely, African Americans saw citizenship as the opposite of annihilation; it was instead the dawning of political visibility and autonomy.

Yet the Snakes and other Creek dissidents who tried to recruit sympathizers among the freedmen indicated that blacks had little to hope for in a white-dominated state. They recruited black collaborators into the short-lived Sequoyah movement, which tried to create a separate Indian state of the remnants of Indian Territory in 1905, and accepted blacks into the Snake movement that was resisting allotment.[39]

The failure of the 1901 and 1905 resistance movements had not ended the struggle. Followers of Harjo continued to refuse their allotments. In July, 1908, Creek freedmen and black migrants came together at the traditional Snake "stomp" or meeting grounds, Hickory Ground. They were still there when a large group of Snakes came to the place for their annual council. With some Afro-Creeks in the Snake police, the presence of a large group of armed and organized blacks and Indians alarmed nearby whites.

After this council, apparently some of the Creek freedmen and the "state negroes," that is, the southern black migrants, remained on Hickory Ground, intending to create a permanent town. They erected some twenty-five tents, each with a stone chimney, along with a wooden store, and a restaurant near the Indian Council House. Both white and other black townspeople labeled the group ruffians, fugitives from the law, and troublemakers.[40] White Indian agents trying to avoid conflict advised Harjo to distance his group from the new black settlement. He readily complied. He had apparently already taken literal steps to do so, holding his 1908 council a mile from the encampment. Despite his efforts, the presence of a black encampment on Snake grounds would offer whites a useful opportunity to blur lines.

The crucial context for the blurring of lines was the simultaneous deterioration of black-white race relations in Oklahoma. While Boley's booster paper boasted of black freedom and enfranchisement when soliciting more southern migrants, whites in the same county swiftly acted to minimize potential black political power even before statehood. Whites forced blacks from white-dominated mixed communities, sometimes with only twenty-four-hour notice; in 1905, Guthrie crowed over the triumph of an all-white ticket in city elections. A mixed-race Republican coalition enjoyed one last flowering and disintegrated. In 1906, Boley, which held the balance of power in the county, helped carry the Republican candidates to victory. The Republican county convention elected a white president and a black secretary, O. H. Bradley, former editor of the *Boley Progress*. Several whites then broke with the convention and formed a rival slate. When the official convention went further and nominated two blacks for county offices, the *Weleetka American* warned its readers "STOP! LOOK! LISTEN! TO A RAILROAD DANGER SIGNAL! THE COUNTY IS IN DANGER OF NEGRO DOMINATION—WHITE VOTERS, CRUSH THE INSOLENCE OF THE NEGRO! PROTECT YOUR HOMES WITH YOUR BALLOT."[41] The Democrats won that election. Whites feared black political and economic encroachment at least as much as Indian resistance.

The Democrats' triumph signaled the beginning of open violence against blacks in the county.[42] The next year, in late 1907 the new state witnessed its first lynching, at nearby Henryetta. A black man killed a white livery stable owner for refusing to rent him a rig. A white mob hanged the black man from a telephone pole and riddled his body with bullets. Many blacks fled Henryetta for other towns. In the same month, the legislature required Jim Crow cars on all railroads operating in the state and, in May, 1908, enacted a law forbidding marriage between blacks and whites. Many white towns prohibited blacks from being in the town after dark.[43] Boley blacks, secure in their black town, remained enfranchised, but well before Oklahoma's 1910 grandfather clause, violence, white-controlled registration, and gerrymandering had destroyed any greater black political power.[44]

What does all this have to do with Creeks? In March of 1909, a little more than a year after Washington's article in the *Outlook* and eight months after Harjo's council meeting, a constable from Henryetta came to the southern migrant and Creek freedmen encampment at the Snake meeting place, Hickory Ground, looking for thieves who had robbed a neighboring white farmer's smokehouse. A most unfriendly reception forced him to leave. He returned to Henryetta to form a posse, and armed skirmishes began almost immediately. Before dawn the next day, a posse of fourteen attacked the encampment, forcing some blacks to flee and arresting forty others, including some Creek freedmen, one person labeled "white," and one labeled a mixed blood of "unsavory reputation."[45] They killed one black man. The local sheriff and his men then occupied the campsite and ordered the remaining women and children to leave within an hour. The next day the Snake Council House, an emblem of Creek, not southern freedmen, presence in the area, was torched. The sheriff denied responsibility but was seen leaving the scene. Similarly, an "unknown" arsonist burned all the wooden structures, tents, and household effects. The grounds, Hickory Ground, were just east of racist Weleetka and south of Henryetta, the site of the lynching. Whites had succeeded in literally redrawing the map and erasing the settlement.

By torching the Snake Council House, the posse had encompassed Snakes—allotment resisters—in its attack on disruptive elements at Hickory Ground. Anxious to extend their victories, and as clear evidence of their ability to cast this fight with Hickory Ground "ruffians" onto the Snakes, a group of deputies went to arrest Harjo, holding him responsible for the encampment that he had tried to avoid. When Harjo and his fellow Snakes returned gunfire, two men, including the son of the sheriff, died in the battle. The white newspapers had a field day, vastly inflating the numbers killed and declaring "WAR WITH SNAKES." Posses roamed the countryside arresting Indians and blacks. They burned Harjo's house and looted others, under the guise of putting down a rebellion. White papers demanded "protection and Indian suppression"; the mayor of Henryetta declared, "The Snake Indians and the negroes affiliated with them are a menace to the country and should be captured."[46] The local federal Indian agent maintained that Harjo would have to admit that "this was going to be a white man's country."[47]

The white posse and its allies had strategically conflated freedmen from everywhere, blacks of all sorts, and Creek resisters. Such a conflation created a two-race system—whites and "others." In this case, "blacks" (unlike in the state's constitution) became "Indians." Engaging the script of Anglo western conquest allowed these whites to pose the eradication of a black settlement as a final Indian engagement, a legitimized whitening of the West against a known external enemy.

Most players read the script with hearty skepticism. A federal investigating commission blamed whites for the unrest. The editor of the *Indian Journal* at nearby Eufaula, with heavy sarcasm, wrote, "The Spanish-American war was never more vividly pictured, and the number killed, wounded and captured is generally larger than was Taft's majority."[48] The *Boley Progress* also saw the numbers and the conflict as absurdly inflated but took a different direction, trivializing the resistance to allotment and doubting Harjo ever had more than a dozen followers at any time, whereas sources in the Senate testimony had placed his following in the thousands.[49] Neither white nor black promoters wished to pose this developing section as unduly riddled with violent contestants.

White conflation of Indians and freedmen does, however, raise the question of the relation of the Snakes to the freedmen. Historians Daniel Littlefield and Lonnie Underhill contend that there had been no long-standing alliance between blacks (they do not differentiate between Afro-Creeks and freedmen) and Snakes, and that the "full-bloods" had objected to freedmen's receiving allotments. Another, more recent, scholar claims that "blacks were not allowed to participate in stomp ground activities, and their presence during ceremonial activities irritated many Snakes." Chitto Harjo's testimony before the Senate Committee corroborated this: "They are negroes that came in here as slaves. They have no right to this land."[50]

Moreover, signs of separation were emerging well before the school segregation decision. The Exoduster and migrant towns were not, as it turns out, the only black towns in Oklahoma. In 1903, when Boley was founded, there were already three towns of Creek freedmen (Arkansas Colored, Canadian Colored, and North Fork Colored), itself a significant marker of a degree of preexisting segregation.

And yet, it would be easy to draw these lines more clearly than contemporaries did. Historians Underhill and Littlefield count a Creek freedman among the two men indicted with Harjo for the 1909 shootings. However, they find the man unmentioned as such in the official correspondence.[51] Perhaps categories assigned by contemporaries and historians again break down, and the man indicted with Harjo was actually an Afro-Creek, rather than a Creek freedman. In any case, no simple pattern explains Creek-freedmen relations. The history of African descendants and Creeks detailed mergers, alliances, and also friction. There was, however, little room for that complexity in a dualistic racial schema, where Creeks would either have to be "white," as the Oklahoma Constitution mandated, and accept allotment and the end of Creek nationhood, or be labeled as non-white, which, at the time, translated to mean disruptive, unruly, and unready for civilization—a target for eradication or colonization.

It is important, in this context, to look briefly at iconography. A cartoon, "War in Oklahoma," from the *Oklahoma City Times*, of March 31, 1909, depicts a band of white easterners that echoed Teddy Roosevelt's look, including the "Indiana Rough Riders," the name of Roosevelt's Spanish-American War troops. They are all men, and all but the journalist wear Stetsons as they triumphantly march out of Hickory Ground, now for rent to picnickers, parading their captured Indian, clearly depicted as black. The meaning of the West in 1909 was clearly inseparable from national racial issues as recodified in the wake of the Spanish-American War (see figure 4.3).

Where Were the Women?

The absence of women in the picture raises some final questions about citizenship and manhood in the events surrounding Boley, and in the polity of the New West. Despite the earlier arrival of women's suffrage in the West than in the East, signs indicate that whites, Creeks, and blacks in Oklahoma differed in their notions of gender as in so much else. The paucity of the sources makes it impossible to do more than venture some hints and suggestions in this regard.

For whites, posing Oklahoma as militarized terrain, as in the cartoon, identified it as undoubtedly male space (despite the presence of journalists and actual homesteaders who were white women).[52] Whites, the conquerors, intentionally selected one of their own to play the groom in the inaugural pageant of Oklahoma Territory's marrying Indian Territory. The rhetoric

WAR IN OKLAHOMA

"They walked right in and turned around and walked right out again."

Figure 4.3. In this cartoon, from the March 31, 1909, edition of *The Oklahoma City Times*, the vigilantes who attacked the Hickory Ground campers became Rough Riders, heroes of the Spanish American War, and the "Indians" they vanquished became a degraded stereotype of African Americans. In other words, white Oklahomans' triumph over Indians and African Americans became inseparable from the nation's new imperial identity and its racial codes.

around the Spanish-American War illustrated that asserting authority and dominion over "lesser" races bolstered white American manhood. It is clear how whites used the West as a site for deploying these notions of manhood, but it is less clear how shifting notions of manhood and political participation played out in non-white communities in the West in the first decades of the century.

White reports of the attack on the encampment at Hickory Ground and the burning of the tents mention only male fighters and passive women and children. Similarly, reports of the aftermath of the pitched battle with Harjo and his supporters in 1909 only depict non-combatant women and children as opposed to male warrior-citizens. Yet when Chitto Harjo was struggling to evade the white troops after the 1909 fracas, women were among those who aided him, and while the men fled their homes to avoid arrest, the women stayed, though being female offered them no protection. Investigators reported tales of "brutality in the treatment of blacks and Indians—mostly involving women," because the men were in hiding.[53] The complicity of women in Harjo's escape and the presence of women at the black tent colony would argue that these were more participatory communities than the depictions allow. As in the cartoon, these depictions largely omit women from the actors in the drama. The frontier remains a place where men fight for territory and women keep the home fires burning.

Did Harjo restore a measure of female power in the Creek community? Had it ever been lost? What bits of evidence there are on Creek women show that at least those women vocal in Harjo's support were savvy commercial farmers.[54] Court cases also prove that Creek women insisted on controlling their own allotments, and on what would happen to the property after they died. They retained the system of Creek casual marriage and serial monogamy to a degree that virtually forced U.S. courts, at least well after statehood, to accept it. Formal legal marriage would have meant that the current partner, rather than the children, inherited the allotment.[55]

Similarly, in Boley, women not only ran the Ladies Commercial Club (not open to single and divorced women), they bought allotments, ran businesses, and participated in political meetings. Amidst its Victorian-style appeals to women's higher moral character and its declaration that in Boley "every man is a man" because he raises and is free to dispose of the entirety of his own crop, Boley's paper also promoted commercial opportunities that would "allow our boys and girls to become business men and women." Even Booker T. Washington, though he only mentioned "men" coming out to build up the country, when referring to the African commercial heritage, chose the word "foreparents"—not "forefathers."[56]

Women could not vote in Oklahoma, but Boley's leaders called open meetings to debate issues or gauge public opinion. All adult members of the community, of whatever sex or economic standing, took part in the general discussion.[57] Such a system echoes Elsa Barkley Brown's description of Reconstruction-era black political meetings in Virginia, where women and children as well as men instructed their elected representatives in equal measure; descriptions of Cherokee council meetings identified women participants as well as men. Similarly, in 1900, representatives of the Creek Nation sent a document to the federal government protesting against the ratification of the agreement with the United States. It argued that ratification by the Creek National Council (men elected by a male electorate) was "not right. Every man, woman, and child among the Creeks has a right to be heard upon the question."[58]

In 1900, few whites clamored for business opportunities for their women in the same breath they did for their men, and Oklahoma would be far from the first western state to offer women the vote. Indeed, whites often considered not only battle but commerce and development explicitly manly, as when the [white] Commercial Club of Muskogee, Indian Territory, referred to itself as "the most virile and progressive commercial organization of the Southwest" in an address to the Senate.[59] The triumph of the imperial United States in Oklahoma may not have been as complete in its gender as in its racial order.

The Twentieth-Century West

Black town builders had dreamed of a black county or even a black state; Indians had been given to understand Oklahoma was their territory. With the twentieth century those dreams gasped their last breath. In 1905 at a summer carnival in Boley, a black band and Indian ball games between Creek and Seminole players had entertained the crowds.[60] By 1909 that picture of a multicultural Oklahoma was hard to find. Historians Lonnie Underhill and Daniel Littlefield report that Snake bands without black allies, such as that of Eufala Harjo's, as opposed to Chitto Harjo's, experienced no violence during the rebellion.[61] The black press's dream of a united front of people of color in the state may have presented local whites a sufficient nightmare that white actions concentrated not only on blacks but on blacks with Indian allies.

In any case, it is crucial to see Jim Crow as a western and not just a southern phenomenon, to see the differently disenfranchised "Indians" and "blacks" as securing a white man's West. With the eradication of Creek autonomous government and the restrictions on black suffrage, Indians and blacks were excluded from the polity more thoroughly than they ever had been in the second half of the nineteenth century. Like the denizens of the newly acquired territories after the Spanish-American War, they were a subjected people.

It was a twentieth-century, not a nineteenth-century, system. Born with the turn of the century, in the Spanish-American War and the Curtis Act of 1898, it was the system under which western history would be lived until the system began to disintegrate with the Second World War and the Fair Employment Practices Commission in 1942 that guaranteed access to lucrative employment across racial lines. Until 1942, the black population west of the Mississippi would hover at two percent of the region. There was a reason: it was not a "natural" phenomenon. Two sizable streams of migration had been cut off—one in the 1870s by white southerners, and one in the 1900s by white westerners. In World War I, blacks would go North and not West.

All these groups—Creeks, blacks, and whites—were themselves hybrid groups, invented ethnicities/races: the Creeks invented two hundred years earlier in the Southeast, blacks a mélange of African groups intermingled with Europeans and Indians, and whites from various parts of Europe and the United States. None of them was native to Oklahoma, itself an invented concept. The fact that all the racial categories in the story have to be put in quotation marks is itself significant. Booker T. Washington's search for and/or creation of the "genuine" Indian, the elision of Afro-Creeks but the depiction of Creek freedmen, and the creation of categories like "full blood," and "native" versus "state" Negroes mark the striving for a clearly racialized world essential to the early-twentieth-century imperial United States. The particular contests over and constructions of these categories in the West had everything to do with the meaning of establishing settlements in Oklahoma for the various groups and individuals involved.

Notes

1. For examples of Indian cattle ranchers see Donald E. Green, *The Creek People* (Phoenix, Ariz.: Indian Tribal Series, 1973), p. 78; on market savvy, see Senate Report no. 5013, *Report of the Select Committee to Investigate Matters Connected with Affairs in the Indian Territory with Hearing, November 11, 1906–January 9, 1907*, 59th Cong., 2nd sess. (Washington, D.C.: Government Printing Office, 1907), throughout, for example, vol. 1, p. 441, J. Coody Johnson on Creek freedmen and p. 589, Dana H. Kelsey; and in vol. 2, p. 1299, David Hodge; pp. 1304–1305, Legus Perryman; p. 1311, Mrs. Lila D. Lindsay; p. 1312, S. W. Brown. And see *Congressional Record*, 55th Cong., 2nd sess., vol. 31, part 6, pp. 5552–53 on how lease money went to enrich "men who are really white men and not Indians."

2. See Gail Bederman, *Manliness and Civilization: A Cultural History of Gender and Race in the United States, 1880–1917* (Chicago: University of Chicago Press, 1995); Kristin L. Hoganson, *Fighting for Manhood: How Gender Politics Provoked the Spanish-American and Philippine-American Wars* (New Haven: Yale University Press, 1998); and Amy Kaplan and Donald E. Pease, eds., *Cultures of U.S. Imperialism* (Durham: Duke University Press, 1993).

3. Robert Rydell, *All the World's a Fair: Visions of Empire at American International Expositions, 1876–1916* (Chicago: University of Chicago Press, 1984), pp. 106–209.

4. Ibid.

5. David Glassberg, *American Historical Pageantry: The Uses of Tradition in the Early Twentieth Century* (Chapel Hill: University of North Carolina Press, 1990), p. 140; Rydell, pp. 106–209.

6. Jacquelyn D. Hall, "Landscapes of the Heart," *Ideas* 6 (1999): 18–19, including quotation from Michelle Wallace, *Invisibility Blues*.

7. Mary Jane Warde, *George Washington Grayson and the Creek Nation, 1843–1920* (Norman: University of Oklahoma Press, 1999), p. 175; John Thompson, *Closing the Frontier: Radical Response in Oklahoma, 1889–1923* (Norman: University of Oklahoma Press, 1986), pp. 77–79, 83. In response to the demands of poor, disenfranchised whites in Indian Territory, the Populists lobbied for joint statehood of Indian and Oklahoma Territories.

8. On the failure allotment when tried by other tribes, see *Report of the Select Committee*, vol. 1, p. 623, Pleasant Porter. Eufala Harjo added to his testimony on education, "It seems there isn't any room in school for the Indian children, and they are the schools of the Indians too, and that is the way it will go. We are pushed out of all that we had. The full-blood Indian people are pushed out today, and they have left their homes and taken what they have, and everything, and are camped out in the woods to-day. The half breeds and negroes are the ones that have taken all the land, and there is nothing left for the full-blood Indian at all." *Report of the Select Committee to Investigate Matters Connected with Affairs in the Indian Territory*, vol. 1. And on this history, see Warde, *George Washington Grayson*, pp. 186–208.

9. Katja Helma May, "Collision and Collusion: Native Americans and African Americans in the Cherokee and Creek Nations, 1830s to 1920s" (Ph.D. dissertation, University of California, Berkeley, 1994), p. 320 [also available in published form by Garland Press]; "Statement of J. Coody Johnson," pp. 440–41. Johnson held that few Creek freedmen spoke English and that two-thirds had been induced to sell their lands "for a very inadequate consideration." See also, from the *Report of the Select Committee*, vol. 1, pp. v and 620–21, Pleasant Porter; and pp. 1263–64, 1267, 1271, Mr. M. L. Mott.

10. Booker T. Washington, "Boley, A Negro Town in the West," *Outlook*, Jan. 4, 1908, p. 31.

11. May, "Collision and Collusion," pp. 315–16.

12. Washington, "Boley," p. 31.

13. Ibid., p. 28.

14. Norman L. Crockett, *The Black Towns* (Lawrence: Regents Press of Kansas, 1979), p. 35.

15. Washington, "Boley," p. 28.

16. Ibid., p. 29.

17. Ibid.

18. Ibid., pp. 30, 29.

19. Ibid., pp. 30–31.

20. Oklahoma Constitution, article 23 section 11; Linda Williams Reese, *Women of Oklahoma, 1890–1920* (Norman: University of Oklahoma Press, 1997), p. 61; *Report of the Select Committee,* vol. 1, p. 697, Miss Alice Robertson.

21. Reese, *Women of Oklahoma,* pp. 76–77.

22. *Report of the Select Committee,* vol. 1 p. 1973, J. George Wright, U.S. Indian inspector, provided a table listing of those enrolled by the Dawes Commission as 6,692 full blood, 3,371 mixed blood, and 5,636 freedmen, with 1,017 Indian children and 569 freedmen's children, for a total of 17,285 Creeks.

23. Joel W. Martin, *Sacred Revolt: The Muskogees' Struggle for a New World* (Boston: Beacon Press, 1991), p. 73, citing Current-Garcia, ed., *Shem, Ham and Japheth,* p. 37. Africans had come to the Creek Nation in the East as traders, escaped slaves, and enslaved people well versed in Euro-American technology. Because Creeks at that time did not organize themselves by color or ethnicity, even slaves could travel freely, own property, and marry into the owner's family; often the children of the enslaved were free. See also Daniel F. Littlefield and Carol A. Petty-Hunter, *The Fus Fixico Letters* (Lincoln: University of Nebraska Press, 1993), p. 56, n. 2.

24. Martin, *Sacred Revolt,* pp. 72–73; Warde, *George Washington Grayson,* pp. 200–201, regarding Legus Perryman, Grayson, and Pleasant Porter, though the latter in 1904 joined a Cherokee man trying to organize a political party limited to "Indians by blood," which "explicitly excluded blacks"—probably freedmen rather than Afro-Creeks, who would, by matrilineal descent, have been "Indians by blood" rather than Indians by grant of citizenship after the Civil War.

25. *Pacific Reporter,* vol. 220; *Oklahoma,* p. 876; *Blake* v. *Sessions et al.* (1923).

26. For an example of a positive statement, see "Statement of J. Coody Johnson, A Creek Freedman, Member of the National Council of the Creek Nation," in *Report of the Select Committee,* vol. 1, pp. 440–41.

27. *Report of the Select Committee,* vol. 1, pp. 697–98.

28. Angie Debo, *The Road to Disappearance* (Norman: University of Oklahoma Press, 1941), pp. 290, 331–33; *Report of the Select Committee,* vol. 1, p. 648. Pleasant Porter, reputedly himself having some African descent, wealthy cattle rancher, and Creek chief, used derogatory language to refer to Creek freedmen and the increase in their numbers.

29. Theda Perdue, "Indians in Southern History," in *Indians in American History,* ed. by Frederick E. Hoxie (Chicago: Newberry Library, 1988), pp. 150–52.

30. Statement of Mr. J. S. Murchison, referring to 1866 treaties and distinguishing between Creek and Cherokee relations with freedmen, in *Report of the Select Committee to Investigate Matters Connected with Affairs in the Indian Territory with Hearings, November 11, 1906–January 9, 1907* Senate Report no. 5013, part 1, vol. 1, Senate Reports 59th Cong., 2nd sess., vol. 3 (Washington, D.C.: Government Printing Office, 1907), p. 308.

31. Grant Foreman, *The Five Civilized Tribes* (Norman: University of Oklahoma Press, 1934), pp. 213, 216.

32. Statement of Redbird Smith, *Report of the Select Committee,* vol. 1, p. 97; May, "Collision and Collusion," p. 239.

33. Crockett, *The Black Towns,* p. 76, using quotation from Boley's newspaper in 1905.

34. For example, *Boley Progress,* Mar. 9, 1905, p. 1; Washington, "Boley," p. 30.

35. As quoted by Sigmund Sameth, "Creek Negroes: A Study of Race Relations" (Master's the-

sis, University of Oklahoma, 1940), p. 56, quoted in Norman L. Crockett, *The Black Towns* (Lawrence: The Regents Press of Kansas, 1979), p. 28 n52.

36. Crockett, *The Black Towns*, pp. 39–40.

37. *Report of the Select Committee*, vol. 1, p. 92.

38. Daniel F. Littlefield, Jr., and Lonnie E. Underhill, "The 'Crazy Snake Uprising' of 1909: A Red, Black, or White Affair?" *Arizona and the West* (winter, 1978): 307–24, especially 309.

39. William F. Swindler, ed., *Sources and Documents of United States Constitutions*, vol. 8 (Dobbs Ferry, N.Y.: Oceana Publications, Inc., 1979), p. 47; Arrell Morgan Gibson, *The American Indian: Prehistory to the Present* (Lexington, Mass.: D.C. Heath and Company, 1980), p. 502; Warde, *George Washington Grayson*, p. 204.

40. Littlefield and Underhill, "The 'Crazy Snake Uprising,'" p. 311, on whites; Crockett, *The Black Towns*, on blacks.

41. Crockett, *The Black Towns*, p. 92.

42. Ibid., pp. 91–92.

43. Littlefield and Underhill, "The 'Crazy Snake Uprising,'" pp. 322, 324; Crockett, *The Black Towns*, p. 98.

44. Crockett, *The Black Towns*, p. 94; Thompson, *Closing the Frontier*, p. 134, notes that only 4 of 500 blacks in Boley could vote; Jimmie Lewis Franklin, *Journey Toward Hope: A History of Blacks in Oklahoma* (Norman: University of Oklahoma Press, 1982), pp. 39, 108–109, notes that Guthrie's district was predominantly black, leading to the first and only black legislator (1908) to sit in Oklahoma until the 1960s and leading the governor to call the legislature into special session to find ways to disenfranchise black voters. At the constitutional convention, 100 of 112 seats were held by Democrats, and the delegates were virtually all white men, regarding which the *Guthrie Leader* declared Oklahoma now a "white man's country"; Reese, *Women of Oklahoma*, pp. 179–80; See also *Report of the Select Committee*, vol. 1, pp. 681–82, 687, on the Creek candidates for the convention.

45. Littlefield and Underhill, "The 'Crazy Snake Uprising,'" pp. 311–12.

46. Quoted in Littlefield and Underhill, "The 'Crazy Snake Uprising,'" pp. 323–24.

47. Kelsey quoted in Kenneth Waldo McIntosh, "Chitto Harjo, The Crazy Snakes and the Birth of Indian Political Activism in the Twentieth Century" (Ph.D. dissertation, Texas Christian University, 1993), p. 136. The troops never found Harjo, who had sought refuge among the Choctaw Snakes and died in 1911.

48. From April 2, 1909, quoted in Littlefield and Underhill, "The 'Crazy Snake Uprising,'" p. 316.

49. *Boley Progress*, Apr. 18, 1809, p. 4, editorial. Of course, this view was self-serving to those promoting to black newcomers the ease of acquiring allotments of land from hospitable Creeks. See *Report of the Select Committee*, vol. 2, p. 1255, Cornelius Perryman; p. 1261, Robert Johnson; p. 1308, Legus Perryman.

50. Littlefield and Underhill, "The 'Crazy Snake Uprising'"; McIntosh, "Chitto Harjo," p. 121; *Report of the Select Committee*, vol. 2, p. 1252.

51. Littlefield and Underhill, "The 'Crazy Snake Uprising,'" p. 322.

52. Reese, *Women of Oklahoma*, pp. 6, 16.

53. Littlefield and Underhill, "The 'Crazy Snake Uprising,'" pp. 312, 317.

54. Alexander Posey, "Journal of Creek Enrollment Field Party 1905," *Chronicles of Oklahoma* 46 (1968): 13–14; Debo, *The Road*, pp. 305–306.

55. For examples, see *Pacific Reporter*, vol. 230, pp. 753–54, *Proctor et al. v. Foster et al.* 1924; vol. 220, p. 881 *Davis v. Reeder et al.*, 1924; vol. 215, p. 792 *Smith v. Lindsay et al.*, 1923. The law accepted that, among the Creek, a man and a woman who lived together as husband and wife were considered married; when they separated, they were considered divorced. Cf. Wendy Wall, "Gender

and the 'Citizen Indian,'" in *Writing the Range: Race, Class, and Culture in the Women's West,* ed. by Elizabeth Jameson and Susan Armitage (Norman: University of Oklahoma Press, 1997), pp. 202–29, particularly pp. 215–17. On other aspects of male/female relations such as education and games, see Posey, "Journal," p. 7, *Report of the Select Committee,* vol. 1, p. 239, Mr. D. F. Redd; vol. 2, p. 1311, Mrs. Lila D. Lindsay. Note also that the constitution that emerged from the Sequoyah movement's convention in 1905 declared that the real and personal property of a femme covert acquired before or after marriage by any means, as long as she chose, remained her separate estate and property as if she were femme sole, *Sources and Documents of United States Constitutions,* vol. 8, p. 71.

56. *Boley Progress,* Aug. 4, 1905, p. 1; Mar. 16, 1905, p. 1; May 10, 1906, p. 1, and Washington, "Boley," p. 28, cited above.

57. Crockett, *The Black Towns,* pp. 63, 81–82.

58. Senate document 443, "Memorial from Ho Tul Yaholla and Hu Tul Kee Fixico, representatives of the Creek Nation of Indians in Indian Territory, protesting against the passage of the bill (HR 11821) to ratify an agreement with the Muscogee or Creek Tribe," 56th Cong., 1st sess., p. 2. See Elsa Barkley Brown, "Negotiating and Transforming the Public Sphere: African American Political Life in the Transition from Slavery to Freedom," *Public Culture* 7 (1994): 107–46.

59. Address to the Senatorial Committee of the Commercial Club of Muskogee, Indian Territory, *Report of the Select Committee,* p. 1989.

60. Crockett, *The Black Towns,* p. 38.

61. Littlefield and Underhill, "The 'Crazy Snake Uprising,'" p. 323.

CHAPTER 5

Partly Colored or Other White

Mexican Americans and Their Problem with the Color Line

NEIL FOLEY

"Race relations," until very recently, has usually meant relations between blacks and whites. Since the 1960s, however, the rising number of Asian and Latin American immigrants to the United States has challenged the abiding and historically important black-white binary. In Miami, Florida, tensions exist between the black and Cuban communities. Throughout the Southwest, conflicts between Anglos and Mexicans predate the War with Mexico in 1846. English-only initiatives, continued physical violence against Mexican immigrants, and the 1994 Californian proposition to deny medical, educational, and other benefits to undocumented workers attest to these ongoing conflicts. In Los Angeles, Koreans and blacks have longstanding grievances against one another; in Houston, Mexicans and Guatemalans struggle for low-paying jobs while many blacks and whites call for immigration restriction and tougher border controls.

In seven of the ten largest cities in the United States—New York, Los Angeles, Houston, San Diego, Phoenix, Dallas, and San Antonio, in that order—Latinos now outnumber blacks. In Los Angeles, Houston, Dallas, and San Antonio, Latinos outnumber Anglos, or non-Hispanic whites, as well. Latinos in Chicago now account for twenty-seven percent of the population, and their votes determine the outcome of most elections. To view the browning of America in other terms, in eighteen of the twenty-five most populous counties in the United States, Latinos now outnumber blacks. Where regions are concerned, both the Pacific Northwest and New England now have larger Spanish-surname populations than black populations. Already U.S. Latinos comprise the fifth-largest "nation" in Latin America, and in fifty years only Mexico and Brazil will exceed the number of Latinos living in the United States. Put another way, the United States will be the second-largest "Spanish-language-origin" nation in the world.[1] In short, we live in a multiracial society that can no longer be viewed in black and white, because it has always been much more racially diverse than one encompassed by the stark simplicity of the black-white racial paradigm. Yet the black-white binary stubbornly continues to shape thinking about the racial place and space of Latinos in the United States who are often compared to, and sometimes equated with, either whites or blacks.

It must be stated from the outset that blacks themselves have been exasperated by the idea that their ethnic backgrounds—as Irish, Mexican, German, etc.—are obliterated by the necessity to maintain "blackness" as the unalloyed touchstone for determining who is white and who is not. In other words, anyone with any African ancestry is automatically "black"—a racial default sometimes referred to as the "one-drop" rule. In U.S. society, according to the racial formula by which mixed-race persons of African descent are denied any identity other than black, it would be impossible for a black woman to give birth to a white baby. By the same cultural rule, it is as impossible for an African American to claim to be "part Irish" as it is for a white person to claim to be "part black." Historian Barbara Fields relates the insightful, though probably apocryphal, anecdote of a white American journalist who asked the late Papa Doc Duvalier of Haiti what percentage of the Haitian population was white. Duvalier had answered that it was about ninety-eight percent white. The journalist assumed that Duvalier had misunderstood the question and put it to him once again. Duvalier assured the journalist that he had not misunderstood the question and repeated his answer. The journalist then asked, "How do you define 'white'?" Duvalier answered this question with one of his own: "How do you define 'black' in your country?" The journalist obligingly explained that anyone in the United States who has any black blood was considered black. Duvalier nodded and responded, "Well, that's the way we define white in my country."[2]

Historically, the one-drop rule of black racial construction fulfilled the need of white southerners to maintain the color line between white slave owners and black slaves even as the South, and the nation, had become a highly polyglot, miscegenated society in which both "whiteness" and "blackness" were cultural fictions, however devastatingly real were the social and political consequences of the "color line." Thus after 1920 "mulatto" ceased to be a racial category in the U.S. census as part of a larger racial project to maintain the color line between monolithic whiteness and blackness.

The dyadic racial thinking of white southerners and northerners encountered some challenges in the mid-nineteenth century as European whites began their westward march across the continent. In the trans-Mississippi West whites encountered Mexicans in the present-day states of Texas, New Mexico, and California. From their first encounters, Anglos (the term used by Mexicans for white Americans) did not regard Mexicans as blacks, but they also did not regard them as whites. Neither black nor white, Mexicans were usually regarded as a degraded "mongrel" race, a mixture of Indian, Spanish, and African ancestry, only different from Indians and Africans in the degree of their inferiority to whites. Indeed, many whites considered Mexicans inferior to Indians and Africans because Mexicans were racially mixed, a hybrid race that represented the worst nightmare of what might become of the white race if it let down its racial guard. Where whites encountered groups who were neither black nor white, they simply created other racial binaries (Anglo Mexican; white Chinese, and so forth) to maintain racial hierarchies, while the quality that made whites superior—their "whiteness"—assumed a kind of racelessness, or invisibility, as they went about reaping the spoils of racial domination.

The persistence of the black-white binary has had some bizarre and unfortunate consequences for the shape of early Mexican American civil rights struggles. The period roughly from the 1930s to 1970 represented a particular strategy of civil rights activism among middle-class Mexican Americans who stressed the importance of assimilation and Americanization. But they also sought to construct identities as Caucasians by asserting their Spanish and "Latin American" descent. These second-generation Mexican Americans were reacting to the racial ideology, forged mostly between 1830 and 1930, that Mexicans constituted a hybrid race of Indian, African, and Spanish ancestry incapable of undertaking the obligations of democratic government. This chapter explores how Mexican Americans, beginning around 1930, when the census counted more U.S.-born Mexicans than Mexican immigrants, sought to overcome the stigma of being Mexican by asserting their Americanness. In the process, they equated Americanness with whiteness and therefore embarked on a strategy of dissociating themselves from African Americans as potential coalition partners in their early civil rights struggles. They came to the realization that being a U.S. citizen did not count nearly as much as being white, the racial sine qua non of Americanness.

Yet understanding the ways in which Mexicans have pursued the privileges of whiteness is not enough. In 1980 the U.S. census officially adopted the term "Hispanic," and many Mexican Americans and other Latinos have accepted the use of this term. As demographers and government officials sought to distinguish Anglos from Hispanics identifying as whites in the census, they have conceived the phrase "non-Hispanic whites" which implies the opposite category of "Hispanic whites," or simply Hispanics. This positioning of Hispanic as an ethnic subcategory of any race, and particularly its deployment as a separate class of whites, poses questions. How did Mexicans, a group historically racialized as nonwhite, arrive at their present status as ethnic whites, not unlike Italian or Irish Americans? As Hispanics continue to identify themselves as whites, what are the implications for

African Americans and the continued dismal state of U.S. race relations, especially as the percentage of African Americans declines in proportion to the population of Latinos? Although this chapter does not fully answer those questions, in uncovering the Mexican American response to the black-white racial binary, it reveals the contradictions and ambiguities in the limiting vocabulary of race in our nation. Moreover, the experience of Mexican Americans in twentieth-century racial politics reflects how the long history of black-white racial thinking has not only impinged upon the freedom of Mexican Americans and other Latinos, but it has also stifled the ability of all Americans to reconsider and reconfigure racial discourses in new and productive ways.

The earliest and most persistent debates on race in the United States centered not on "the Negro problem" but on the boundaries of "whiteness"—who was white and who was not. The 1790 naturalization law was enacted to ensure that only "free white" persons—not Indians or Africans—could become U.S. citizens. However, the flood of immigrants from Ireland in the mid-nineteenth century—and later Jews, Slavs, Mediterraneans and other non-northern Europeans—altered the boundaries of whiteness to exclude all but those from northwestern Europe, the so-called Nordics. Whiteness thus fissured along *racial* lines, which culminated in the Immigration Act of 1924. This act established immigration quotas according to the national origins system, which greatly curtailed immigration from eastern and southern Europe. Asian immigrants were ineligible to become citizens, because they were not members of the "Caucasian race"; moreover, their immigration had been curtailed by the Chinese Exclusion Act of 1882 and the so-called Gentleman's Agreement with Japan in 1908 to limit Japanese immigration.[3]

Mexicans, however, continued to pose a problem to immigration restrictionists because the national-origin quotas of the 1924 immigration act did not apply to immigrants from the Western Hemisphere. Industry and large-scale agricultural farms throughout the American Southwest had so thoroughly relied on Mexican labor that immigration restriction would have meant nothing less than economic disaster for the entire region. As Mexicans continued to pour across the international border with Mexico in unprecedented numbers during the boom years of the 1920s, restrictionists argued that most Mexicans crossed the border illegally, often did not return to Mexico, took jobs from white people, and, most significantly, constituted a threat to the purity of the white race. For many Anglos in the Southwest, Mexicans were not whites and could not be assimilated into white American society.[4]

By the middle of the 1930s it was clear in Texas and other parts of the American West that African Americans did not constitute the number one race problem, as they had historically in the states of the South, including East Texas. In the West the threat to whiteness came principally from Latin America, particularly Mexico, not from Africa or African Americans. African Americans, after all, were not "alien" or foreign, and whites had a long history of dealing with blacks. In Texas and other southern states, whites and blacks had grown up together in the same towns, even if Jim Crow laws prevented them from sitting at the same lunch counters or attending the same schools. Blacks, for their part, shared much of southern culture with whites, whether on cotton farms or in Baptist churches. Indeed, African Americans in Texas shared with whites the experience of being displaced from their farms by Mexican immigrants whose language, religion, and customs differed from those of both blacks and whites.

Blacks, whatever else they might be to whites, were therefore not "alien," a word reserved by nativists to describe immigrants. Although many Mexicans had lived in Texas long before Stephen Austin established the first Anglo settlement in 1822, Anglos still regarded Mexicans as alien culturally, linguistically, religiously, and racially. Their status as racially in-between, as partly colored, hybrid peoples of mixed Indian, Spanish, and African ancestry, made them suspect in the eyes of whites, who feared that Mexicans could breach the color line by marrying both blacks and whites. Although laws existed against race mixing for whites and blacks, no such laws prevented the mixing of Mexicans with both blacks and whites.[5]

Most Anglos in the Southwest did not regard Mexicans as white, but they also did not consider them to be in the same racial category as "Negro." Before 1930 many Mexicans themselves simply thought of themselves as "Mexicanos"—neither black nor white. In 1930 a sociologist, Max Handman, commented: "The American community has no social technique for handling partly colored races. We have a place for the Negro and a place for the white man: the Mexican is not a Negro, and the white man refuses him an equal status."[6] As Handman explained, "The Mexican presents shades of color ranging from that of the Negro, although with no Negro features, to that of the white. The result is confusion."[7] No one has been more confused than whites themselves over the racial status of Mexicans, because some Mexicans look undeniably "white," while others look almost as dark as— and sometimes darker than—many blacks. "Such a situation cannot last for long," wrote Handman, "because the temptation of the white group is to push him down into the Negro group, while the efforts of the Mexican will be directed toward raising himself to the level of the white group." Mexicans, according to Handman, would not accept the subordinate status of blacks and instead would form a separate group "on the border line between the Negro and the white man."[8] Indeed middle-class, mostly urban Mexican Americans would invent themselves as a separate group after 1930, but it would not be "on the border" between black and white. They would come to insist that all Mexicans, citizens and non-citizens, were whites or Caucasians, albeit of Latin American descent.

Anglos, for their part, had long recognized that not all Mexicans were equally inferior. Immigrant Mexicans who were poor, non-English speaking, uneducated or illiterate, and often dark-skinned were inferior to a small class of Mexicans—U.S. citizens, English-speaking, educated, and often, but not always, light-skinned—who could be accorded certain privileges extended to other whites, such as voting, holding public office, sending their children to white schools, and even allowing for intermarriage, although usually in the case of an Anglo man desiring to marry a Mexican woman. Intermarriage was possible precisely because Anglos had "de-mexicanized" a privileged class of Mexicans who had been transformed into "Spanish Americans" or "Latin Americans"—into, in other words, a separate class of whites.[9]

Mexican Americans sought to have their status as whites recognized socially and politically in a region that had practiced Jim Crow segregation of both Mexicans and African Americans. They challenged attempts by state and federal governments to classify Mexicans as nonwhite and to maintain segregated schools in the aftermath of *Plessy* v. *Ferguson* (the 1896 Supreme Court decision that helped to entrench legal segregation throughout the South).

The first legal attempt to determine the racial status of Mexicans occurred in 1896 in Texas federal court when Ricardo Rodríguez, a long-time resident of San Antonio and legal Mexican immigrant, applied for U.S. citizenship. Anyone born in the United States is automatically a citizen, but immigrants who desire citizenship status must become "naturalized," a bureaucratic process by which immigrants fulfill residency requirements and forswear allegiance to their homelands. Two white politicians in San Antonio worried that Mexican immigrants might become citizens and exercise their right to vote. Consequently, they filed a law suit against Ricardo Rodríguez on the grounds that he was "Indian Mexican" and therefore not "white." The naturalization law, enacted in 1790 and amended in 1870, stipulated that only "free white persons" and "persons of African ancestry" were eligible for citizenship. Because Native Americans and all Asians were barred by naturalization law from becoming U.S. citizens, the lawyers hoped to prove that Rodríguez, a dark-skinned Mexican who freely admitted he was probably of Indian descent, was racially unfit for citizenship. In one of the many briefs filed in the year-long case, one of the attorneys opposed to granting citizenship to Rodríguez cited, as evidence, the findings of a French anthropologist who compiled a classification of race according to the variety of human skin color. It was impossible to distinguish with any degree of certainty between Indian Mexicans, African Mexicans, and "Spanish" or white Mexicans; therefore, the attorneys essentially argued that the boundary of whiteness be drawn on the basis of skin color. Rodríguez was, according to the attorneys, a "chocolate brown" Mexican. The judge in the case conceded, "If the strict scientific classification of the anthropologist should be adopted, [Rodríguez] would probably not be classed as white." Nevertheless, the court ruled that all citizens of Mexico, regardless of racial status, were eligible to become naturalized U.S. citizens. The fact that Mexicans, unlike Chinese immigrants or American Indians, could be become naturalized citizens of the United States, however, rested less upon the assumption that they were white than on the obligations imposed upon the United States by Article VIII of the Treaty of Guadalupe Hidalgo. The treaty that ended the U.S. war with Mexico, signed in 1848, stipulated, among other things, that Mexicans could become U.S. citizens. From the legal standpoint, Mexican immigrants who were primarily "Indian" in appearance and ancestry could thus be granted U.S. citizenship, although Indians born in the United States were not eligible for citizenship, at least not until the Indian Citizenship Act of 1924.[10]

Second, *Plessy* v. *Ferguson* did not apply to Mexicans, inasmuch as they were officially recognized as "white." In Texas, for example, the legislature passed a law in 1893, six years before the Supreme Court mandated "separate but equal" facilities for blacks and whites, that required separate schools for the state's white and "colored" children. The statute defined colored as "all persons of mixed blood descended from Negro ancestry."[11] Thus Mexicans in the state were segregated by custom rather than by law, and school districts defended the practice on the grounds that Mexican children did not speak English and spent part of the school year with their families as migrant agricultural workers. When Mexican American civil rights activists were able to show that Mexican children were arbitrarily segregated, regardless of English-language facility, the courts generally ruled in favor of the plaintiff Mexican Americans.[12]

Third, the U.S. census had always counted persons of Mexican descent as whites, except in 1930, when a special category was created for "Mexicans." The question of Mexican racial identity became especially acute during the immigration restriction debates of the 1920s. This broad exemption from immigration quotas led to the historic congressional debates in the 1920s by restrictionists determined to close the door to Mexicans. The Bureau of the Census decided that beginning with 1930 it would establish a new category to determine how many persons of Mexican descent resided in the United States, legally or illegally. Before 1930 all Mexican-descent people were counted simply as white persons, because the racial categories at that time included Negro, White, Indian, Chinese, and Japanese. The 1930 census created, for the first time in U.S. history, the separate category of "Mexican," which stipulated that "all persons born in Mexico, or having parents born in Mexico, *who are not definitely white,* negro, Indian, Chinese, or Japanese, should be returned as Mexican." This meant that census workers determined whether to record a particular Mexican household as "white" or "Mexican." About ninety-six percent of Mexican-descent people were counted under this new category of Mexican; only four percent were counted as white.[13] Mexicans had, for the first time in U.S. history, been counted as a nonwhite group. The government of Mexico as well as numerous Mexican Americans protested this new classification. Bowing to pressure, the U.S. government abandoned the category of Mexican in the 1940 census but sought other means of identifying the Latino population, by identifying those with Spanish surnames or households whose dominant language was Spanish.

Although Mexican Americans were accorded de jure white racial status in naturalization law, school segregation statutes, and in the census, they nevertheless endured de facto discrimination in their everyday lives: they lived in segregated neighborhoods or *barrios,* their children attended segregated schools, and they were prohibited from using some public facilities, such as swimming pools, or sitting in the white section at movie theaters, eating in white-only restaurants, or staying in white-only hotels. Nevertheless, Mexican Americans remained vigilant in monitoring local laws, customs, and racial protocols that might limit their claims to the rights and privileges of whiteness. Whenever local officials challenged their claim to whiteness, Mexican American civil rights activists sought redress from the federal government—sometimes through the courts—to prevent officials from classifying, categorizing, or otherwise consigning them to the non-white side of the color line.

In 1936, in El Paso, Texas, white city officials challenged the traditional classification of Mexicans as whites in the city's birth and death records. The county health officer, T. J. McCamant, and Alex K. Powell, the city registrar of the Bureau of Vital Statistics, adopted a new policy of registering the births and deaths of Mexican-descent citizens as "colored" rather than "white."[14] Both McCamant and Powell claimed that they were simply following the regulations established by the Department of Commerce and Bureau of the Census and that officials in Dallas, Fort Worth, Houston, and San Antonio used the same classification system.[15] McCamant also acknowledged that changing the classification of Mexicans from white to colored automatically lowered the infant mortality rate for whites in a city where Mexicans comprised over sixty percent of the population, most of whom were poor and suffered higher rates of infant mortality than did whites. Because the El Paso Chamber of Commerce had hoped to market El Paso as a health resort for those suffering from tuberculosis and other ailments, it became necessary to disaggregate Mexicans from the white category on birth records and to move them into the colored category, thereby automatically lowering the infant mortality rate for "non-Hispanic whites."

The Mexican American community of El Paso, as well as Mexicans across the border in neighboring Juarez, became furious over this racial demotion and mobilized to have their whiteness restored. Members of the El Paso council of the League of United Latin American Citizens and other community leaders immediately filed an injunction in the Sixty-fifth district court. Cleofas Calleros, a Mexican American representative of the National Catholic Welfare Council of El Paso, wrote to the attorney representing the twenty-six Mexican Americans who had filed the injunction, "Is it a fact that the Bureau [of the Census] has ruled that Mexicans are 'colored,' meaning the black race?"[16] Calleros argued that classifying Mexicans as "colored" was not only incorrect but illegal. Texas civil and penal codes classified Mexicans as "white," because "colored" referred only to those persons of "mixed blood descended from negro ancestry." He added that Mexicans "as a race are red if they are Indians and white if they are not Indians," essentially negating the historical presence of African ancestry among Mexicans.[17] An editorial in a Spanish-language newspaper argued simply that a Mexican who is not "pure Indian" is of the "Caucasian race," thereby implying that a "one-drop" rule applied to Mexicans: any amount of white blood rendered an Indian or a mestizo white, an interesting inversion of the one-drop rule of the U.S. South that rendered all those with the smallest African ancestry as black.[18] While praising the high civilization of the Aztec, Maya, Olmecs, and Toltecs, often as a defense against frequent Anglo insinuations that Mexicans were little more than mongrelized Indians, Mexicans nonetheless began to insist that they belonged, according to one Spanish-language editorial, "to the racial group of their mother country, Spain, and therefore to the Caucasian race."[19]

Alonso Perales, president of LULAC, writing to Cleofas Calleros to congratulate him for his "virile stance" on the classification issue, explained that he never protested the fact that Mexicans had their own category in San Antonio because "we are very proud of our racial origins and we do not wish to give the impression that we are ashamed of being called 'Mexicans.' Nevertheless," he continued, "we have always resented the inference that we are not whites." If Mexicans had to have their separate category for statistical purposes, he believed that the category of white ought to be subdivided into "Anglo American" and "Latin American."[20]

The campaign to restore their status as whites in the birth and death records in El Paso did not end with local classification schemes. Mexican Americans also learned that the U.S. Department of the Treasury and Internal Revenue Service had instructed applicants for social security cards to check either the "white" or "negro" box on the application forms. If applicants were neither white nor Negro, they were instructed to write out the "color or race" to which they belonged and gave as examples: "Mexican, Chinese, Japanese, Indian, Filipino, etc."[21] Once more Mexican Americans in El Paso and elsewhere in Texas wrote indignant letters to the Treasury Department complaining bitterly that Mexicans were white and should not be included in the same category with nonwhite groups like the Chinese and Japanese. The storm of protest led federal officials to acknowledge the error and to promise to reprint new forms. Tens of thousands of the old forms had already been mailed to numerous states, however, and could not be recalled. The commissioner of Internal Revenue suggested that Mexicans could simply check the "white" box. One Mexican American attributed the confusion surrounding the racial status of Mexicans to the influx of "white trash" into Texas who were ignorant of the fact that the "first white explorers and settlers in the State of Texas were Spanish speakers." Long-term Anglo residents of the region, he seemed to imply, knew better.[22]

The real issue over racial classification was clearly as much about Mexican racial pride as it was about fear over discrimination. In Texas, Mexicans endured the injuries of discrimination daily. Middle-class Mexican Americans needed to believe that segregation stemmed from Anglo ignorance of Mexico's history and the fact that many middle-class Mexican Americans, like their Anglo counterparts, actually believed that whites were superior to both Indians and Africans. Mexican Americans did not necessarily acquire a belief in white racial supremacy in the United States, although it was certainly reinforced there whenever one encountered blacks and Indians in the United States.[23]

These mostly middle-class Mexican Americans were not simply content to deny any "negro ancestry." For many Mexicans and Mexican Americans, "colored" meant racial inferiority, social disgrace, and the total absence of political rights—in short, the racial equivalent of Indian and Negro.[24] In their injunction against the El Paso city registrar, for example, they cited an Oklahoma law that made it libelous to call a white person "colored."[25] Mexican Americans in San Antonio, who joined the campaign to change the classification scheme, sent a resolution adopted by various LULAC councils to U.S. Representative Maury Maverick, a liberal Texas Democrat, to register their "most vigorous protest against the insult thus cast upon our race."[26] Maverick wrote to the director of the Census Bureau in Washington, D.C., that "to classify these people here as 'colored' is to jumble them in as *Negroes,* wich [sic] they are not and which naturally causes the most violent feelings." He urged the director to include another category called "other white," and argued that the classification of Mexicans as "colored" was simply inaccurate, because "people who are of Mexican or Spanish descent are certainly not of African descent."[27] An irate Mexican American evangelist wrote that if Mexicans were colored, then Senator Dennis Chavez of New Mexico, who was the first U.S senator of Mexican descent, "will have his children classified as Negroes. Then Uncle Sam can hang his face in shame before the civilized nations of the world."[28]

Amidst all the protests that classifying Mexicans as "colored" insulted Mexicans on both sides of the border, little was heard from the African American community of El Paso, which, although small (less than two percent), could not have appreciated the Mexican community's insistence that being classified in the same racial category as "negro" was the worst possible affront to Mexican racial pride. However, one El Pasoan, J. Hamilton Price, who was either African American or posing as one, wrote a long letter explaining how both blacks and whites in El Paso were roaring with laughter over the Mexicans' exhibition of wounded dignity.[29] Price wrote that local blacks did not consider Mexicans white, nor did they consider them to be superior to blacks. Furthermore, if Mexicans considered themselves superior to blacks, he wanted to know why Mexicans in El Paso ate, drank, and worked with people considered racially inferior. He went on to list the numerous ways in which Mexican behavior departed radically from Anglo-white behavior with respect to blacks. "One sees daily in this city," he wrote, "Mexican boys shining the shoes of Negroes. If Mexicans are racially superior to Negroes," he continued, "they shouldn't be shining their shoes."[30] It is worth listing all the behaviors Price described to indicate how ludicrous he found the Mexican claim to whiteness:

—Some of the Mexican men had their hair made wavy to look more like the curly hair of Negroes.
—In local stores Mexican clerks addressed Negro clients as "Sir" and "Ma'am."
—In local streetcars Mexicans occupied the seats reserved by law for Negroes.
—Many Mexicans in El Paso preferred Negro doctors and dentists to those of their own race.
—Many Mexicans were employed on ranches and in the homes and commercial establishments of Negroes.
—Mexican boxers competed with Negroes in Juarez and would compete with them in El Paso, if it were permitted.
—Mexican soccer players avidly played against Negroes, and many of the players on the Mexican teams were Negroes.
—In some of the Mexican bars and small restaurants Negroes were as well received as Mexicans themselves.
—Four out of five clients of Negro prostitutes were Mexicans.
—In El Paso and Juarez many Mexican women were married to Negroes.

Price wrote that the offspring of Mexican and black marriages were so numerous in El Paso that they were called "negro-burros," literally, "black donkeys." In Mexico, according to Price, many of these mixed-raced persons were considered Mexican and occupied important positions in Mexican social circles. They often frequented the best theaters, restaurants, and Mexican hair salons, married Mexican women, and, if Democrats, were able to vote in the Democratic primaries in Texas, which otherwise barred blacks from voting. His point was that the vast majority of El Paso Mexicans, who were not of the middle class, did not think of themselves as white and that El Paso blacks also did not regard Mexicans as white. Price, angered by the manner in which Mexicans objected to being labeled as "colored," ended his long letter with some racial invective of his own: "Though once pure Indians," he wrote, "Mexicans had become more mixed than dog food—undoubtedly a conglomeration of Indian with all the races known to man, with the possible exception of the Eskimo."[31]

Price's letter brought a series of angry rebuttals from Mexicans who denounced Price as a coward for using a pseudonym—they could not find his name in the city directory. One writer, Abraham Arriola Giner, accused Negroes of deserving their inferior status for having tolerated oppressive conditions that no Mexican ever would. He boasted of the high level of culture attained by his Indian ancestors and belittled Negroes as descendants of "savage tribes" from Africa where they practiced cannibalism and did nothing to improve their lives. He reminded Price that American Negroes, as former slaves, did not have their own country or flag and that there was no honor for those who did not understand the meaning of liberty. In a final stroke of racial arrogance, Arriola Gina wrote that Mexicans would never tolerate any race claiming to be superior to Mexicans because "such superiority does not exist."[32]

These middle-class Mexican Americans in El Paso sought to eliminate once and for all the ambiguity surrounding Mexican racial identity. First, they recognized that any attempt to define them as "nonwhite" could easily come to mean "noncitizen" as well, because many Anglos did not regard Mexicans, particularly of the lower class, as truly American or fit for American citizenship. Second, middle-class Mexican Americans themselves drew distinctions between themselves and lower-class Mexicans whom they often regarded as "Indios" or "Indian Mexicans" and used terms like "mojados" ("wetbacks") and other terms of class and racial disparagement. Hamilton Price, the black El Pasoan, pointed out as much when he reminded El Pasoans about the close, even intimate, relations that existed between blacks and lower-class Mexicans in El Paso, from Mexican men shining the shoes of African American men to African American men marrying Mexican women.

Many middle-class Mexican American elites in El Paso, men like Cleo-fas Calleros, immigration representative of the National Catholic Welfare Conference; LULAC president Frank Galván; Lorenzo Alarcon, "presidente-supremo" of United Citizens' Civic League, and many others were well connected to the white elites of the city and drew their power, in part, from being representatives of "their people." They believed that any act of discrimination against any member of their community, or any attempt to deny full citizenship rights to any Mexican American, constituted a threat to all Mexican Americans. They understood that basic citizenship rights—such as the right to vote, sit on juries, hold public office, and so forth—depended less on their citizenship status, important to them as this was, than on their right to claim status as white citizens of the United States.

Virtually the only groups that could not lay claim to white racial status were African Americans, Native Americans, and Asian Americans, whom the government classified as separate and distinct races for purposes of census enumeration. Therein lies the beauty of a word like "white" or Caucasian: it is broad enough to include Jews, Italians, the Irish, and Greeks, so why not Mexicans as well? It was not the color line per se that was the problem in American life and culture, many Mexican Americans reasoned, but the way in which they were consigned to the nonwhite side of the line. In short, Mexican American civil rights organizations sought to expand the civil rights of Mexicans by expanding the boundaries of whiteness to include, to use their own phrasing, "the Spanish speaking people," Americans of Spanish-Speaking descent, and Latin Americans.

As whites of a different culture and color than most Anglo whites, many middle-class Mexicans learned early on that hostility to the idea of "social equality" for African Americans went right to the core of what constituted whiteness in the United States. Whether or not they brought with them from Mexico racial prejudice against blacks—and certainly many Mexicans did—middle-class Mexican leaders throughout the 1930s, '40s, and '50s went to great lengths to dissociate themselves socially, culturally, and politically from the early struggles of African Americans to achieve full citizenship rights in America.

A few years after World War II ended, another Mexican American civil rights organization was founded, the American GI Forum. Significantly, the name of the organization did not include any reference to its being an organization for Mexican American war veterans. Hector García, a medical doctor who founded the American GI Forum, achieved a degree of national attention in 1949 when he challenged the Anglo owner of a funeral home near San Antonio for refusing the use of the chapel to the Mexican American family of a deceased veteran, Private Felix Longoria. Dr. García organized a statewide protest that attracted the attention of U.S. Senator Lyndon

Baines Johnson who offered to have Private Longoria buried in Arlington National Cemetery in Washington, D.C., with full military honors, which the family graciously accepted. The incident established the American GI Forum as an effective civil rights advocate for Mexican Americans, even though Dr. García himself insisted, years after the Longoria incident, that the American GI Forum was not a civil rights organization but rather a "charitable organization." As late as 1954 Dr. García claimed, "we are not and have never been a civil rights organization. Personally I hate the word." What did Dr. García have against the phrase "civil rights"?[33]

Here it is worth noting that the phrase "civil rights" was so firmly linked in the post–World War II imaginary to the civil rights struggle of African Americans that Dr. García perhaps thought it best not to acknowledge too forcefully the American GI Forum's own civil rights agenda. He was in good company, if one includes the Kennedy brothers in the pantheon of civil rights advocates. In 1960, Robert Kennedy, who at the time was the campaign manager for his brother's presidential race, told campaign aides, who were in charge of efforts to secure the votes of black Americans, to change the name of their campaign section, which they had called the "office of civil rights." Robert Kennedy believed that making Negro civil rights a central concern of the Kennedy presidential campaign would alienate white voters in the South. He also asked them to change the name of a Harlem conference on civil rights to a conference on "constitutional rights."[34] Robert Kennedy, like Dr. García, did not wish to alienate whites in Texas—or anywhere else— by appearing to join the struggle of black people for civil rights.[35]

By the early 1950s the American GI Forum, while still denying that it was a civil rights organization, sought to end discrimination in Texas schools, in employment, and in the use of public spaces. The core strategy depended on educating Anglos that "Americans of Spanish-speaking descent" or Latin Americans were Caucasians and that to identify them as anything but white, whether on birth certificates or traffic citations, was illegal. Making any distinction between Latin Americans and whites, he wrote, was a "slur," an insult to all Latin Americans of Spanish descent.[36]

A decade later, Vice President Hubert Humphrey made the mistake of writing the American GI Forum to announce the government's new program to offer summer jobs for teenagers, especially, he wrote, for "the nonwhite teenagers." The AGIF Auxiliary chairwoman, Mrs. Dominga Coronado, rebuked the vice president: "If everyone in the government takes the position emphasized in your letter ([that Mexicans are] nonwhite), then it is understandable why the Mexican American is getting 'the leftovers' of the Federal programs in employment, housing, and education."[37] White people, she seemed to imply, do not eat leftovers.

Educating Anglos to acknowledge the white racial status of Mexican

Americans represented a major political goal of the American GI Forum. To become white—and therefore truly American—required members to distance themselves from any association, social or political, with African Americans. When the AGIF *News Bulletin,* for example, printed an article in 1955 titled "Mexican Americans Favor Negro School Integration," Manuel Ávila, an active member of AGIF and close personal friend of Hector García, wrote to state chairman Ed Idar that "Anybody reading it can only come to the conclusion [that] we are ready to fight the Negroes' battles . . . for sooner or later we are going to have to say which side of the fence we're on, are we white or not. If we are white, why do we ally with the Negro?"[38] Mexicans were learning to act like white people in Arizona, he reported, where Mexican restaurant owners, who normally served Negroes, had recently placed signs in the windows that Negroes would not be served. If Mexicans refused to serve Negroes, Ávila wrote, Anglo restaurants might begin serving Mexicans. Mexican Americans, he argued, must say to Negroes, "I'm White and you can't come into my restaurant."[39]

A sympathetic white woman from rural Mississippi, Ruth Slates, who owned a store that served many Mexican and Mexican American cotton pickers, wrote to Dr. García in 1951: "My blood just boils to see these farmers . . . trying to throw the Spanish kids out of the schools . . . and into negro schools." She pointed out that although some of the "Spanish kids" "hate negroes," others, unfortunately, "mix with them." She then advised Dr. García that Mexicans needed a strong leader to teach them "right from wrong," because some "even marry negros and some white girls." Slates was giving Dr. García a quick lesson in southern racial protocol: if Mexicans want to be white, then they cannot associate, much less marry, black folk, and she also implied that marrying white girls, in Mississippi at least, might not be a prudent thing to do.[40] Ruth Slates liked "Spanish kids" and hoped that Dr. García would provide the kind of leadership required, as it is now fashionable to say, to perform whiteness.

The American GI Forum thus faced a major dilemma: if it acknowledged that it was a civil rights organization rather than a patriotic veterans organization or a charitable organization, whites might regard it as part of the ideological and political struggle of African Americans for equal rights. How could the American GI Forum argue that Mexicans were white if its agenda included the struggle for civil rights, including, presumably, those of blacks? Put another way, if Mexican Americans were white, why did they need a civil rights organization in the first place? If being white meant anything, particularly in a state like Texas that once belonged both to Mexico and the Confederacy, it meant being not Mexican and not black. Both LULAC and the American GI Forum eliminated the word "Mexican" from their vocabularies precisely for this purpose. In seeking to equate the word "Mexican" with nationality and not race, members of LULAC and the American GI Forum asserted their identities as white Americans, although of Mexican ancestry.

The American GI Forum became the principal source of financial and political support in the only civil rights case involving Mexican Americans to reach the U.S. Supreme Court. This case highlights the irony of a civil rights strategy that is rooted in a claim that Mexicans are members of the Caucasian race. In 1954, the U.S. Supreme Court handed down a ruling that acknowledged the white racial status of Mexicans at the same time that it ruled that Mexicans represented a "separate class" of whites who had been systematically prevented from exercising their constitutional rights. An all-Anglo jury convicted the defendant, Pete Hernandez, of murder. AGIF and LULAC challenged the ruling on the grounds that Hernandez had been denied his constitutional right to be tried by a jury of his peers, because not a single Mexican American had ever been selected for jury service in the last twenty-five years in a county that was twelve percent Mexican American. The Texas Court of Appeals, however, agreed with the lower court that the "equal protection" clause of the Fourteenth Amendment to the constitution applied to "negroes and whites" and that, because Mexican Americans were legally white, Hernandez was indeed tried by a jury of his peers. The Texas courts basically reasoned that Mexican Americans could not have it both ways: they could not insist that they were white and, at the same time, that an all-white jury constituted an violation of the "equal protection" clause of the Fourteenth Amendment forbidding discrimination on the basis of race.[41]

The Mexican American attorneys appealed the decision to the Supreme Court in *Hernández* v. *the State of Texas.* Two weeks before the historic decision *Brown* v. *Board of Education* the Supreme Court ruled that Mexican Americans had been discriminated against as a "separate class" of white people, acknowledging, in effect, the differential treatment accorded to whites and Hispanics in Texas and elsewhere in the Southwest. Even the county courthouse, where the original trial was held, had segregated public bathrooms, one for whites and one for Negroes and Mexicans. This decision was a major triumph for Mexican Americans who had argued in other cases that Mexicans constituted a separate class of white people, in effect, "Hispanic whites."[42]

The American GI Forum, like LULAC, represented a narrow band of educated, English-speaking Mexican Americans that recognized that racial status counted more than citizenship in achieving full citizenship rights as Americans, as white Americans. For the masses of working-class Mexicanos, however, many of them first generation, the idea that they were members of the white race would have struck them as somewhat absurd. Anglos were white; mexicanos were, well, mexicanos—raza, and later, chicanos. Perhaps that is why Manuel Ávila was so upset about the American GI Forum *News Bulletin* article favoring Negro school integration. The article reports, "Whether it is because they know what segregation of their own children means or because traditionally people of Mexican and Spanish descent do not share in the so-called doctrines of white supremacy and racial prejudice, the Mexican-American population of Texas . . . is in favor of doing away with the segregation of Negro children in the public schools."[43] It seems that the lure of whiteness, and all it implies, did not exert as powerful a hold on the majority of Mexican Americans as it did on the civil rights strategists of the American GI Forum.

The claim that Mexican Americans constituted a "separate class" of whites—a kind of "separate but equal" whiteness—formed the basis of the legal strategy of Mexican American civil rights activists from 1930 to 1970 and culminated in the creation of the "Hispanic" category in the 1980 census, replicating once again the part federal policy has played in Mexican American racial politics. Significantly, the extension of "other whiteness" to Mexican Americans and other Latino groups is deeply implicated in the maintenance of blackness as the racial touchstone for determining who is white and who is not, as well as the maintenance of blackness as the racial barrier impeding the advancement of African Americans in white, mainstream society.

In 1980 the U.S. census created the official category of Hispanic, but not as a racial category on par with the category of white, black, Asian, and Native American. The census bureaucrats and politicians were aware of the sensitivity of Latinos to being regarded as nonwhite, and consequently they made the category of Hispanic an ethnic subcategory of race. In other words, one can be of any race, including black or white, and still be Hispanic. As a census category and ethnoracial identity, it has thus come to signify a whiteness of a different color, a darker shade of pale, a preference for salsa over ketchup. Many identifying themselves as white and Hispanic, whether consciously or not, are implicated in the government's erasure of the Indian and African heritage of Mexicans. The journey of mixed-race Mexicans thus ends at the doorstep of Hispanic whiteness where no blacks or Indians are free to enter.

African Americans, for their part, have sometimes been guilty of playing the "citizenship card" in their dealings with Mexicans. During the 1920s many African Americans enthusiastically endorsed immigration restrictions aimed at Mexican Americans, believing that Mexicans took jobs from African Americans and lowered the standard of living. Black Texans in Houston, for example, expressed their bitterness in 1934 over a municipal decision to set aside a ten-acre tract of land for recreational purposes for the growing population of Mexicans in Houston. Black civic leaders had purchased property from the city a year before to serve the recreational needs of African Americans in Houston and complained bitterly that the city had not appropriated any money either for its purchase or upkeep. According to one complaint, "Mexicans are aliens who swear their allegiance to a foreign power. But when it comes to spending a little money for recreation purposes, it seems to be all for aliens and nothing for citizens."[44] More recently, nearly half of all African Americans in California voted for Proposition 187 to deny educational and health benefits to undocumented Mexican workers and their families.

Tensions clearly exist today in the United States between the growing Latino population and African Americans, whose percentage of the total population continues to decline in many states with each census, particularly in key electoral states. For many blacks, hard-fought gains won during a century of struggle and suffering are now being overshadowed by the prospect of majority Latino populations in major urban areas and large states, like Texas and California. For example, the Latino population in California will increase from thirty-two percent today to about forty-three percent in the next twenty-two years, while the population of blacks in the state will go from the present seven percent to just over five percent. Their percentage of the population will actually be declining over the next twenty-two years. In Texas the Hispanic population will increase from the present thirty-two percent to about thirty-seven percent in 2025, or well over one-third of the state's population, while the percentage of African Americans will increase only about two percent over the same period.[45]

The declining percentage of African Americans in major urban areas has already led to some bitter disputes in Dallas between black and Latino members of the school board. Dallas Independent School District board meetings during the 1997–98 school year degenerated into angry accusations between Hispanics and blacks over filling the post of school superintendent. The warring factions settled on Bill Rojas, a black man of Puerto Rican descent. The source of the tensions between blacks and Latinos in Dallas and in other cities is that while the Latino population surpasses that of blacks, African Americans still retain control of school boards, local politics, and other levers of power. In Dallas, for example, blacks hold more teaching and administrative jobs than Hispanics, although slightly more than fifty percent of the students are Hispanic, compared to thirty-nine percent for black students.[46]

In Los Angeles' Watts district, blacks and Latinos constantly feud over staff hiring at the county-operated Martin Luther King, Jr.–Drew Medical Center. The hospital was built in the late 1960s in response to blacks' complaints that they were medically underserved in Watts, which was predominantly black. Now, however, Latinos outnumber blacks in Watts and are demanding that the hospital hire Latino doctors and administrators. Blacks, of course, believe that they are being pushed out by recent immigrants, who demand the rights and privileges that blacks have won only after decades of civil rights struggles.[47] Tensions are not limited to competition between the two groups. In 1995 in Lubbock, Texas, two Hispanics and a white were convicted of a federal hate crime for driving around the town shooting black men with a shotgun, leading many blacks to wonder whose side Latinos are on.[48]

The rapid increase in the Hispanic population has not, however, complicated the black-white binary of U.S. race relations to the extent one might have expected. In part, this is because middle-class Hispanics—with the assistance of the Census Bureau in 1980—have redrawn the boundaries of whiteness to include both Hispanics and "non-Hispanic whites." Mexican Americans, like other Hispanic groups, are at a crossroads: one path, slouching toward whiteness, leads to racial fissures that harden the color line between blacks and whites. Hispanic whites express their new sense of white entitlement often by supporting anti-affirmative action laws, English-only movements, and other nativist ideologies on the backs of immigrants and African Americans. Another path welcomes the shared responsibility of defining and bringing into existence a transnational multiracial identity that acknowledges the Indian and African heritage of Latinos and their ancient ties to the Western Hemisphere, an identity that author Richard Rodriguez calls simply "brown."[49] By examining how whiteness constructs and maintains racial boundaries, often in conflicting and contradictory ways, we can better begin to understand the ways in which the black-white racial paradigm masks the liminal spaces and racial places that are home to increasing numbers of Americans.

Notes

1. Mike Davis, *Magical Realism: Latinos Reinvent the U.S. City,* revised edition (London and New York: Verso, 2001), pp. 2–16.

2. Barbara J. Fields, "Ideology and Race in America," in *Region, Race, and Reconstruction: Essays in Honor of C. Vann Woodward,* ed. by J. Morgan Kousser and James M. McPherson (New York: Oxford University Press, 1982), p. 146. On the legal construction of whiteness in the United States, see Ian F. Haney López, *White by Law: The Legal Construction of Race* (New York: New York University Press, 1996); and Cheryl I. Harris, "Whiteness as Property," *Harvard Law Review* 106 (June, 1993): 1709–91. See also Thomas C. Holt, "Marking: Race, Race Making, and the Writing of History," *American Historical Review* 100 (Feb., 1995): 1–20.

3. See Mathew Frye Jacobson, *Whiteness of a Different Color: European Immigrants and the Alchemy of Race* (Cambridge: Harvard University Press, 1998); and Neil Foley, *The White Scourge: Mexicans, Blacks, and Poor Whites in Texas Cotton Culture* (Berkeley: University of California Press, 1997).

4. The debate can be traced through the numerous congressional hearings by the Immigration and Naturalization Committee during the 1920s. See, for example, U.S. Congress, House Committee on Immigration and Naturalization, *Immigration from Countries of the Western Hemisphere,* 70th Cong., 2nd sess., 1930; idem, *Immigration from Countries of the Western Hemisphere,* 1928; idem, *Immigration from Mexico,* 71st Cong., 2nd sess., 1930; idem, Naturalization, 71st Cong., 2nd sess., 1930; idem, *Restriction of Immigration,* 68th Cong., 1st sess., 1924, Serial 1-A; *Seasonal Agricultural Laborers,* 1926; *Temporary Admission;* and idem, *Western Hemisphere Immigration,* 71st Cong., 2nd sess., 1930. For scholarly analysis of the immigration debate, see David Gutierrez, *Walls and Mirrors: Mexican Americans, Mexican Immigrants, and the Politics of Ethnicity* (Berkeley: University of California, 1995); and Mark Reisler, *By the Sweat of Their Brow: Mexican Immigrant Labor in the United States, 1900–1940* (Westport, Conn.: Greenwood Press, 1976).

5. Peggy Pascoe, "Miscegenation Law, Court Cases, and Ideologies of 'Race' in Twentieth-Century America," *Journal of American History* 83 (June, 1996): 44–69. Mexicans, who were legally "white," were rarely prosecuted for marrying blacks. For the only case in Texas of a Mexican brought to trial for marrying a black, see *F. Flores v. the State,* 60 Tex. Crim. 25 (1910); 129 S. W. 1111. I am indebted to Julie Dowling for bringing this case to my attention. See her paper, "Mexican Americans and the Modern Performance of Whiteness: LULAC and the Construction of the White Mexican," presented at the American Sociological Association annual conference, Anaheim, Calif., August, 2001.

6. Max Sylvius Handman, "Economic Reasons for the Coming of the Mexican Immigrant," *American Journal of Sociology* 35 (Jan., 1930): 609–10.

7. Handman, "The Mexican Immigrant in Texas," *Southwestern Political and Social Science Quarterly* 7 (June, 1926): 27.

8. Ibid., p. 40.

9. See David Montejano, *Anglos and Mexicans in the Making of Texas, 1836–1986* (Austin: University of Texas Press, 1987); and Foley, *The White Scourge.*

10. *In re Rodríguez,* 81 Fed. 337 (W. D. Texas, 1897); Arnoldo De León, *In Re Ricardo Rodríguez: An Attempt at Chicano Disfranchisement in San Antonio, 1896–1897* (San Antonio, Tex.: Caravel Press, 1979), p. 8; Tomás Almaguer, *Racial Fault Lines: The Historical Origins of White Supremacy in California* (Berkeley: University of California Press, 1994), pp. 162–64; Fernando Padilla, "Early Chicano Legal Recognition, 1846–1897," *Journal of Popular Culture* 13 (spring, 1980): 564–74; Martha Menchaca, "Chicano Indianism: A Historical Account of Racial Repression in the United

States," *American Ethnologist* 20 (Aug., 1993): 583–601; Haney López, *White by Law*, p. 61; Gary A. Greenfield and Don B. Kates, Jr., "Mexican Americans, Racial Discrimination, and the Civil Rights Act of 1866," *California Law Review* 63 (Jan., 1975): 693. See also Mae M. Ngai, "The Architecture of Race in American Immigration Law: A Reexamination of the Immigration Act of 1924," *Journal of American History* 86 (1999): 88, 93. For an analysis of the legal decisions that barred numerous groups from claiming white racial status, see Stanford M. Lyman, "The Race Question and Liberalism: Casuistries in American Constitutional Law," *International Journal of Politics, Culture, and Society* 5 (Winter, 1991): 183–247. For a fascinating personal history involving the legal and cultural complexities of racial identity, see Ernest Evans Kilker, "Black and White in America: The Culture and Politics of Racial Classification," *International Journal of Politics, Culture, and Society* 7 (Winter, 1993): 229–58.

11. C. H. Jenkins, *The Revised Civil Statutes of Texas, 1925, Annotated,* (Austin: H. P. N. Gammel Book Co., 1925), vol. 1, p. 1036.

12. See Guadalupe San Miguel, Jr., "The Origins Development, and Consequences of the Educational Segregation of Mexicans in the Southwest," in *Chicano Studies: A Multidisciplinary Approach,* ed. by Eugene E. García, Francisco Lomeli, and Isidro Ortiz (New York: Teachers College Press, 1984), pp. 195–208.

13. See Gary A. Greenfield and Don B. Kates, Jr., "Mexican Americans, Racial Discrimination, and the Civil Rights Act of 1866," *California Law Review* 63 (Jan., 1975): 700.

14. *Herald-Post,* Oct. 6 and 7, 1936; *La Prensa* (San Antonio), Oct. 10, 1936; and *New York Times,* Oct. 21, 1936, in Cleofas Calleros Collection, University of Texas at El Paso, hereafter cited as CCC. All references from this collection are from box 28, folder 1 ("Color Classification of Mexicans"). See also Mario García, "Mexican Americans and the Politics of Citizenship: The Case of El Paso, 1936," *New Mexico Historical Review* 59 (Apr., 1984): 187–204. García, who based his article on the same file from the Calleros collection, argues that Mexican American leaders used the controversy over racial classification of Mexicans "to show Anglo leaders that Mexicans would not accept second-class citizenship." (p. 201). While that is no doubt true, García mistakenly argues that Mexican Americans used the politics of citizenship rather than race in forging racial identities as whites. As Caucasians, Mexican Americans asserted their own racial superiority over African Americans and other "people of color."

15. Mr. Calleros to Mr. Mohler, memo, Oct. 9, 1936, p. 1, CCC.

16. Ibid., p. 2.

17. *Herald-Post,* Oct. 7, 1936, CCC.

18. *El Continental,* Oct. 6 and 25, 1936, CCC.

19. Ibid., Oct. 25, 1936, CCC. Author's translation.

20. *La Prensa,* Oct. 12, 1936, CCC.

21. Form SS-5, Treasury Department, Internal Revenue Service, instructions for filling out form, item number 12, CCC; *Herald-Post,* Oct. 8, 1936, CCC.

22. *Herald-Post,* Oct. 8, 1936, letter of M. A. Gomez; *El Continental,* Oct. 8, 1936, CCC.

23. García, "Mexican Americans and the Politics of Citizenship," p. 189.

24. *El Continental,* Oct. 18, 1936, CCC.

25. *Collins* v. *State,* 7. A. L. R., 895 (Okla.) in petition presented to the District Court of El Paso, *M. A. Gomez et al., v. T. J. McCamant and Alex Powell,* Oct., 1936, CCC.

26. LULAC Resolution, San Antonio Council no. 16 and Council no. 2, Oct. 14, 1936, CCC.

27. Maury Maverick to William L. Austin, Oct. 15, 1936, CCC; see also Calleros to Mohler, Oct. 9, 1936, CCC.

28. *Herald-Post,* Oct. 8, 1936, CCC.

29. *El Continental,* Oct. 14, 1936, CCC. An editorial appearing opposite Hamilton's letter

stated that the letter appeared to be written "por un negro" and that although vulgar ("grosera"), the editor decided to publish the letter to express a different point of view.

30. *El Continental,* Oct. 14, 1936, CCC.

31. Ibid.

32. Ibid., Oct. 16, 1936.

33. Hector García to Gerald Saldana, Mar. 13, 1954, box 141, folder 13, Hector P. García Papers, Texas A&M University, Corpus Christi, hereafter cited as HPG.

34. Taylor Branch, *Parting the Waters: America in the King Years, 1954–63* (New York: Simon and Schuster, 1988), p. 341.

35. While not promoting the American GI Forum as a civil rights organization in 1949, García nevertheless wrote to the Texas governor that "Texas is in immediate need of a Civil Rights Program." Hector P. García to Allan Shivers, Dec. 4, 1949, HPG.

36. Hector P. García to Editor, *Lubbock Morning Avalanche,* July 18, 1956, HPG.

37. Humbert Humphrey to Dominga Coronado, June 12, 1967; Dominga Coronado to Hubert Humphrey, June 26, 1967, HPG.

38. Manuel Ávila, Jr., to Ed Idar, Feb.7, 1956, box 26, folder 28, HPG; *News Bulletin* 4, nos. 1 and 2 (Sept.–Oct., 1955): 1, HPG.

39. Manuel Ávila, Jr., to Ed Idar, Feb.7, 1956, box 46, folder 28, HPG. See also Isaac P. Borjas to Hector P. García, June 2, 1940; Newspaper clipping, *Caracas Daily Journal,* [1960?], box 114, folder 22; and Ruth Slates to Dr. Hector García, Mar. 23, 1951, box 59, folder 33, HGP.

40. Ruth Slates to Dr. Hector García, Mar. 23, 1951, box 59, folder 33, HGP.

41. *Hernandez* v. *State,* 251 S. W. 2nd 531 (1952); *Hernandez* v. *Texas,* 347 U.S. 475 (1954). For an extended analysis of the legal construction of racial identity in the Hernandez case, see Ian F. Haney López, "Race, Ethnicity, Erasure: The Salience of Race to LatCrit Theory," *University of California Law Review* 85 (1997): 1143–1211.

42. Neil Foley, "Becoming Hispanic: Mexican Americans and the Faustian Pact with Whiteness," in *Reflexiones: New Directions in Mexican American Studies,* ed. by Neil Foley (Austin: University of Texas Press, 1998). See also Carlos M. Alcala and Jorge C. Rangel, "Project Report: De Jure Segregation of Chicanos in Texas Schools," *Harvard Civil Rights–Civil Liberties Law Review* 7 (Mar., 1972). Carl Allsup, *The American G. I. Forum: Origins and Evolution* (Austin: University of Texas, Center for Mexican American Studies, Monograph 6, 1982).

43. *News Bulletin* 4 (Sept.–Oct., 1955): 1.

44. Houston *Informer,* May 5, 1934, cited in Arnold Shankman, "The Image of Mexico and the Mexican-American in the Black Press, 1890–1935," *Journal of Ethnic Studies* 3 (summer, 1975): 52.

45. http://www.census.gov/population/projections

46. *USA Today,* Sept. 10, 1999.

47. Ibid.

48. Bill Piatt, *Black and Brown in America* (New York and London: New York University Press, 1997), p. 9.

49. Richard Rodgríguez, *Brown: The Last Discovery of America* (New York: Viking, 2000).

Contributors

WILLIAM D. CARRIGAN is assistant professor of history at Rowan University. He is revising his dissertation, "Between South and West: Race, Violence, and Power in Central Texas, 1836–1916," for publication with the University of Illinois Press. He is also the author of "Slavery on the Frontier: The Peculiar Institution in Central Texas" in *Slavery & Abolition* 20 (1999).

STEPHANIE COLE is associate professor of history at the University of Texas at Arlington. Her book, *Servants and Slaves: Domestic Service in the North/South Antebellum Border Cities,* is forthcoming from University of Illinois Press. She is also co-editor of *Women and the Unstable State in Nineteenth-Century America* (Texas A&M University Press, 2000).

SARAH DEUTSCH is professor of history at University of Arizona and the author of *No Separate Refuge: Culture, Class, and Gender on an Anglo-Hispanic Frontier in the American Southwest* (Oxford University Press, 1987) and *Women and the City: Gender, Space, and Power in Boston, 1870–1940* (Oxford, 2000), as well as numerous articles on race relations in the American West.

LAURA F. EDWARDS is associate professor of history at Duke University. She is author of *Gendered Strife and Confusion: The Political Culture of Reconstruction* (University of Illinois Press, 1997) and *Scarlett Doesn't Live Here Anymore: Southern Women in the Civil War Era* (University of Illinois Press, 2000).

NEIL FOLEY is associate professor of history and American studies at the University of Texas at Austin. He is the author of *The White Scourge: Mexicans, Blacks, and Poor Whites in Texas Cotton Culture* (University of California Press, 1997), which won the Frederick Jackson Turner Award of the Organization of American Historians and other awards. He is editor of

Reflexiones: New Directions in Mexican American Studies (University of Texas Press, 1998).

NANCY HEWITT is professor of history and women's and gender studies at Rutgers University. She is the author most recently of *Southern Discomfort: Women's Activism in Tampa, Florida, 1880s–1920s* (University of Illinois Press, 2001) and editor of *A Companion to American Women's History* (Blackwells Publishers, 2002).

ALISON M. PARKER is associate professor of history at the State University of New York, Brockport, and is the author of *Purifying America: Women, Cultural Reform, and Pro-Censorship Activism, 1873–1933* (University of Illinois Press, 1997). She served as co-editor and contributed a chapter to *Women and the Unstable State in Nineteenth-Century America* (Texas A&M University Press, 2000).

CLIVE WEBB is a lecturer in American history at the University of Sussex at Brighton, England. He is the author of *Fight Against Fear: Southern Jews and Black Civil Rights* (University of Georgia Press, 2001).

ISBN 1-58544-319-0

9 781585 443192

90000